HOWL: of Woman and Wolf

HOWL

of Woman and Wolf

SUSAN IMHOFF BIRD

TORREY HOUSE PRESS, LLC

SALT LAKE CITY • TORREY

This is a work of nonfiction though some names have
been changed to avoid confusion.

First Torrey House Press Edition, October 2015
Copyright © 2015 by Susan Imhoff Bird

Published by Torrey House Press, LLC
Salt Lake City, Utah
www.torreyhouse.com

International Standard Book Number: 978-1-937226-47-3
E-book ISBN: 978-1-937226-48-0
Library of Congress Control Number: 2014945479
Author photo by Allegra Imhoff
Cover design by Rick Whipple, Sky Island Studio
Interior design by Jeffrey Fuller, Shelfish.weebly.com

. . . spirit howls and wildness endures.

– TERRY TEMPEST WILLIAMS

contents

HOWL
of Woman and Wolf

big mountain

Three weeks into April, winter eases. Snow pulls back from soil and road, melting underneath itself. My belly is lean, muscles on fire. Each breath hurts. The road tilts up, more so than last fall, and with each push on the pedals my quads quiver. I will ride to where the snow stops forward progress. I've cycled up a gradually climbing canyon, down a short descent, alongside a crystal-edged reservoir, and around a metal gate stretched across the road, its Closed to Motor Traffic sign chipped and rusty. The road is mine alone on this late winter morning. I've skirted narrow strips of ice, and navigated slick black pavement. Rivulets of snowmelt follow the path of least resistance, which sometimes angles left, sometimes right, rarely flowing straight toward me.

I'll be halted soon. I know that when the road curves again it will position me due east, where the sharp hillside on my right blocks sunlight. I will gain the shady stretch where winter's blanket lies thick and frozen on the ground, its blunt edge confrontative, where my skinny tires become useless.

I dismount. Snow covers the road and lies on gray branches and leans against boulders. It clings to clumps of autumn's late grasses. I walk my bike from the last clear patch of asphalt to the road's edge. I lean it against the trunk of a gnarled scrub oak, its bark cracked and scarred.

Below my handlebars, attached by a loop of zip-tie, dangles a small, metal cylinder. The container is just over two inches tall, an inch in diameter. I peel off my gloves to unscrew the lid. I hold the open tube and walk to the snowy edge of the road where scrub oak grow thickly down the hill. I shake some of Jake's ashes into my hand, then send them floating out over the crusty snow. *I love you, Jake. I miss you.* He is everywhere here. I walk to the other side of the road where the red dirt hillside soars, and scatter the rest of the ashes over the scarlet earth, the snow patches, a stream of meltage running in the berm.

He's been gone three years and three months. He would have turned twenty-two today. He is twenty-two.

This is my third observance of this ritual, my solitary ceremony. Me. Jake. We meet here surrounded by what appears dormant but is filled with life. Moose and deer stand motionless, hidden by willows and pines. A beaver silences its gnawing, a squirrel pauses, a magpie gazes my way and keeps its peace. All I hear is trickling water; even the wind has calmed its constant whistle through bare branches. These gray trees, not a bud in sight, will burst into thousands of leaves unfolding with green life in mere weeks. I breathe in crisp air, then let it go. The silence is broken by birdsong, a solo.

The canyon walls press, constrict. My lungs no longer burn, but my chest aches. A whisper, *somewhere else. Go, leave. Head north.* True north.

When I married Daniel eight months ago I thought we would share this, that he'd be here beside me. But instead, I am more alone than before. I ache today for Jake. But I'm devastated by my failure to create the relationship I crave and need—the profound connection I thought was finally in my life.

I sprinkle ashes.

I write Jake's name with my finger in the snow at the edge of the road.

1. seed

Wolf stands with forelegs planted, head lifted, as the wind ruffs her smoke gray fur. The land rises behind her—shrubs and bunch-grasses as tall as her chest, a valley and rising hill beyond, aspen and willow throughout—she is host. Her eyes lock on mine and I stare. I am a guest in her land. I bow my head, and she lifts her nose. Our exchange complete, she turns and sniffs the air before moving off, loping, her long legs moving the grass as does a summer wind, a burst, here and gone.

As we drive along the narrow road into Lamar Valley I see this part of Yellowstone for the first time. I've visited West Yellowstone, and driven up to Old Faithful from Jackson in the south, but I've never been on this northernmost road that sweeps east to west, from entry gate at Gardiner, Montana, to entry gate in Silver Gate, Montana, moving through Wyoming in between. Immense and verdant in early June, the valley cradles the surging Lamar River, hundreds and hundreds of bison, lolloping black bears, and countless eagles, cranes, coyote, and other smaller creatures. And a pack of wolves, the well-known and beloved Lamar Canyon pack, a pack trying to survive its decimating losses of the winter. The alpha female—well known throughout the wolf-watching world as the 06 female—and the beta male, 754, had both been shot by hunters in Wyoming, outside park boundaries, just months before.

Bison, large as cars, plod with massive shoulders hunched

around their necks, eyes blinking, gargantuan heads swinging side to side. A herd crosses the road. A dreadlock-bearded bull, its horns ridged and curving into its wooly mane, leads the leisurely procession, two younger bulls following, neither as filled out, as wooly, or as impervious as the first. A few cows, three or four calves that bound and weave between the plodders. Hooves pound the ground, deadened clomping, the sound of two hundred years ago.

Our eyes dart left and right searching for movement or at least familiar, recognizable shapes. Cars halt in each paved pullout along the road, and people stare into the river-split valley, some with binoculars, others with cameras, and the serious wildlife viewers with tripod-mounted scopes. We drive past a collection of cars and small buses and I want to tell Mark to stop, to let me out, let me see what's going on, but I hesitate from the sheer unfamiliarity of it all. I've never done anything like this.

Mark drives on, and I squash the voice inside that says go back, fearing I might have missed something important, a once-in-a-lifetime opportunity. I don't want to be wrong. Nerves tighten my gut, and I perch on the edge of the back seat in our rented Dodge Durango. People litter both sides of the two-lane road, scanning for wildlife, and we continue west toward the heart of the valley, North America's Serengeti. Another mile, two. None of us know exactly where to start. I begin to release my worry over the spot we didn't choose, when Kirsten's words register.

"Gray thing running," she's said, pointing to our left, out in the midst of the valley.

A small shape, moving. Wolf?

We're approaching a pullout where thirty people stand, looking out at the grasslands. Mark angles into a narrow slot and we pile out of the car.

"What are you seeing?" I ask a tiny, dark-haired woman. She wears a black fleece vest and hat. She stands next to a scope.

"A wolf, eating a baby bison that died. It's Middle Gray, one of 06's daughters. Would you like to look?"

"Yes, thanks," I eagerly nod, and move to the scope. I lean in to the eyepiece and see my first wolf. It's far away, but I can see it tearing at the honey-colored carcass, then moving away, circling, returning for more. She tears flesh, looks right, left, then moves in for another bite. A mouthful, a lift of head. The carcass at her feet retains its shape, a bison calf, legs outstretched, neck extended. Its torso is half eaten, and an animal I've never seen except in films and photographs is lowering her head to rip more flesh from its bones.

Cool morning air brushes my cheek. I tug my hat over my ears. Voices blend and soften. A coyote approaches the wolf; the wolf turns and snarls. The coyote leaps backward, then paces ten feet from the calf. An eagle circles. Adult bison stand, immobile, a dozen feet away. I straighten, move away from the scope, and the valley expands. I find the partially eaten calf. Twenty yards to the right, another calf lies on the ground, a cow bison standing guard. From the hum of voices comes explanation: the calf being eaten was killed by a coyote kick. The calf at the adult's feet, stillborn. Is the cow its mother? She stands alone, unmoving. There must be an understanding that what lies before her is wrong. I don't dare suggest she feels something for her dead baby. But I wonder. A group of bison, ten or so, drift over to join the solitary mother, and they all stand around the calf on the ground, occasionally nibbling the grass at their feet. Camaraderie, some kind of bovine mourning process.

"Would you like to look through my scope?" The quiet voice enters my reverie, and I turn to see a woman with short, well-cut gray hair looking at me.

"Yes, thanks," I reply, and move over, place my eye against

the eyepiece. She is taller than me, and I lift to my toes to look through her Swarovski scope, positioned to allow view of both bison calves. A coyote darts in to take a bite of the by now well-eaten calf. Mom and company continue to guard the other. A few sandhill cranes prance in the marshland to the right, and I watch as a golden eagle circles, then dives down to the calf, driving off the coyote.

To my left is the Pied Piper of wolf watchers, Rick McIntyre. He sits on a camp stool, watching the wolf. The hair under his cap is a faded red, his skin is pale, and he is so thin I wonder how frequently he bothers to eat. Wolf watchers envelop him. He ducks his chin to speak into a recorder and I catch a handful of words: Middle Gray, calf, road. He's been here since the beginning, since the first wolves were brought back into the park, almost twenty years ago. Photographer, author, a man who's followed his passion from park to park for more than thirty years. His job here is to help park visitors see wolves. He utilizes telemetry—tracking collared wolves via radio signal—a scope, and information collected by dozens of park visitors and dedicated wolf watchers, some of whom live right outside the park's eastern border and watch wolves almost every day of their lives.

He responds to my greeting with a gentle smile.

"Are you getting to see some wolves?"

"This is my first morning, my first wolf," I reply.

"Ah," he nods. "I hope you'll see more. I need to pack up and move down the road, clear a space for Middle Gray to cross as she heads back home."

He places his stool in the back of his SUV, hops in, and drives onto the road. I search the valley for Middle Gray, who is no longer eating, nor is she circling the carcass. She is a dozen feet away from it, heading east. She trots smoothly, in a straight line across the ochre earth.

A million years ago—a blink of the earth goddess's eye—the dire wolf lived in North America. From matter had come insectivores and creodonts. As time passed and each evolved, the ancestors of animals on earth today emerged. They lived in a world untamed. Rocky hills and uplifted moraines, flowering plants, scrubby grasses. Conifers, dense and dark, covered the land. Screeches split the air, howls echoed. Thundering hooves, death screams as prey lost to predator. Not a word spoken, just lapping of windblown water, splashing creeks, the steady drum of rain on dusty soil.

The dire wolf, toes splayed wide, trots between far flung trees, seeking her pack. Separated during the last hunt, distracted by a stream and seduced by her thirst, she trails the others by half a mile. In the far distance are moving bodies, and she increases her speed. Maybe they've closed in on a bison, maybe they need her. The pack works together, sometimes as many as twenty, thirty, trapping a horse or bison then attacking, their teeth razor sharp and quick to draw blood. Five feet long from nose to tail, her shoulders are more than two feet from the earth, and she weighs 115 pounds. Her mate is ahead but she's drawing near. A bison is besieged. He butts the wolves with his huge head, unable to stop them from tearing at his flanks. She reaches the pack and jumps at the dark animal's rear leg, her teeth ripping skin and muscle to scar the bone underneath. When the bison topples, the whump of his body hitting earth vibrates beneath her feet and echoes across the rimrocked plateau.

Tens and hundreds of thousands of years elapsed, her progeny roaming the plateau, crossing hills and plains, continually in search of prey. Bison and horses, and occasionally a giant ground sloth, a mastodon. Then 750,000 years ago, *Canis lupus*, the gray wolf, traveled from Eurasia to North America. It settled onto tundras, mountains, and plains, from the Arctic to the southwestern tip of the continent, existing alongside the dire wolf. The gray wolf was well established before Native American and Inuit peoples arrived, and hid amidst the tall pines, watching as human beings moved onto its land. Near the close of the Pleistocene epoch, over eleven thousand years ago, the dire wolf began to die off as the number of large prey animals decreased. The gray wolf, which ate small as well as larger mammals—perhaps because it was less dense than the dire wolf, more agile, able to dart and sprint—adapted better to these harsher conditions and by seven thousand years ago, became the primary canine predator in the Northern Hemisphere.

The world of the gray wolf's dominance is large and stark, naked of human beings, flush with foliage, trees, rocks, water, predators and prey. Animals rove, den, and spend their lives dodging those that pursue them, or pursuing those that dodge. Species and plants evolve, and the land matures. Weather dictates behavior, cycles govern existence. Life emerges, and ceases.

A gust of wind throws hair across my face. I brush it away, clear my eyes, scan the sightseers for Mark and Kirsten. They both look toward the river, where it bends and overflows its banks, where cranes high-step and birds erupt from hidden swales and swirl into the sky. We traveled here together, spent last night in Cooke City, will camp tonight in the park. They had planned the trip, then asked if I wanted to join them. Daniel, too. Mark would fly his old Cherokee, and we'd visit Idaho, then Yellowstone, then Missoula. I'd said of course, but Daniel couldn't take time away from work. I packed everything I thought I might need, threw in more socks, and asked if my bicycle would fit in the plane. Mark's brow furrowed. He said maybe, if all the camping gear and our bags left enough room. A seven-day trip was too long for me to go without cycling. Mark had planned a stop in Pocatello, Idaho, then a night's stay in Rexburg, seventy-five miles away. I could ride between the two towns, could probably ride in Yellowstone, too. I packed my cycling gear—helmet, shoes, granola bars and electrolyte chews—in hopes that all those sleeping bags, tents, mattress pads, and cooking supplies would squish.

The bike fit.

We'd flown from Salt Lake City to Pocatello, where I hopped on my bike and pedaled north. Before I left home I'd called the Idaho Department of Transportation to ask about a bike-safe route, and the clerk suggested I call the Pocatello Chamber of Commerce, where I was directed to Birgitta, who owns a bike and might know more about that kind of thing. I left her a message, and an hour later received a call from a young man at the local bike shop, who helped me map out my route. Most of it was on the old Yellowstone Highway. Red-winged blackbirds burst from fields, flapping and coasting high above my head as I pedaled. A line of cars waited to pay admission fees and drive through Bear World. The Snake River flowed wide and opaque as I rode over it, grateful for the fact that everyone isn't like me, and every place isn't like my own neighborhood. The entire way, I'd been gifted with a tailwind that smelled, at times, of baking potatoes. I arrived in Rexburg sweaty and starved.

The next morning we'd flown to Bozeman, Montana, rented the Dodge Durango, and driven to the park, and now we stood, gazing at the immense valley known around the world for its wolf-viewing.

This morning's wolf has left the baby bison. She is headed east. She trots across the shrub-dotted land and up toward the road, a good half mile from us, where she crosses the tarmac and lopes up the hillside, north, to her home. Everyone at the pullout watches, electricity charging the air, until her tail disappears from view. Then the valley becomes again an immense expanse of earth, speckled with bison and cranes. An eagle soars high above, scouring the land for movement.

Absence. Void. My teeth chatter and under my skin, muscles echo the vibration. My legs tremble so hard my feet jump in the footrests. The nurse wraps another blanket over me, hot from the warmer, its waffled texture under my fingertips up and down, here and gone.

I woke to drizzle, angry drops slipping down the window, nothing but gray. From the bare trees lining the hospital drive, to rooftops and high-rises five miles away, to the foothills of the Oquirrh Mountains on the far edge of the valley, their peaks hidden, perhaps stolen during the night.

My belly is empty. Bob walks alongside as the nurse pushes me from the outer edge of the hospital to a room in its heart, a room dangerously close to the spot where I, six hours before, gave birth to two boys, one alive, one dead, each connected to the other by a meandering blood vessel woven through their shared placenta. We pass through wide wooden doors that open at the press of a square metal button. My legs jump. I clench my jaw. I am wheeled down a hallway of shiny linoleum. I press down against my legs. This void is larger than me.

He lies on an open table, lights hot and bright eighteen inches above his body. He has no fat, cannot keep himself warm. Eyes covered by a strip of cloth, he is naked but for a miniature diaper. He is attached to machines by wire leads and a tiny pulse oximeter around his foot. Heart rate, respiration, oxygen saturation, temperature. Each vital has an acceptable range, and the machines shriek an alarm when a limit is breeched. His Apgars, three and seven, are not terrible for a thirty-two-weeker, and he is, at three pounds thirteen ounces, one of the largest preemies in the room. I tuck my index finger into his hand, which curls loosely around it, and tears spill. I cannot look at Bob. Beeps assail me, assorted volumes and pitches. Lights—green, blue, red, soft white—flash, or hum steadily. For a moment my body is calm—my jaw relaxed, my legs at rest. Jake looks nothing like any baby I've ever seen. No chubby cheeks, just scrubby skin over toothpick bones. His head too large, his nose a dot, the skin of his feet and hands translucent. An IV sticks in his left hand, the needle as fine as thread.

It's mid-morning and the day is warming, though the wind holds a chill. We've erected our tents, tossed sleeping bags and pads inside, stored our food in the bear-safe lock boxes, and come back into the valley. Wolves are crepuscular animals, hunting at dawn and dusk. We may not see a wolf, but black bears, bison, and deer are abundant. The park itself, its towering conifers, massive walls of stone, thundering rivers, gives me more than enough to ponder, and I am silent as we drive back along the Lamar Valley road.

Mark parks by twenty other cars, and we join those who stand where grass meets pavement. I recognize a woman from earlier, the one with short gray hair, a Swarovski scope.

"Any wolves?" I ask.

"No," she says, "but the calf's body is still there. A coyote's been eating. Would you like to look?"

I peer out into the valley, see the concave body, then look to the right where mama bison stands over the other dead calf.

"I'm Kris," she smiles. "I love the wolves. You watch long enough, you get to know some of their personalities. They all have stories. We watched 06 for years—she was amazing, dynamic. Our rock star."

"She was killed in December?" I ask.

A wince, a nod. Kris's eyes spark green. "She was born back in 2006—that's why the name—and became the alpha female of the Lamar Canyon pack, which has been so visible, most everyone who watches wolves knows of her. She had her first pups in 2010, and a second litter the next year. She was so charismatic, just beautiful, full of fire. Thousands of people watched her, took pictures, read about her. Then last December, 2012, she left the park, probably on a hunt, and was killed by a hunter. Legally. She was fifteen miles outside the park."

Kris is silent as we search the valley before us. I imagine 06, think of her daughter tearing at the bison calf carcass this morning.

"The alpha male's brother had been shot just weeks before she was, and the pack has struggled. It's fallen apart. If people knew the stories of these wolves, that they are parents, children, that they teach their pups, play with them. That they're beings, filled with life, history, families. They could never kill these wolves, not if they knew."

Jake was born in April of 1991, when wolves were, for most of us, creatures of fairy tales and magazine articles. Gray wolves, at that time, claimed territories in upper Wisconsin, on Isle Royale in Lake Superior, and in the wild hills of northwestern Montana. Every other state in our nation—except Alaska—cleared them out a century ago. Wolves had been vilified by early settlers, and this wild canine that had inhabited land across all but the Southeast was virtually extirpated by the 1920s. However, while Jake lay in the hospital biologists and politicians were working to legislate the reintroduction of wolves. The proposal took form in the 1970s, shortly after the Endangered Species Act was signed into law, and after nearly two decades, was moving closer to a congressional vote. The gray wolf was to be returned to its former home, beginning in the central Idaho wilderness, and in Yellowstone National Park.

Opponents argued against this reintroduction—bringing wolves from across the border in Canada, letting them acclimate, then setting them free under legislative protection—by pointing out that wolves were already recolonizing, reestablishing themselves in America. Making their way down from Canada a few at a time, settling in the high hills. In 1986, a wolf den was discovered in Montana's Glacier National Park—the first wolf den found in the West in over fifty years. This example of recolonization, a natural process, became an argument against reintroduction, an artificial method of reestablishing wolf populations in their former territories. Proponents of reintroduction countered that recolonization would take an unpredictable, lengthy journey, while suitable habitats could benefit from wolves right away. The latter argument prevailed, and the reintroduction was set to begin as soon as plans were solidified, and the right people signed the right forms. It was only a few years away.

Just a mile down the Lamar Valley road, we stop again. The viewing area is filled with cars and we squeeze into a spot half gravel, half weeds. A bear of a man wearing a thick mustache and bright yellow fleece taps on my window.

"Come look," he says. "I've got a grizzly in my scope; she's over on the hill up there." He points across the valley to a hillside thick with massive clumps and stretching fingers of snow.

I squint, the dusky cinnamon bear emerges. Her hump glistens in the sunlight filtering through the trees. She moves, a lumbering roll, fur sparking. She's five hundred feet away, thank God.

"I'm Michael, Michael Powers," he says, offering a hand. "And this here's my son, Hayden."

Hayden's cheery face peeks from underneath a fishing hat. He turns back to his own scope, fixed on the grizzly.

Not a soul is frugal with his scope here. Everyone wants to share the joy of seeing the bear, the eagle, the wolf, the playful coyote pups. Michael Powers is from Arizona. He spends two weeks each summer in the Yellowstone area with his wife and son. His personalized license plate is DRUID21, for the alpha male of the Druid Peak pack that, during the first dozen years of Yellowstone's wolf reintroduction, was one of the most viewed wolf packs in the world.

"It's like going to see a movie knowing there's no script, until the moment something happens. You may come in with an outline, but all that's there are the main ideas—yes, there are so many bison, this many wolves and packs, this many black and grizzly bears. But the details come as you interact with the place. Optics play an important role in this—wildlife here is accustomed to people, and pretty aware, so I believe if you want to see them as naturally as possible, it's better to view from a distance. That's why I love sharing the scopes. That's why I tapped on your window."

Wildlife viewing takes time and a wallop of patience—lots of standing still and squinting into scopes. I can't reconcile cycling, here, with looking for wolves. I try not to think about my bike stashed in the car as Michael continues.

"My job is high stress, and I can just feel that peeling away from me when I'm out here watching wildlife. It just slips away. One day I watched a big male grizzly make his way along the hillside north of Soda Butte. Then he disappeared behind the hills, and I knew where he was going. I said to my wife, let's get in the car and go to the Trout Lake pullout, and Hayden was in the back in his car seat—he was three. We parked, facing where I thought the grizzly would appear, and suddenly there he was, cresting one of the hills right in front of us, and Hayden shouted *dog*! He hadn't yet learned the word bear. No one else was there. Just us.

"Then one time Hayden and I were watching the Cottonwood pack on an elk kill. The wolves had eaten and were mostly just lying around when I saw a coyote trying to sneak in. I got Hayden on the scope and said, watch this—I knew what was going to happen. The coyote appeared in the scope and then a blur of two wolves shot out of the grass, chasing the coyote away. For a moment it was quiet, and then Hayden said, Dad, that was amazing.

"I want this experience to be available for everyone. There's nothing like it, anywhere. And Hayden's picked up on that too. He'll go looking for people who haven't been able to see the wolves or the bears, and offer them a look through our scopes."

I lean into his scope and look again at the grizzly. Her cubs are not in sight. She lifts a paw to her mouth, chews, shakes her head. She could kill me with the swipe of a paw. Could tear me apart in seconds. Would kill anyone, anything, do whatever she had to do to protect her cubs.

A dozen years ago I received as a gift a cookbook titled *Wild Women in the Kitchen*. A collection of recipes and stories and folklore, it's packed with brief tales about infamous women throughout time, from Joan of Arc to Sarah Bernhardt to Cher. I ignored the book for years, mainly because cooking is not one of my passions. Five years ago—long after Bob and I divorced—I decided to open it and read some of the stories. Who were considered wild women, and how are they different from me? The recipes I skimmed or ignored, but I read one, then another, then a dozen of the biographical paragraphs before I paused to contemplate. These women dared to be themselves, they made decisions based on their own needs and desires. They moved across countries and oceans, they followed their hearts, they lived bravely, their lives affected others. They spoke up. They trusted their paths. From Jane Austen, who dared to wittily write of society's conventional restrictions upon women, to Alice B. Toklas who in 1907 fell in love with Gertrude Stein and later published a cookbook with a scandalous recipe for hashish fudge, to Eleanor Roosevelt with her famous Sunday evening salons. These women were courageous. True to themselves. I considered my own life, realizing how far from wild I was. Not only were these women wild, most seemed to have found—or created—their own tribes.

It rains during the night, and in the morning I discover I'd planted my tent on top of a natural drainage. My sleeping bag, on top of a pad, is damp. I tug a hat over my hair, some pants over my long johns, a jacket over my top. Mark and Kirsten are already at the splintering wooden picnic table. Water boils. Coffee is imminent.

"Sleep well?" Mark asks.

"Mm-hmm, you?"

"Good, great," they nod.

I don't tell them I woke up in midnight dark, remembering the artificial sugar packets in my duffle bag, terrified a bear would sniff them out and I'd be exposed as a fool. A maimed or possibly dead fool, who couldn't follow simple rules. I'd slept poorly after that.

We drink coffee. Kirsten makes oatmeal. Mark jots in his journal, I open my own and try to pluck thoughts from the ether and write them down. I can't. I expand here, and my mind is a galaxy filled with words, concepts, ideas, possibilities. But I can't pin one down. I belong here, I'm of this land, I share a trace of origin with these creatures—the crane, the grizzly, the wolf—yet I am foreign, out of place. When those wolves, almost twenty years ago, were released here in the park, they stepped into the unknown. Transplanted, they were allowed time in one-acre pens to adjust to the climate, the smells, the air. And when the gates fell open, some clung to the familiar and wouldn't leave. But eventually, all the wolves left wire fences behind and ranged over the 3,400 square miles of the park. They mated, formed packs. They created families. They explored new land. Attacked prey. These early wolves were invited interlopers, running free, carving out territories in land taken from them decades before. In the pens they'd been restrained. Released, they struck out and reclaimed everything they'd once been.

Mammoth Hot Springs was once an army post. In the park's early years, poachers, souvenir hunters, and entrepreneurs who set up camps and tours, outmanned and outmaneuvered the park's gamekeepers and wardens. Park administrators sought federal help to protect the beauty and stability of the ecosystem. The army arrived in 1886—fourteen years after the park's official opening—and stayed for thirty years. Mammoth, now, is soldier free, but remains Yellowstone's official hub. Mark, Kirsten, and I walk past log cabins, graceful two-story brick and frame buildings, a sandstone chapel constructed by Scottish masons, all built during the army's tenure. We head to the Yellowstone Center for Resources, to see Doug Smith, head of the Wolf Project.

Doug Smith is a Paul Bunyan. His stride is twice that of mine, and were we not inside a grand building constructed in 1897 he'd be ducking as he passed through doorways. He is a man larger than life, his energy traveling in an aura disturbing electrons and protons throughout his environment. Jumping and sizzling, they mix and reform and change the air, the furniture, those around him, me. As with the teacher who magnetically engages his student and the actor who hooks and hypnotizes his audience, Doug captures his visitors' attentions and I sit, mesmerized, noticing little of his office other than a wall of bookshelves to his right and a huge map of the park replete with hand-drawn odd-shaped circles and ellipses delineating wolf pack boundaries, labeled with pack initials and written in dry erase marker, pinned to the wall directly behind him. A plaid shirt on a hanger is hooked to a high shelf of his bookcase. A large computer monitor sits on a credenza behind his back, and at times during our discussion he turns to it, locating visual aids to illustrate his words.

A scientist, Doug relies on observation and its resultant charts and graphs. But Doug is anything but dry and didactic; his tall, tightly muscled form is in constant motion, and his voice moves from exultation to solemn respect in split seconds. Doug eats an unpeeled carrot while we talk, occasionally dipping it into a pot of grainy brown hummus—lunch. His blue eyes flash and his chiseled jaw and cheekbones are unsettling in their rawness. A pure, male energy seated behind a desk, munching a carrot and explaining bar graphs. Although his intensity makes my nerves flutter, I wouldn't miss this for the world. This man knows more than anyone about the reintroduction of wolves to Yellowstone National Park.

"I'd always been light on the enjoyment aspect," Doug says. "But lately I've shifted from a wholly scientific view to seeing the human piece, the gift of nature to man and our need for that."

We discuss the story Doug and Gary Ferguson write of in *Decade of the Wolf,* about a wolf crossing the road one morning in Lamar Valley that stopped to stare at a park visitor who was sitting, roadside, in his wheelchair. Watching the interaction through his scope, Doug saw the wolf pause and make eye contact with the man, who, Doug says, was visibly moved. The inquisitive wolf, the curious human visitor, coming together in a moment that is likely to have forever changed the human. This, Doug says, is what national parks are all about. They are places created for human enjoyment, places where humans are offered the possibility to explore the magnificence of the natural world.

"Wolves are totemic, iconic. They are intelligent, capable, complex. There's much about them we don't know—we can't know—and we're intrigued by that. We have a desire to access this understanding."

Doug meets my eyes with his own, and his energy overwhelms me. Yet he has that plaid shirt hanging in his office. He's a plaid shirt guy.

I've known, ever since Bob and I divorced, that I have a love out there somewhere, and that he has a plaid shirt. Not a thick wool but a soft, well-worn flannel. A shirt that suits his gentle manner. In marrying Daniel I had decided he was that love—maybe not exactly my plaid-shirted vision—for how many of us can predict the person we end up loving? My eyes move to that shirt on its hanger. Doug is married, but I find the shirt curious. Maybe it's a sign along my path: don't give up, you get to have your plaid shirt guy. Either our marital therapy will work, or it won't, but regardless, there's a plaid shirt in my future. I drag myself back to reality, and ask how Doug's fascination with wolves began.

He was eleven or twelve, he says. Growing up in Wisconsin, Doug was not as distanced from wolves as most were in the 1970s: Minnesota, Wisconsin, and Michigan were the only states that hadn't exterminated wolf populations earlier in the century, keeping at least a few alive until 1960. At that point, all that remained were on Isle Royale, near the Canadian border, and in remote parts of Minnesota. Wolves lived only in truly wild places, stimulating dreams and fantastical visions in young boys' heads. Dangerous, powerful, magnetic, the wolf was mysterious, a thing of legend and folklore. Wolves to Doug were also symbolic of something greater: the scapegoat, the unloved. The unloved have a romantic allure—that ever-doubting piece within is inexplicably drawn to those who are looked down upon and persecuted for reasons that defy logic and offend sensibilities.

As a young man, Doug worked with wolves on Isle Royale under the tutelage of Rolf Peterson, one of the world's best known wolf researchers. Rolf was the first biologist to feed

Doug's growing passion for wolves. Doug has worked for the National Park Service since 1994, with wolves the entire time. He's continually researching wolf behavior: predation patterns, kill rates, social norms, the influence they have on elk herds in the park.

Doug has spent thousands of hours in planes, mostly in a tiny yellow Cessna, viewing thousands of wolves, and has spent countless hours hiking, tracking, and processing wolves for research purposes. Throughout his twenty years in Yellowstone, Doug has learned the stories of these wordless wild animals, stories he labels fascinating and enriching. Magical, even.

"When wolves are present they have this power to take control," Doug pauses and his hands are, for once, at rest. "You feel the power of the wolf blowing through."

Doug tells us that wolves in the more secluded packs act differently from those whose territories include well-traveled park roads, that their behavior patterns are much more complex, sophisticated. Wolf packs whose territories are well within park boundaries are substantially less likely to have a member killed by a hunter, affording greater stability in the pack's structure, which in turn allows for better communication, generational learning, and long term relationships. In other words, the less interaction with humans, the more effective and stable the family, or pack. Although the mother wolf cares for her pups almost solitarily for the first few weeks, the entire pack pitches in during the rest of the pups' early lives. Packs that lose members lose teachers and role models. It can create chaos.

Doug admits he's learned a few parenting tips from his study subjects.

"They're infinitely patient, and use positive reinforcement to shape behavior of the pups. They model behavior, they nudge the pups along, and they repeat this over and over again. Mothers, fathers, uncles, aunts, siblings—the entire pack participates in teaching the young ones how to be a wolf."

But the biggest lesson he's learned from the wolves is to never feel sorry for himself. Wolves are resilient, intelligent, and tenacious. He's seen a wolf with an obviously broken leg still take down and kill a bison. The wolf does what he needs to do to feed himself and his family. He doesn't dwell in self-pity.

I wonder what it's like to work with an animal that stirs such intense feelings, and I ask him how he balances the science, the conflicting viewpoints, and the politics.

"I believe very much in what I'm doing. I believe in the Park Service, in their mandate, which rests on the concept of preservation. I believe in the responsibility and mission of increasing understanding through research and connecting with this knowledge, using science as the underpinning of action." He also understands that people—the citizens, landowners, ranchers, farmers and hunters—who live on lands bordering wolf habitat have a legitimate concern about wolf populations. They want their voices heard. They want to know that they are a part of wolf management decisions.

"Extremists consider the wolf-reintroduction just one more form of government pushing policies down their throats, while most others sit somewhere between that position and a place of, Hell, if you make me deal with those damn wolves, how are you going to make it up to me? Few people who actually live in wolf-populated land are begging for looser control."

While he's first and foremost a scientist, Doug is also concerned about what he calls massive, seemingly unsolvable problems regarding wolves and humans. When I ask Doug if he ever gives up hope, he responds with a slight shrug, "Yeah, I do."

At present, wolves who step foot outside Yellowstone Park boundaries during hunting season are unprotected, a situation many find ludicrous. A buffer zone with limited hunting is one suggested compromise, coming from park personnel such as

Doug who find an unlimited hunt right up to the border to be counterproductive to the efforts of the National Park Service. Doug himself is a recreational hunter, and has no issue with hunting for food or even sport. But to kill wolves just because they're wolves is against everything he stands for. As Doug's Canadian colleague, author of *Wolves of the Yukon*, Bob Hayes states, "We've been killing wolves for a hundred years; let's try something else."

I need to try something else. I want to be a wild woman. To follow my passion, to take care of myself first, to speak my mind. Find my tribe. To not evoke descriptions dominated by the word nice. Nice is a fine trait, but wild and passionate means adventure and movement, a release of what's been contained, a heartswelling connection with soul. I've been moving toward wild for years, riding my bike through canyons and scrambling up red rock cliffs. The outer wild is gradually working its way inward, fueling my journey. I'm closer to releasing the wild creature who has always lived within me, who has always been told to behave herself—who has been crying to be let loose. She's of the earth, and of me. But she's been squashed.

Here in Yellowstone I'm entranced by one of the wildest things on our earth, an animal we tried and failed to tame, the wolf. During the last century, we wouldn't allow wolves to be part of our environment. Now people and organizations throughout the country are working to live in the same space with wolves. Wildness can coexist with my more tame self, just as wild creatures can coexist with humanity in the same landscape.

We look for wolves the next day, early morning, late in the evening. We see none.

2. lope

Snow lies thick on the ground, frozen on pine needles. She sleeps in a curl, nose tucked under tail. Her body warms her body. Last spring's pups are almost yearlings, nearly as large as Sophie. Almost capable of joining the hunt. Elk forage for food in the valley below. A calendar would say it's January, 2008. A map would place her in west-central Idaho, near the Sawtooth Mountains. And biologists would say she was a two-year-old female that belonged to the Timberline pack. Her stomach is full of yesterday's elk, and she rises on stiff legs, sniffing the air in the pre-dawn dark. She straightens her forelegs and bends chest to ground, her pelvis high. She arches her back and lifts her nose. She howls. The sound floats on the frozen air. It slips into the trees. Walking from pup to pup, she nudges shoulders. She nudges each yearling, her mother, her father. They sleep. She steps away. She moves into a trot, and runs steadily west.

She turns north, then west again. She traverses a mountain, arrives at a cliff. Far below, a river. Chunks of ice pile on both banks, and the swift water flows green under thin sheaves of ice growing in from the edges. She picks her way down, paws finding purchase on a rock, in a crevice, on a wind-buffed shelf. She reaches bottom and she swims the frigid river, its current pressing her body downstream. She hauls herself onto the frozen bank. Shakes. Water flies a dozen feet, freezing as it lands on snow, on deadwood tossed from the river, on the rocks that have tumbled down the cliff. Up. She climbs the other face of the deepest river gorge in the country, pausing only once to look back upon what she has left. A cartographer would label this Hell's Canyon, would neatly print Snake River on the twisting ribbon of blue. He would print Idaho on the right side, Oregon to the river's left. She continues west, then north, follows curves of land. The river here is less strident. She scents elk. She stops. A researcher for the Oregon Department of Fish and Wildlife would document her as one of the first wolves to step foot in Oregon in over sixty years, would know her river as the Imnaha. And when she finds her mate and gives birth to pups just months from now, the researcher will call her new family the Imnaha pack.

Green shoots crouch beneath winter-gray sage and shrub. A mist, white and translucent, rolls over a ridge, hovers, and disappears into the morning. Later the cloud of fog returns, then rolls away as I turn my back. It's June, but the fifty-degree weather feels like I'm in some mysterious, mountainous land where the inexplicable can happen at any moment. I'm in the Lamar Valley, searching a hillside of hummocks for coyotes.

"See that tree?" Pete says. "Follow that line to your left, where you see that green vale, then follow it up, about halfway up that sagebrush rise, then there's that little dirt patch; there's the den."

I find the tree easily, but the dirt patch eludes me. Pete's scope is mounted on a tripod, and he beckons me over. I put my eye to the eyepiece—squint the other shut—and lean close to eliminate peripheral light. Coyote pups seem to leap into existence from the grassy hillside, their light brown limbs tangling and separating and finally sorting themselves into six different bodies. They frolic, nip and push, halt, turn a head to an elder. They run and leave the frame of the scope, rendering the hill green once more. I turn from the scope and scrutinize the hillside. I try to find them unaided, and fail. I still can't find that dirt patch.

"They're out of sight again," I say, and Pete hops over to scan for the pups. He finds them within seconds, and adjusts the scope. He steps back, offering views to the rest of us.

We lucked into Pete this morning. Doug Smith had told me Pete was out here working with Rick McIntyre, somewhere. What Doug hadn't told me is that Pete Mumford is young, energetic, and gorgeous. Mark says he's a nice young man, but Kirsten and I have nicknamed him Jesus, for his curling longish blond locks, his piercing blue eyes, and his manner, gentle yet authoritative. Disciples would follow this man anywhere.

Those blue eyes are steadfast and focused as he responds to questions, and a few days' beard growth runs cheekbone to exquisitely formed chin. A thick headband holds back golden hair, sunglasses perched atop, and his acid green down-filled jacket shows a month's exposure to pollen, wind, and weather. His tan Carhartts are battle marked, and he wears brown-laced hiking boots and a communication device velcroed into the harness strapped across his t-shirt-covered chest. Slim-hipped with a skier's physique, lean and muscled, he radiates energy and enthusiasm.

A member of the Wolf Project team for only the past month, he describes his job much like McIntyre's, to help people see the wolves, to manage crowds and traffic situations when needed, and to stay on top of what's termed citizen science—opportunistic data collection from the near-constant supply of wolf watchers. (In addition to the daily crowd of wolf watchers who provide information, a number of wolf watchers use radios to communicate their sightings to Rick, providing location and behavior information that adds to Rick's immense collection of wolf observations.) A native New Yorker, Pete graduated Cornell in the winter of 2011 with a degree in Natural Resources, then moved west to work on a bison vegetation study in Yellowstone. The following winter he volunteered to help with the annual winter wolf study—he describes this animatedly, his arms up, hands pointing to his head and shoulders, "look, free labor"—and got his foot in the door.

I peek again at the coyote pups, then step back from the scope to let another watcher look. Squealing erupts on the hillside, a veritable yip-fest, and we all smile at each other.

As the yips fade I turn back to Pete and ask what he likes about being part of the Wolf Project team. His eyes grow huge.

"Are you serious? Who wouldn't be excited to be doing this? Wolves? For me it's the total package—they can run forty miles an hour, they're graceful, can go three weeks without food, they're amazing. The eccentricities in their dynamics keep us curious, and guessing, and what a great way to work."

Pete moves to the back of his truck and brings out his wolf-finder divining rod. He waves it around in every direction. The antenna searches for signals emitted by the collars that many of the park wolves wear. Each collar has a separate frequency, and Pete scans for the wolves of the Lamar Canyon pack. No beeps. The antenna goes back in the truck.

Pete talks science, biology, and his eyes lift skyward momentarily before he responds to my more politically probing questions.

"The work isn't about liking wolves—it's about law, and science, and best practice. Do you know the McKittrick story?" Pete asks.

"No," I shake my head.

"He shot one of the first collared wolves released in the reintroduction, Number 10, back in April of 1995. It was barely a month after the wolf and his mate had been released from their holding pen. The day before the shooting, Chad mired his truck on a muddy hillside where he'd planned to hunt for black bear. The next morning a friend helped him free the truck, but before they left the area they noticed a large animal uphill, some kind of canine. Chad grabbed his gun and even though his friend said hey, maybe it's a dog, Chad shot and killed the animal. They hiked up to the body, and when they reached Number 10 and saw the radio collar, they panicked. They dragged the body downhill, then unbolted the collar from the wolf's neck.

"Chad wants the skull and the pelt, so he skins the carcass and dumps the body in the brush. The friend wants Chad to turn himself in, promising to support the defense that it was an accident. Chad refuses. The friend worries about the collar, that it might still be transmitting, and eventually throws it in a creek not far from his home. He has no idea that these collars send a mortality signal if the wolf has stopped moving for a specific number of hours, nor that the collar is waterproof.

"Pretty soon McKittrick was caught, thanks to the radio collar—which was quickly located—and a few people who weren't willing to lie to protect him. He was charged and found guilty of killing a member of a threatened species, possessing its remains, and transporting those remains. After a few appeals, he finally served a three month sentence in 1999."

Pete tells the story matter-of-factly, but I hear what sounds like empathy for both sides. McKittrick was a barely employed, unsubstantially educated man who made a poor decision, and Yellowstone lost an animal on which they'd spent ten thousand dollars to bring into the park. The alpha female lost her partner, and numerous park and law enforcement personnel spent hours attempting to ameliorate the consequences of McKittrick's decision. It's part of wolf history in the park. McKittrick isn't evil and wolves aren't to be glorified. Interestingly, this case resulted in a Department of Justice directive—the McKittrick Policy—that requires prosecutors to prove that the defendant knowingly killed a protected animal. The word "knowingly" is at issue, its definition not clearly stated, which places a higher burden of proof on the prosecutor. As such, the policy has effectively hobbled prosecutors and drastically reduced the number of criminal prosecutions against people killing protected animals.

"This work is complicated. We have to balance protection with leaving the wolves alone, and we have to work with state and federal agencies, and people, too, ordinary people. As a scientist I can objectively approach wolf interactions. If a wolf were impacting my livelihood, my business, I'd want some kind of control. No matter our level of awe about them, there are limits to what we as a society can allow, can tolerate. I'm okay with that."

Pete has been steadily scanning the hillside. Coyotes howl from somewhere beyond sight, and we all fall silent, listening. Seconds later we hear an answering chorus, drifting toward us from another direction. The volley of howls and yips seems to suspend time, but it is over almost instantly. I ask Pete what else drew him to the study of wolves, besides their charisma.

"The complexity. The dynamics still aren't well understood, the lifestyle, pack organization. We know a lot, but not with certainty. Wolves, like us, are cultural learners. They pass knowledge down through generations. Each wolf in the pack plays a part in its social structure. A beta male may be the alpha male's brother and key lieutenant, while another brother might be the omega, bottom of the social ladder. Young adults often disperse to start their own packs. But when packs fall apart, like when an alpha gets killed, the structure doesn't work as well. Young wolves, without enough training, can get overly aggressive or go after livestock instead of sticking with what they know, elk and deer, wild game.

"There's always some surprise, something cool, something that makes you go wow, that was amazing. I'm curious, I like to learn, and they're always teaching us something new."

I release Pete to the rest of the wolf watchers, and turn away from the coyote hillside and toward the Lamar River. I inhale air from miles away, air that has traveled here over small valleys, skimming lake surfaces, rolling up mountain peaks and swooping down their craggy sides, leap-frogging over the bison by the river to brush past me before skimming the next rise of hillside. Sun-warmed, river-fresh. I've left my bicycle behind for three days now, and am operating at a lower frequency than usual, breathing in peace and breathing out tranquility. My day is structured only by the movements of the wolves that live in the canyon, the wolves that seem to be hiding from us this afternoon. There's a crinkled brown paper bag with two cinnamon rolls from the Bearclaw Bakery in the car and my water bottle is full. I look out at cranes high-stepping through marshy river edges. I am possibly the hundred millionth person to stand here and whisper, thank God this place exists.

Emerson's words echo: *the landscape belongs to the person who looks at it.* I possess this beauty, me alone, as I breathe it in and store it in my cells. I color it with my past, seeing mountains I skied as a girl, rivers I splashed through, meadows where I ran and swung on tree limbs. I place myself inside it all. I move into vrksasana, tree pose. I am balanced. A breath, two, five, then I become human again and walk back to the car.

I haven't always been balanced. I toddled like most children, and earned each bruise and scrape. As I grew I became more steady, learned to skateboard, ride a bike, ski. I earned a degree, worked a corporate job, got married. Stable, settled, tethered by a house and a bank account and a husband. And then the pregnancy, the loss, the death. I lost every bit of balance I'd ever possessed.

My feet are spread so far apart, I'm immobilized. One is planted in the cemetery—with Little Joe, and the other at the hospital—with Jake. I lose equilibrium with the slightest shift toward one or the other, and crash noiselessly into a netherworld. Grieving is impossible when I navigate by clinging desperately to a thread of hope.

On Jake's second day of life we're told he had a seizure during the previous night.

"A seizure?" Bob asks.

"Yes, so he's on phenobarbital to suppress them. But we have an ultrasound scheduled, they should be here soon with the machine." The nurse is small, short dark hair, olive skin. Her eyes are walls. She doesn't smile.

"An ultrasound?"

"They want to look at his brain. Seizures usually indicate some kind of injury to a section of the brain, so they want to look, see if they can determine why he had the seizure."

I look at Bob. I'm in my wheelchair again this morning. I cannot walk all the way from my room to the Newborn ICU. I have another heated blanket on my lap, a plastic band on my left wrist stating that I am the mother of Jake Imhoff. I do not have a band for Little Joe.

Each day in the newborn ICU is a week in normal life. I assume the babies in the incubators to be worse off than those under lights on warming tables, until I'm told the opposite is true: on a warming table the baby is available for immediate intervention should he or she suddenly retrogress. Crises erupt and resolve, blood is drawn, tests are performed, diagnoses pronounced and options presented. What is life-threatening in the morning can disappear by evening. What appears normal can indicate severe distress. And just when I think Jake is stable, I'm told of some new complication. He hasn't urinated, he might have necrotizing enterocolitis, he isn't alert enough. Hourly I'm presented with something new to absorb and incorporate. *You must keep hope.*

There is a room off the hallway with a single reclining chair and a machine that pumps milk from my breasts. I hide here.

Alone in this room I am protected from beeps and severe expressions, from bad news, from terror of the unknown, from others.

Sympathy pours toward me, and I can't bear it. *Believe. Hope.* Each expression demands a reaction I can't give because I am hollow.

Why are you keeping him alive, my mother asks. The fury of my netherworld leaps from me, pulsing, and shoves itself between the two of us. I don't know who this woman is. Jake is keeping himself alive. His heart beats, his lungs compress and expand, his stomach digests, his kidneys filter. I say nothing.

I see pain darken the green of her eyes. My mother doesn't believe in medical heroics. But she's never given birth to a preemie, and she doesn't understand that there's nothing heroic about feeding and keeping warm a newborn baby boy—even a baby boy who's suffered cerebral hemorrhages in both hemispheres of his brain. Bleeds, they're called. A grade IV in his left, a grade III in his right. There's nothing heroic about this. Nothing heroic about placing one foot in front of the other. Feeding and changing diapers, cradling and kissing my baby, hoping and praying—all while operating almost by rote, my entire belief system in pieces, my sense of self in shards.

I sit with eyes closed on the wooden deck that runs along the entry doors of the Elkhorn Lodge in Cooke City, Montana. Clear skies brought a brisk morning and a cool day, and I welcome the slender slice of sunlight hitting my body. The hill before me is naked and yet covered with trees: these are trees that burned during the town's terrifying fire of 1988, trees that stand tall, lean precariously, and lie on the ground, dead, none able to leave this death knoll. The sun is ready to drop below the mountains though the sky remains bright on this June evening. Tomorrow morning we leave Yellowstone. Part of me will stay here, just like these trees. Will eventually decompose, will become part of the soil. Will give life to what comes next.

And how much of this landscape will come with me when I leave? I look within, searching for wild, for what's been reignited. And suddenly I'm thinking of Daniel, our relationship flat, lifeless. I see us in our house, in shorts and t-shirts, a project.

I am on a stepladder. I jam the putty knife under a corner of paper, shove it up, between wall and ancient wallpaper paste. The grasscloth is dated, has been on the foyer walls for decades. I'd lived with it for six years, and am excited that Daniel and I are stripping it, replacing the bumpy, stringy stuff with smooth, taupe paint. It hadn't been easy to settle on a color. Daniel wanted the sage green gone—he thought my house entirely too green—and we'd tried eighteen shades of gray-tan-beige before finally choosing this taupe. He and his fifteen-year-old son had moved into my house when we married a few months before. I'd lost more of my space than just that inside closets and cupboards.

He preps an un-papered wall, I soften old glue and scrape dusty paper from another era.

"I was stripping old wallpaper the week that Jake was born," I say.

"Oh?"

"This puts me back there—I haven't scraped old wallpaper in a long time. I'd taken a week off work, and was just home, nesting I suppose."

I pause between sentences, sometimes between words.

"I'd had an ultrasound a few days before, and on that Monday morning my doctor called, told me he wanted me to have a non-stress test to check on the babies. They were concerned about the growing size discrepancy. I said sure, any day, I'm off all week. He suggested Thursday. I said okay."

I scrape distractedly. I tear a strip of stringy paper free, and toss it in the trash pile before continuing.

"I hung up the phone, climbed back onto the stepladder, and kept scraping. And then by Thursday, Little Joe had died, and then on Saturday Jake was born. Wallpaper will probably always put me right back there."

"Mm." He tapes his wall. I sit.

Silence.

I don't need much, but I need more than an "mm." His back is to me and I watch him stretch, measure, press blue tape against the ceiling. He finishes that corner and moves to the next wall. I sit on my stepladder. Then I scrape some more. I squeeze my eyes against the tears.

Three months later, I bring it up when we begin therapy, how I'd hoped for some supportive words, some display of empathy. Oh, he says. I didn't know you wanted me to say anything.

The therapist suggests I'd given Daniel a "love test," expecting him to know what I wanted. Instead of simply asking.

We leave Cooke City after buying another bag of cinnamon rolls and sticky buns at the Bearclaw Bakery. We head west, a final drive through Lamar Valley, then on to Missoula. Our eyes are peeled for wolves. Mark brakes for bison, for black bears, for tourists who are too focused on taking pictures to think about driving. We get stopped by bear jams: tourists pausing half-way and no-way off the road to watch a bear amble, munch berries, or otherwise occupy itself within sight of a road. An eagle soars over Soda Butte River. A deer hides in an aspen copse, his antlers sliced by the tall, narrow trunks.

Once outside the park, we pick up speed, dry brown land changing to lush hillsides of greening shrub and tree as we enter Paradise Valley. Voluptuous growth. Delicate lady's slippers and thunderous sequoias. Creatures both meek and predatory. Hares. Wolves. Pounding waterfalls, deer and bears and muskrats. Wilderness, untrammeled, roadless. And border lands, where roads snake through wildness, where we're allowed glimpses of creatures in their own spaces. Places where I pedal my bicycle as dawn breaks, letting the world seep into my consciousness.

It's slightly before five and predawn hovers, resting on the surface of the road and rising upward as far as I can see until it touches the remnants of a night sky, Venus hanging low, a flare of light just a finger, maybe two, above the hills at the mouth of the canyon. The birds are wide awake, exchanging messages, declaring their intentions for the day, and I am an interloper, eavesdropping. This portion of the world is dark and asleep yet wildly vibrant. Dew-moistened grass is slick and the breeze rustling over it releases a wet whisper that I hear beneath the slapping of tree leaves and the creak of weakened branches soon to be torn from limbs by the next violent windstorm. The early mornings here are always blustery, the cool air rushing down-canyon into the warmer city. By mid-morning the pattern reverses as the heat of the city searches for escape and pushes its way up between the sloping canyon walls. But I ride during the dawning of the day, wind against my body, clapping the flag's thick white cord against the flagpole at the top of the street just before the canyon's entrance, warning me that I will have to work hard these next six miles before the sweeping switchback in the canyon places the wind at my back.

I hear the water crash over the rocks of the creek bed—I cannot see it—just as I hear a critter, a squirrel or a magpie, move through the coarse undergrowth beside the road. I've barely entered the canyon, am no more than half a mile in, and everything inside me has shifted. The two miles I've ridden to reach the canyon mouth are urban, the roads mildly steep and most houses midnight dark. With entry into the canyon my world becomes wild and untamed, the grasses high and irregular, the hillside artistically barren then lush. I breathe better here.

I round a curve and approach the spot I once heard coyotes howl. I was new to riding, new to the canyon's predawn milieu. I'd heard the howl—a brief one—then immediately convinced myself I hadn't, when another howl tumbled down the hillside. I sucked in a breath. I was spooked. No streetlamps dot this two-lane road, no fence runs resolutely along the shoulder. Not a single house sat within a mile of me in either direction. Coyotes won't attack me, of course not. I'm much too big. But shivers flew up my spine, the way they do when a wild animal's howl leaps from the dark and you are solitary, exposed, ignorant of what wild creatures truly are.

I pedal past the spot of those long-ago howls—it's been five years since that morning—and follow the curve of the road. It rained last night and every fragrance is intensified, released and flung by brush and shrub. I inhale deeply, relish the mix of all I do not know. I am the happy wanderer. I don't need to know the name of every plant and bird and tree. I learn a few more each year, research new sightings, try to single out a unique bird call and determine its owner. I temporarily name what I do not know but intend to learn: full-petaled yellow flower in bunches, gnarled trunk twisted brown tree. Ah, arrowleaf balsamroot, a bristlecone pine. I'm often torn between making up my own name for a thing, and researching its official name. Naming is an act of creation, of possession, an act that forges a bond. But even in learning a name bestowed by someone else, I tighten the connection. The purple-red reed-like shrub in thick bunches I love—they line creek banks, they are munched by moose—the separation between us evaporates when I learn its name: ah, red twig dogwood.

As I ride I search the hillside to my left, a meadow on my right, combing the tall grass for an indication of life, a brown back, movement not attributable to wind. I anticipate a call, a throaty bark, a deep whistle or a delicate scampering through dry twigs. Wildlife is here. But the rare appearances of the deer—four foraged by the roadside yesterday, a doe hurrying along three smaller companions, their coats mangy and uneven in this late spring—the porcupine, the raccoon, tell me either that I must begin earlier, before rays of sunlight begin lighting the world, or that wildlife is better at watching me, than I it. How many sets of eyes might that be, hidden by thick trunks and fields of vibrant yellow balsamroot? The thoughtful hunter knows his quarry stalks him, just as he does it. I am a hunter of wildlife, but my weapons are none. A gently whispered good morning and my slowly moving body on a bicycle are the worst with which the deer and porcupine must contend. My hunting results only in my own deep gratitude for each brief sighting of bird or beast. And what do I miss when I blink, turn my head at the moment something flits by in the opposite direction? The more aware I become, the more I will see.

This canyon I claim is not my own but is Emigration Canyon, the Donner-Reed party's path of entry into the Great Salt Lake Valley, now speckled with homes. The road winds gently upward for eight miles before reaching the crest, long ago named Little Mountain. The final mile-and-a-half climb is uninhabited by humans, though parcels with water rights are for sale. Were I wealthy, I would buy them all so that the deer and owls, the rabbits and raccoons and hawks could retain their stomping grounds. From the summit on, the land is governed by multiple agencies—and one corporation—with plans and leases: two different counties, the federal government, Chevron, and a watershed. To my delight and benefit, the result of this confused management arrangement is a peaceful land devoid of homes.

Following the road down, now on the eastern side of the crest, I coast toward Little Dell Reservoir, a body of water barely large enough to kayak or canoe in—perhaps a mile from dam to distant shore and a quarter mile across. I sometimes see a fisherman quietly contemplating life or nothing at all as his line dangles into the gray or blue or green water, depending upon the clouds, the sun, the fickle wind. Some days the reservoir is Caribbean blue at its edges, other days it is glass-like, mirroring the pine-covered hillside to the south. Wind can chop its surface into millions of white caps. Predawn mornings render it glossy and iridescent as a gray pearl.

In the hollow of a curve halfway down, between summit and reservoir, deer graze then hearken, heads lifting, eyes alert. A moose munches willows in the pocket where snowmelt collects in the spring, and I grin in delight as rabbits and chipmunks dash across the road before me. A few summers ago I saw fox kits, leaping and jumping upon each other, full of energy and mischievousness in this same hollow. Hawks swoop and soar, and the rare peregrine falcon sits, regally, in a stark gray tree not yet lush with spring's buds. My soul is damn happy, awash in a delight that springs loose and bubbles to my surface.

After riding past the reservoir, I skirt over dirt around the edge of a still-locked snow gate and begin the climb up Big Mountain. I'm still following the path of the Donner-Reed party, yet in reverse. I continue east, an anti-pioneer emigration route.

While Little Mountain is beautiful and a beloved place to visit, Big Mountain is wild. Pine and aspen coat north-facing hillsides, while those that face south are sagebrush-speckled red rock and dirt. Hawks circle, porcupine amble, deer dart and bounce and hide behind willow and dogwood and gambel oak. It is at once arid and richly riparian. A beaver dam impedes the creek, its sticks, twigs, and logs gray, weathered, and organized in that complicated way only beaver know, instinctively, to arrange. Nests rest in meeting place of trunk and limb, and when

I pause to listen, at least one winged or fleet-footed critter is always calling or chattering. And all of this wildness I see from the two-lane blacktop road I travel. It is far from truly wild, yet more wild than any other place I intimately know. It is here I connect with something more genuine, more authentic, than almost any other piece of my life.

When the Mormon settlers walked and rode from the Midwest to Utah, they determined the best route into the Salt Lake Valley to be one that the Donner-Reed party had broken in 1846, a path that led from the Wyoming territory south and west through Echo Canyon. The pioneers then traveled up a long, rather gentle grade to a hill called Hogsback—a short, steep climb and descent. Next came a few miles of creek-laced path, until Big Mountain jutted into view. The final trial. The name came from Shoshone who lived nearby, and was uttered with respect. At its base they circled left, choosing the most manageable path up the side of the steep, dramatic ridge. For the next half century, wagon tracks dug deep into the earth were scars traveled by those who followed. Today the hillside is brush-covered, those tracks all but healed, and a paved road climbs a different face of the mountain. At the mountain pass, 7,400 feet above sea level, the original pioneer path and the tarmac meet in a graveled parking lot where cyclists and motorists often pause to absorb the view. Hill after hill fall away, each layered with growth both ancient and new. As far as one can see to the east, the south, the west, statuesque mountains—snow-capped peaks luminous for much of the year—rim the horizon.

At Big Mountain's crest, the pioneers tied logs to the backs of handcarts and wagons. They descended a steep ravine that wound past rocks and trees, the descent easing after a tense mile. Logs were removed. They could now proceed downhill without fearing gravity's speed would spill or overturn their carts.

Today's two-lane road takes a different route down, switching back and forth, hairpin turning a time or two or three. Red dirt hillsides, scrub oak, grasses as tall as my waist. Tightly woven nests hide in branches, creek water trickles over mossy rock. It is this, the western side of Big Mountain, that I cycle up and down most often, that fills me with wonder, that I still consider wild. Half of the year, the top six miles on either side of the pass are gated and closed—no winter maintenance. These months, from late November to mid-May, are the months I find myself most in love with Big Mountain. I am often the only human on the road, surrounded by the intensely un-quiet quiet of this environment that is almost untouched, whether astride a bicycle before snow buries the road, or on snowshoes or skate skis once the asphalt disappears. No, Big Mountain isn't truly wild, but it's the closest thing to wild that I'm able to access an hour away, by bicycle, from home.

Mark is driving again, and we're miles northwest of Yellowstone, far outside park boundaries, traveling through a state that loves, hates, and spends a great deal of time and energy managing wolves. Montana.

Snow-tipped mountains edge the plains, their valleys rocky and steep. The road rises through a pass chiseled into umber rock. Where sheer faces aren't exposed, where soil has burrowed into cleft and crevasse, the hills sprout green. Grasses, brush, pine, leafy aspen. Soon Hellgate Canyon winds narrow, each larch-covered hillside leaning into us. Sunlight barred, duskiness presses as we drive alongside the tumbling Clark Fork River and cross the Blackfoot River's crashing core. I suppress my breath. Around the bend light shatters the gloom and Missoula beckons. Rooftops glint. I blink. We cross the Clark Fork again, again, each time whetting my appetite. We hug a brown dust hillside, then exit the freeway and enter a city that borders land inhabited by more than forty packs of wolves.

The next afternoon, Mark, Kirsten, Liz Bradley, and I are in Montana Fish, Wildlife and Parks' tiny Missoula office building, in the conference room because Liz's office is so packed with desks, chairs, and cabinets that there isn't room for all of us. We sit in large wheeled chairs around a boat-sized table, the space behind each of our chairs only enough to squeeze through, one hip against chair, the other touching wall. Wolf packs, forty-five of them, are depicted on the large wall map by black stars. Liz is one of six wolf biologists in the state. Her job is partially funded by the federal government, a funding stream that will be phased out in 2015, as dictated by state and federal agreement.

A tall brunette with straight, shoulder-length hair, Liz is athletic and unpretentious. If she's wearing makeup it's invisible. However, I'm not sure of her real feelings about anything we discuss. Liz says the bulk of her job consists of outreach and education in an effort to help people adjust to the 2011 law that removed wolves in Montana from the endangered species list. With the delisting came management plans that include hunting and trapping. And a lot of politics. But Liz isn't worried about the wolves' overall numbers.

"Wolves have great long term viability—they breed quickly, and travel great distances. They're going to continue spreading, they're going to survive."

"What about the hunters? They are quite vocal in their opposition—do they have a valid argument? Do ranchers?" I ask.

"As for the effect on the total game population, there have been local impacts, for sure. Wolves are a part of that. We've added one more mouth to feed out there. However, weather has an even greater impact on game populations, always has. You really have to look at every small area, case by case, before you can label the cause of the population change. We've gone through waves of panic, and of depredation—some cattle, sheep—but now things are settling a bit."

She speaks calmly and her statements are thoughtful, rational. It's difficult to imagine anyone on either side of the argument taking offense, or even disagreeing with her.

"What do you, though, Liz, think about wolves coming back onto the land?" I ask.

She makes it clear her response is personal, not Montana FW&P's position. "We're trying to make a place for wildlife on the landscape. To do that, we need to build tolerance for wolves, which means setting hunting and trapping guidelines, allowing that for hunters. There also has to be some control. Some way for ranchers to feel supported, heard. And we do all of this both for perception, and for real management needs."

I feel her walking a line, a line every state wildlife agency employee understands. She knows where her agency's funding comes from: hunting tags. Montana hunting and fishing licenses brought in forty-eight million dollars to the state in 2014. Liz knows it's hunters who provide the bulk of funding for her miniscule, overcrowded office, this cramped conference room with its exposed brick walls, and the helicopter which takes her out on observation and collaring missions, where she's able to actually put her hands on those loved, feared, and hated canines. She admits the department is missing input from wildlife lovers and watchers. Almost all of her interactions are with hunters and ranchers. Hunters who pay for her department's existence and ranchers who side with the hunters, at least as far as wolves are concerned.

I'm curious about the time she spends outside of these walls, away from paperwork and politics.

"I keep learning, all the time," she says, her eyes brightening. "I do observation flights frequently, counting wolves, counting pups. They really are charismatic—they're fascinating animals. And they share so many traits with humans—I think that's why we're so drawn to them. Collaring wolves is an experience without equal—there's nothing like it I've ever done in my life."

Doug Smith had described experiencing the same excitement Liz feels. After twenty years in the park, researching, studying, and processing wolves, he's never lost the thrill, that powerful response to seeing a wolf, let alone touching and working with one.

"What would it be like if wolves were to move into Utah, Oregon, Washington, Colorado, in a significant way?" I ask Liz.

"Going through the public uproar is just part of the process," Liz replies. "Most Montanans really value their landscape; they love the land and the wildness of it. Take the Bitterroot Valley, as an example. It's well-populated, diverse. Ranchers, hunters, retirees, people living in trophy homes—they're there because of the beautiful landscape. But you know, if you're going to live there, you won't be able to let your dog roam, or keep chickens out. When people feel that we as an agency are managing the wolves, it helps them create a better long-term approach to co-existence. If we're purely pro-wolf, they feel discarded. We need to let them know we understand their needs. We've been able to do great proactive work in the Blackfoot watershed, utilizing a range rider and other tools, because keeping ranchers around is really a community goal."

Doug had said the same thing, but shared concern about the "social carrying capacity," the level to which we as a society are willing to tolerate and live with wolves, and wondered if we've already surpassed it. When wolves were stripped of their protection in 2011 in Montana, Wyoming, and Idaho, liberal hunting regulations leapt into place. Already, close to two thousand wolves have been killed in those three states. Thirty-plus years ago they were labeled endangered, twenty years ago they were brought back and allowed to reestablish, and now the governments in states where they live are working hard to bring their numbers back down to the legally mandated minimum. In Montana, that's thirty breeding pairs. In Wyoming, outside of Yellowstone itself, ten. In Idaho, fifteen. In Utah, poised to deal with state management if the federal endangered species classification is terminated, that means two breeding pairs. Some people are in an uproar over this. Others want even more wolves killed. And then there are those who have reached their *caring* capacity, who are tired of the hubbub, who no longer really care about wolves at all. Some people are embittered, angry that their lives are affected by so many outside forces, and scapegoat the wolf. Some shy away from these controversies, overwhelmed by the shifting world—changes in climates and economies—believing the solutions are out of their hands.

Doug believes man and wolf can coexist. The problem, he says, is that not only do we compete for prey, but we are too similar. Wolves form life-long bonds, use highly sophisticated non-verbal communication, parent their young, make use of extended family, defend their territory, and are the top predators in their natural environment. Man's desire to be the hunter places him in direct competition with a powerful, competent creature. In some, Doug says, wolf hatred runs deep.

Unearthing the roots of today's anger toward wolves is something many, from Barry Lopez in his book *Of Wolves and Men*, to Doug Smith, have attempted to do. Ralph Maughan, who hosts the Wildlife News—a website chronicling wolf news from the start of the reintroduction in 1995 to the present day—believes he has one answer. He claims it wasn't until almost a decade into the restoration that a "militant anti-wolf narrative" developed, led by key politicians in wolf-recovery states, and some who aligned themselves with the Tea Party or similar anti-government groups. The wolf became a scapegoat for the recession, any decline in ranching economy, and the fact that a hunter was unable to track and kill his intended prey. Today, Ralph claims, what we see is cultural conflict. He argues that the current controversy over wolf restoration in the West is not really about wolves at all.

It's the end of Liz's work day, and she's stayed late just to talk with us. I don't believe I've accessed Liz Bradley's true feelings about managing wolves in Montana, but I realize she wants to keep her job. She likes working with wildlife, and it's clear that she loves working with wolves. Before we part, she bends forward, tucks a strand of hair behind her ear, and rests her elbows on her thighs. She leans into her words.

"The most important thing we can do today is have our children develop a love and appreciation for the natural world. Once that's established, the rest of the decisions come easy."

Not so very long ago there was a mountain. As mountains go it fell somewhere between Sagarmatha—Nepal's Goddess of the Clouds—and Magazine Mountain, a bump in the flats of Arkansas. It was an ordinary mountain, unnamed and taken for granted by all who lived upon or traveled its sloping sides. That number was significant, from insects and earthworms burrowing in its soil to the bushy-tailed foxes in their earthen dens to the red-tailed hawks and robins, warblers, thrushes, and hummingbirds whose nests dotted the aspen whose roots hugged each other deep below the pine-needle- and brown-leaf-covered soil. At the seam where the mountain met another, where the creek flowed, lived a beaver colony, replete with fish and frogs, water striders, bluebirds, mallards, grebes, and songbirds, whose voices soared from the glade.

If we were to count the flowers, the penstemon, the lupine, all of the balsamroot and Indian paintbrush and wild hollyhock, the lives supported by the mountain would climb to numbers we can barely comprehend. Thick with conifers, aspen, scrubby oak, the occasional twisted and gnarled juniper, the undergrowth is springy and green, gathering sunrays filtered by towering trees. Last fall's leaves and needles carpet the soil which is rocky, nutrient rich, bustling with insects and earthworms that tunnel and commune.

This mountain hosts visitors as well. Those who come to graze, to find sustenance. Those who come to hunt. Those who come to die. Deer, elk, moose, these solid thick-haunched creatures find plentiful saplings, willow growth, grasses, and plants. Hawks, ravens, turkey vultures, and eagles circle above the mountain, searching out what has died. And the mountain welcomes its top predator, the wolves that trot along its flanks and edges, the wolves searching for the wounded deer, the weary elk, the very young, the old.

This is Aldo Leopold's mountain, the one that need not fear its deer, its elk, for it is a mountain well-familiar with the howl of a wolf. It is a mountain in natural harmony, full of life, full of death. Decomposition begets new life, the mountain active in each step of the circular process. Leopold, considered by many a father of the conservation movement, described an ecological ethic that resonates with me for its simplicity and inclusive view of the universe. His land ethic

> . . . simply enlarges the boundaries of the community to include soils, waters, plants, and animals, or collectively: the land . . . a land ethic of course cannot prevent the alteration, management, and use of these 'resources,' but it does affirm their right to continued existence, and, at least in spots, their continued existence in a natural state. In short, a land ethic changes the role of Homo sapiens from conqueror of the land-community to plain member and citizen of it. It implies respect for his fellow-members, and also respect for the community as such.

On Leopold's mountain I share responsibility. Flora and fauna are rife with cellular knowledge telling them how to grow, how to behave, how to participate. Because this is my home, too, I am obligated to sink into my deeper self, to connect with my own cellular knowledge that guides me to think and behave in ways that benefit the earth. I deserve to live among richly varied, healthily functioning, glorious, green mountains, and I accept accountability for their health. I know I am one part of a brilliantly complex, interrelated existence.

Leopold suggested it possible to view the earth as a coordinated whole, its parts—oceans, land, crust, atmosphere, and so on—similar to the organs of a body, each having its own, definitive function. In the 1970s, decades after Leopold's death, chemist James Lovelock took this a step further and presented his Gaia principle, a theory suggesting our planet was indeed a self-regulating, complex system formed by organisms—biota—interacting with their inorganic surroundings. Joseph Campbell, one of the world's foremost authorities on mythology, challenged the biblical condemnation of nature, instead seeing man as part of nature, embracing the Gaia principle. He viewed the entire planet as a single organism, human beings as of the earth, the consciousness of the earth. Campbell was adamant that we must learn to again be in accord with nature, to "realize again the brotherhood with the animals and with the water and the sea."

I am neither biologist, nor chemist, nor naturalist. Nor mythologist. I've never called myself an environmentalist. Politically I often sit on a buck rail fence—I picture my pigtailed ten-year-old self perched there—leaning left but never hopping completely off my perch. I pay taxes. I vote. I use canvas bags at the grocery and turn lights off when I leave a room. I compost coffee grounds and vegetable peelings. But my yard is not xeriscaped, and I don't drive a hybrid.

I care deeply about this earthen world, and passionately about my own small section of it. I ride my bike through canyons and mountain passes in the West that retain some of their wildness. Before daybreak the canyon is dark and mysterious, filled with birdsong, scamperings, chirping, and the silence of a hawk floating through the air, its body silhouetted against a lightening indigo sky. A great horned owl family lives above a bend in the road, and I honor the path where deer cross from eastern hillside to the hollow across the tarmac. The hillside covered in gambel oak where each year I float some of Jake's ashes is sacred.

I don't want to lose one scintilla of this experience. I know I am one with the earth. I've been riding and hiking canyons and mountain passes for years, taking for granted that they will be here for me. That more cabins will appear and a road might be widened, but that overall, these canyons will retain their wildness and bounty. And that wildness includes top predators. Grizzlies and wolverines and mountain lions. Wolves.

Most Americans know wolves only through fairy tale, fable, and myth, and more recently, through the controversy raging over their status as a protected, endangered species, their reintroduction in 1995, and their loss in 2011 of protected status in portions of many western states. We don't know what it's like to live with wolves, but according to polls and surveys, we want them back on the landscape. Whether because we want to hear their howls or because we find them to be charismatic creatures or because we believe they have the right to exist, the majority of us want them back. And they are coming back; the question now seems to be, for how long?

Those who don't want wolves on our landscape are fierce and vocal. Many are backed by well-funded organizations such as the National Cattlemen's Beef Association and the Rocky Mountain Elk Foundation. Stories and fables proliferate, some growing more fantastical as time passes. Facts are bandied about, figures abused. What began in 1966 with the first Endangered Species Preservation Act and manifested in 1995 as a reintroduction of an extirpated species has deteriorated into, at times, a playground battle of name calling, rumors of conspiracies, and figurative if not actual fisticuffs. Legislators vote for increased control, even when state wildlife departments have data proving wolves kill few domestic animals, and reduce prey animals by almost statistically insignificant numbers. Hunters and their organizations argue that wolves are reducing elk numbers, without controlling for weather, where the land is in terms of fire cycle, and other predators on the land. Disheartened, I've studied pictures of men, many triumphantly holding bloody wolf carcasses, one posing in front of a wolf whose leg is caught in a trap, a ten-foot circle in the snow stained pink with its blood.

A century ago we shot, poisoned, and trapped wolves out of existence. *We've always done it this way* is not a justification for abusive practices, whether that abuse is of animals, of other humans, or of the land. We live in an era filled with new discoveries and understandings of that which surrounds us: scientists point to plastics, coal, and toxic wastes as destroyers of our air and land's ability to support us. Fewer trees and less soil mean decreased carbon sequestration. A warmer earth is killing polar bears and pika. To close our eyes and ears to these understandings is both foolish and harmful, and I believe we are too smart, too creative, too capable to continue ignoring good science. When we can find wilderness—even small spots of wildness— and become still, we better understand the importance of our surroundings. We can better hear our conscience.

Humans have always changed and will continue to change the landscape. Historically, Euro-Americans annihilated humans and animals that were in the way, justifying their actions from a platform of "white man was meant to rule." We now face consequences—ecosystems in disequilibrium; a thinning ozone; landfills overflowing with refuse that takes hundreds of years to break down, while leeching toxic chemicals as it does—resulting from that stance. Having wolves back on the landscape won't change the economy, will probably not save the rainforests. It won't stop new fossil fuel extraction, and won't solve water issues in the West. But it is a correction. An apology.

Liz Bradley knows all of this. The history, the current political environment. But her parting words are of hope, echoing Leopold's conviction. Love and appreciation of the natural world guides us toward better decisions.

We're in Montana, and I want to look for wolves, not just talk about them. But we've run out of time. I will return in the fall to explore the Blackfoot Watershed, a community of ranchers, with a range rider. I picture a ruggedly handsome man on a horse, clad in chaps and a big old hat. He slouches in his saddle, crow's feet crunching, the anticipation of a smile dancing on a corner of his mouth. He is dauntless. He searches the watershed for wolves. He gallops over fields and moseys up draws, protecting sheep and cattle from predatory canine teeth, bared and sharp. Out there, somewhere, are wolves.

3. den

Ice recedes at the river. Days grow longer. Sophie gives birth to two pups in her scooped and sculpted earthen hollow. Soon one no longer breathes. She digs a hole. She buries her pup. It will not be eaten by other predators. Another male wolf joins their small pack; they are now four.

Ice builds again, then retreats. Sophie gives birth to six pups— three male, three female—and the pack explodes to ten. A small gray-brown male searches the den, sniffing, pawing, yellow eyes gleaming. Green grasses grow tall, shadows short. Yellow Eyes follows the breezes, a hare's musky scent, nose in the air then to the ground. A spotted snake stops him, hissing, snapping. He jumps and runs back home. The days lengthen. Yellow Eyes trails a red fox kit, a ground squirrel. A magpie crashes through branches, wind sends leaves tumbling. Nose twitching, he runs, captivated, a hundred different scents competing for his attention. His mother's howl sings in the distance. He turns, the sound guiding him home.

The Tetons hold snow like treasure, buried under overhangs, beneath trees, in shadowed gullies. Sheer cliff faces are cold, gray stone. Some drip black with snowmelt. Jagged edges slice the air and mirror what within me is rough, defiant. We're suspended eleven thousand feet above sea level, and the highest crags thrust another thousand feet into the sky. Jackson lies a vertical mile below the belly of our plane. Mark speaks into his headset and Kirsten responds, a muffled blur of sound. I cannot speak, a bubble of awe in my throat. The three main peaks of the Grand Tetons—Grand Teton, Mount Owen, and Teewinot—are the loudest of the range. Its other voices are no less resonant, though, and as we float, I see the sinew connecting them, the vales, the ridges of bone. The discordance gives rise to harmony, and I want to remain here, in this air, beside this massive disruption of earth.

Two hours later the wheels of the Piper Cherokee touch the Salt Lake City runway, and we chug to a stop by the hangar. We unload, pack everything into the back of Mark's wagon, and slide my bike on top of it all. I'm headed home.

There are two in there, she says. I immediately accept this, as if I'd known these past four months that I'm carrying twins. It's February, 1991. Bob leaps up in delight, dances around the darkened ultrasound lab. The technician moves her wand, clicks the mouse, measures, labels. You can clean off your tummy, she says, I'm all done. Bob hugs me and helps me sit; he's glowing. I feel a bit larger than I did before.

They're identical, and one is just a smidgen smaller than the other. Unusual in identicals, but not worrisome. They'll keep an eye on it, and compare the discrepancy with next month's ultrasound. I christen the big one Hoss, the smaller, Little Joe. I loved Bonanza.

The size disparity increases over the next two ultrasounds, but by the time I'm asked to come in for a test, Little Joe's heartbeat is gone. He'd kicked the night before, perhaps performing his final somersault. The following day my body begins laboring, and at just shy of thirty-two weeks, my twin boys are born. Hoss is whisked to the ICU while I hold Little Joe. He is tiny, a few ounces over three pounds. He is dusky, no oxygen to blush his skin. His eyes, behind closed lids, must be blue, like Jake's. I cradle him against me, tears flow. The obstetrician flicks her needle back and forth, repairing my skin, and, when she's done, touches my knee. Tells me the nurse will take Little Joe when I'm ready. Ten minutes, twenty. I eventually release him to Bob, who hands him to a nurse, who carries him to the bowels of the hospital where his small, human form will be collected by the mortuary. We name Hoss, Jake, and name Little Joe, Joseph: he was going to be Andrew, but we've only ever known him as Little Joe.

I'd been in labor all night, and delivered the boys at nine on a gray, rainy morning. The loss, the death, the shock took my voice, took everything I thought I knew about myself and smashed it into pieces, then scattered them throughout the universe, laughing, daring me to find and collect them, to glue them back into a mosaic that might possibly, in small ways, resemble the me I used to be. Pieces float out of reach. Trust. Control. Lightheartedness. Wild abandon. Even today I continue to find small pieces of myself in unexpected places: dancing on a lake surface, looking suspiciously like moonlight. In the flick of a mule deer's ear. In the eyes of my friend whose wife is gradually, almost imperceptibly, being paralyzed by ALS. I add these back, I fill in. I can live with a shattered heart. Like Doug's wolves, I, too, can run with a broken leg.

Four days after the delivery, we stood in the cemetery, the winter-matted grass still dotted with snow. Family, the closest of friends, two dozen of us staring at Little Joe's grave. Bob handed a white rose to each while I stood in a summer dress, arms wrapped around myself. Then we climbed into our car, and drove back to the hospital.

I return home from our Yellowstone and Montana trip the second Saturday in June. I drag my bags into the house I love, put my bicycle in the garage, leave the garage door open. Daniel and I hug hello, exchange a kiss. I look into his amber eyes, see a reflection of myself—wary, self-protective. I go to our room and change into biking clothes. He sits on a stool, in the kitchen. "Do you want to come?" I ask. "I need to head up Emigration."

"No, thanks," he says. "I've already been out, rode a little this morning."

Transitions are difficult for me. This time I arrived home filled with longing for a closer connection to the land, to my earth goddess self. I'd spent a week away from everything I knew, and found that I was more comfortable in those foreign spaces than I was in my own home. My den. My disrupted den. I needed to visit my canyon.

Early in my first marriage I learned to decompress, alone, for ten or fifteen minutes after coming home from work. I was a buyer for Nordstrom, a position, it was said, that ate people like me for lunch. The more cutthroat you were, the more often you were promoted. I had climbed up the food chain by working an associate attorney's hours, by always saying yes, and by learning to ignore pain and disappointment. I carried our medical insurance. It was less expensive than what Bob—a financial analyst—could provide. The coverage was excellent. It covered most bills from my pregnancy, even from the operating room delivery. And when the newborn ICU bills started flowing in, I used a notebook to track what they allowed, what they paid, and what I owed. Neat lines tracked the dollars and cents, columns representing needle sticks, blood draws, monitoring machines, nursing care, assessments from neonatologists, ophthalmologists, pulmonologists, gastroenterologists. The warming table, the incubator. And to keep this insurance, I would keep working. Jake had a preexisting condition, and Bob's company medical policy would not insure him. After my leave, I would head back to my job to keep our family covered. I'd hire a nanny, someone to care for Jake while I was gone.

At the time, I didn't know much about wolf behavior, that the breeding female of a wolf pack is known as the alpha, and that it is often the alpha female who directs the activities of the pack. It is she who chooses her mate and searches the landscape to find the right location for her den, then grows and gives birth to the next generation of hunters. As soon as she has recovered from delivery, she leaves her pups behind with uncles, older siblings, sometimes even the alpha male, while she hunts the rabbits, the elk, the bison, the moose, that will feed her pack. I'm hardly the only mother to head off to work.

The Inuit are one of many indigenous populations who rely on an oral history to teach new generations about the past. One of their folk tales is beautifully illustrated in Tim Jessell's *Amorak*. In a fable of the beginning of the world, the Great Spirit tells the first woman to cut a large hole into the ice of the land. She does, and out of this hole come the animals, one after another, the bears and the seals, the snowy owl and the wolverine, the arctic hare, the red fox and the arctic fox, the lynx and the great auk, and lastly, the caribou. The Great Spirit tells the woman that of all the creatures the caribou is the most valuable, for it will be the animal to provide sustenance and warmth for the people of the land. And this grows to be true, as the caribou population flourishes. The children of the first woman hunt the caribou, obtaining meat to eat and skins to be made into clothing and coverings. The children hunt the biggest and best of the caribou, leaving the ill, the elderly, the small. And soon, the caribou population weakens, with the small producing more small caribou and the weak and ill creating more weakness and illness. One night the first woman asks the Great Spirit what they might do to return the caribou to health so that good meat and skins might again bless them. The Great Spirit tells the woman to return to the ice, to the hole she had made, where she will receive the answer. When she returns to that spot, she sees a great and beautiful animal coming from the hole; it is the wolf, *amorak*. Here, says the Great Spirit, is the animal who will hunt the caribou, taking the ill, the small, the weak. The wolf will keep the caribou healthy so that you and your children will again benefit from what they can give you. And thus the wolf ranges the land, raising pups and teaching them their role in keeping the caribou herd strong, playing their part in the way of the world.

This fable provides insight into the connectedness of the natural world, and suggests that humans may not always possess the innate wisdom they imagine. We are of the earth, but our tendency to overuse and destroy is so robust it overpowers our knowledge of that oneness. Instead of killing only enough buffalo to feed us, and letting them repopulate to feed us again, we shoot them to near extinction. We dam rivers, impeding or blocking salmon migration and decreasing spawning grounds, until events like the Klamath River fish kill of 2002 occur—sixty-five thousand dead adult salmon. We allow domestic cattle to trample streambeds, destroying habitat and food for uncountable wildlife populations. Wisdom about living on the land comes from time spent listening to, watching, and learning from the landscape. Sage advice comes from indigenous peoples, and is found even in fable and myth. Scientists propose action based on data collection, research outcomes. Philosophers consider morality, the ethics of behavior. My greatest strength as a human being is the ability to listen to all of these—the sage, the scientist, the philosopher—and to change my behavior when I learn that I should. To commune with the earth, to return to the hole in the ice, to welcome a new ally.

In 1982, The Talking Heads recorded a song called "This Must Be the Place." Not a hit at the time of release, it has since grown in popularity, now covered by a handful of other bands and a staple on classic alternative rock playlists. An anything-but-typical love song, it has one particular line that hooks me: *home, is where I want to be, but I guess I'm already there.* This line speaks two truths: home as a craving, and paradoxically, home as something that can be found anywhere. Home to me is sanctuary, the two words synonymous, and I am a ruthless protector of this space. In my sanctuary love is the foundation. Peace reigns. And expressed moments of frustration are accepted and forgiven. While most Americans reside in just a handful of homes during his or her lifetime, I am on my nineteenth. Dorm room, squished apartment, sprawling rambler on a hillside. What makes home *home* for me are soft places to curl up and read, private spaces and, ideally, nooks and crannies where surprises hide: a stack of themed books, a clock made of bicycle parts. Table and floor lamps. Framed family photographs perched in bookshelves and on tables and on dressers and on a wall or two or five. Books, everywhere, neatly aligned or haphazardly stacked, and rugs, soft and thick. Home has a strong roof and locking doors and windows that raise and lower to capture breezes and keep out rain and bitter cold. Home is safe for feelings and thoughts, and safe for its accoutrements and occupants. It is a place for respite, for rest, for eating. For nurturing, loving, creating, working, playing, sharing, being. Home expands outward to the yard with its flowers, trees and grasses, and the neighborhood. Home spreads up the hill and down the street and on a day when the sky is heavy with clouds, rain falls, and a rainbow pokes from hillside to distant valley, the entire city is home and my heart expands to encompass it all.

The deer, the elk, the beaver, squirrel, and coyote—all creatures have their own versions of home. Tunnels in the ground that open into dens, or acres of wildness. Aldo Leopold wrote—which strikes me in the heart—that wilderness areas are a series of sanctuaries. Sanctuaries, places of the natural world, places of peace and growth. However, the greatest difference between the homes of wildlife and those of humans is in their level of safety. The deer has no lock, the elk has no walls. Wildlife is constantly threatened by predators, humans near the top of that list. We are constantly intruding and encroaching upon traditional homes that belong to wildlife, forcing these creatures to live in increasingly smaller areas. We take, we confine. We call it hunting, we call it managing, we call it manifest destiny. We consider it ours. And as the human population continues to grow we expand further and further into land that is something else's home.

Wolves live in family groups that stake and mark their territory, and they vigorously defend their land. Yellowstone research shows that most adult wolf deaths in the park are attributed to territorial disputes. However, two- and three-year-old wolves frequently disperse, leaving the pack to find a mate and establish his or her own family. Wolves are fabulous long distance travelers. Migrating wolves face challenges in the Western states because current law protects them in some areas but not others. Even Yellowstone Park wolves, during hunting season, are unprotected once they step outside park boundaries.

A movement afoot recognizes the challenge that humans and wildlife face living together on this planet. The Spine of the Continent Initiative, envisioned by Michael Soulé and supported by scores of other scientists and conservationists across North America, seeks to establish landscape connectivity and migratory corridors throughout our continent, allowing those creatures who migrate north and south to safely navigate their journeys, while also allowing wildlife to flow between our currently separated national parks, wildlife refuges, and other such areas. Without connected corridors, populations can become isolated and diminished, putting them genetically at risk. Imagine expanding our wilderness areas so that in corners and strips and stretches they touch each other, allowing wildlife safe, continuous passage from one area to another. Mary Ellen Hannibal, in *The Spine of the Continent*, explores the story of the pronghorn antelope of Wyoming, showing how multi-generational migratory patterns dictate a herd's activity, and how man's activity can affect these patterns. A narrow road that bisects a migratory path can wreak havoc with a herd's journey, as can fences, because pronghorns, while capable of jumping, will not jump over a fence, preferring to slither underneath if there is enough of an opening. If there isn't enough slithering room, they will often turn away from their path and that fence, and change a migratory pattern. What the pronghorn have done for thousands of years can be undone by a few strands of tightly strung barbed wire.

To establish a safe migration corridor for the pronghorns, two biologists rallied agencies with jurisdiction over the herd's territories—from the Bridger-Teton National Forest and the Grand Teton National Forest to Wyoming Fish and Game and the National Elk Refuge to the U.S. Fish and Wildlife Service and the BLM—and private property owners, as well. The result is a protected pathway for this herd to travel, one free of fences and traffic. Spine of the Continent supporters want to expand this type of effort across the continent. The swath of creature-safe migratory pathways ideally extends from northernmost Canada, through the United States and down into Mexico, following the ridges of five thousand miles of the Rocky Mountains. This contiguous corridor will require hundreds of negotiations to finance and establish wildlife rights-of-way easements, passage over or under freeways, and other innovations in order to succeed. A long, connected path of wilderness protected from automobiles, guns, fences, and other human hazards, this stretch of land will enable safe migration and intermingling for hundreds of species, millions of animals, albeit one fenceless parcel or wildlife overpass at a time.

Yellowstone and other rigidly protected areas become anchors with "overlapping zones of various protection regimes and conservation goals radiating out from them, like petals from the center of a rose," as Emma Marris describes in *Rambunctious Garden*. As humans move further and further into places once remote and difficult to reach, what we consider natural areas tend to contract, able to support fewer and fewer individuals within a species. Since they require greater ranges, large species populations first decrease, then possibly disappear from the area. But many small species will disappear from these diminished natural areas, too, because a difficult year—one of drought, sickness, pestilence—can wipe out an entire, reduced, population. By protecting wildlife in these connected zones, we increase the chances that species will become neither endangered nor extinct.

The Endangered Species Act itself speaks to the need to protect more than just a specific fish, plant, or creature. Its purpose is "to provide a means whereby the ecosystems upon which endangered species and threatened species depend may be conserved, and to provide a program for the conservation of such endangered species and threatened species." The ESA makes explicit that the ecosystem underlies the existence of the individual. To protect the creature, its habitat must be conserved. As federal judge Beryl Howell wrote in her December 2014 decision regarding the continuing protection of gray wolves in the western Great Lakes, the ESA "reflects the commitment by the United States to act as a responsible steward of the Earth's wildlife, even when such stewardship is inconvenient or difficult for the localities where an endangered or threatened species resides."

For wolves, the expanded protection of wildlife corridors will allow for increased interaction between packs, which supports creation of new packs and fosters genetic strength. Although a female wolf will typically not breed with her father, other inbreeding occurs when populations are limited, leading to situations similar to that currently happening on Isle Royale in northern Michigan where, because of the island's inaccessibility, the wolf population is weakened and likely to eventually die out due to lack of diversity. The larger wildlife landscapes of the Spine of the Continent initiative allow for healthier wildlife populations, protecting creatures from genetic demise.

A challenge in promoting connectivity projects such as the Spine of the Continent lies in their use of mapping, however, since maps draw targets by showing areas of potential change, areas presently inhabited by human beings. Viewed as threats to wildlife, people who live in targeted places on these maps are sometimes considered liabilities. Few want to be seen that way, or worse, asked to leave. Those who live and earn their livelihood in places mapped as potential migratory routes are understandably concerned and even angered. Tensions mount over this issue, and discussions of wildlife corridors can quickly become contentious. I sit for a few minutes to slip on the moccasins of those landowners and imagine their world. I find giving up my home and lifestyle for pronghorns and grizzlies a difficult thing to swallow.

Wolves, to retain genetic diversity and healthy social structures, require space to roam. While the typical territory of a wolf pack is approximately ten square miles, wolves can cover up to a hundred miles in a day. A GPS radio-collared wolf, known as OR7, has been tracked moving from his pack in northeast Oregon to California and back. He left Oregon in

2011, and traveled over three thousand miles in three years. He's been nicknamed Journey. Echo, the wolf sighted on the north rim of the Grand Canyon in late 2014, had been collared near Cody, Wyoming, more than four hundred miles away. Though many young adult wolves disperse to begin new packs, the rest remain loyal to their pack and its territory. Those wolves typically roam, then return home. However, when wolves currently protected within national park borders travel outside of those boundaries during hunting season, they are vulnerable to hunters. Radio-collared wolves that are part of long-term research studies within these national parks have been killed while outside park borders, whether two or twenty miles beyond that safety line. The Spine of the Continent plan proposes to reduce the likelihood of such shootings by providing protected space around and between parks, allowing for the natural movement of mountain lions, wolves, and grizzly bears. Enlarging and connecting wilderness allows increased range for animals that have an innate need for space.

My family moved out west when I was eleven, my dad eager to get back to big land where he could ski mountains instead of valleys. The home my parents chose was in an offbeat subdivision at the top of a mountain pass fifteen miles east of Salt Lake City, where not everyone had water rights, but most had garages right next to the road. Snow fell deep and often. Our first year, it snowed September first and June first and on a regular basis in between. The house came with a snowplow, which my dad quickly upgraded, plowing our massive driveway storm after storm. That first winter he began making plans to build an addition that would place a new garage within ten feet of the road, not the thirty-plus where the existing garage currently sat.

Our low-slung, split-level, wood-sided house sat on the western ridge of the development, the back windows looking out over miles and miles of watershed, never to be built upon. Our front windows, facing east, were huge, offering panoramic views of sparsely populated valley down below through which Interstate 80 wove and further beyond, ridge after ridge of majestic peaks of the Uinta range, sixty miles distant. I had no idea skies could be so huge, that I could live on a mountain, that mountains could rim the edges of my world.

A few houses lined the road north of us, and to our south lay an expanse of sagebrush and bare dry earth, the only other houses so encased by pines and bends of the road that only a portion of roof top and the occasional glint of metal gutter were visible. Isolated from city life, even country village life, we were twenty minutes—in good weather—from a grocery store, schools, work, any kind of extra-curricular activity. A gas station and café sat at the interstate exit, one mile and two big hills below my house, and early on I learned that a quick bike ride down to buy a candy bar resulted in a twenty-five minute walk and push back home. My friends were ten- and fifteen-minute walks away, and though a few houses perched in between, most of what I walked past was sagebrush, oak, aspen, and wild native grasses. Grasshoppers clacked and flew past, a dragonfly might magically float along beside me for dreamlike moments. The soil was gray and rocky at the edge of the road. We had moved to something called high desert which was arid and parched when it wasn't arid and covered with snow and ice.

We owned the sky above us in every direction, the air almost always clear and clean, the blue cloudless. I quickly learned the magic of Utah winters: snowstorms blanketing the land, wind whipping snow drifts to heights above my head, the world nothing but a blizzard of white, and then the clouds pass, breaking apart and away, and the skies turn blue as the sun sparkles and bounces from surface to surface, simultaneously blinding and thrilling the eye.

Here I learned the basics of conservation. Take what you need, and utilize well what you take. Never waste water: it is precious. Don't use lights unless you need them, and always turn them off when you're done. Plan ahead and consolidate your errand, work, and school trips. Make use of what you have, and be thoughtful with the earth's resources. Arid land is fragile, wildlife wondrous and to be respected. Today's snow is next spring's wildflower and next summer's drinking water. We are visitors, guests, stewards of the earth supporting and surrounding us. Act accordingly.

Stewardship is a concept espoused by most who work the land, by conservationists, by hikers and rock climbers and explorers, by those who run rivers and guide people on outdoor expeditions for a living. Experiencing changes over time brings home the effect we have on the land, and this effect is magnified in drier, western environments. Cryptobiotic soil illustrates the importance of understanding the landscape. It looks like a dark patch on sandy soil, but is actually alive. Made of lichens, algae, fungi, mosses and cyanobacteria, it not only helps retain moisture, but also stabilizes the dirt and sand, and plays a role in nitrogen fixation. One errant footstep destroys what may take from years to a century to re-form. Step here, don't step there.

New discoveries blossom daily. When I'm introduced to a better way to grow vegetables, cut an onion, pedal my bike, I adopt new behaviors and become more efficient. More effective. When I learn that wild animals are at risk because of roads, fences, hunting licenses, or legislative actions, I want to change our rules and practices. But as a society, we move sluggishly. The fight for women's right to vote began in the United States in the 1840s; the nineteenth amendment, establishing this right, was passed in 1920. In the mid-nineteenth century, sepsis—infection—killed almost half of all surgical patients. When surgeon Joseph Lister realized that infection seeps into patients via germs, he identified chemicals and processes to kill those germs. While he proved that germ-destroying cleansing of hands, tools, and wounds prevented sepsis and saved lives, his observations were greatly ignored, and a generation passed before Lister's recommendations became routine. With their adoption, the practice of medicine changed. Both brilliant and wise, Max Planck once said that scientific truth doesn't convert its opponents by being true, but instead becomes accepted when the naysayers finally die and the next generation grows up accustomed to it. Over time we've learned to build more structurally sound buildings, install smoke detectors, get rid of lead paint and asbestos. We have taken better care of ourselves. We've made our bodies and homes safer. Life expectancy has increased.

But we haven't done as well for our environment. We've sliced away at wilderness, and let former ranch and wildlands be sold to developers. The Keep America Beautiful campaign began in 1953, and anti-littering laws exist in all states—in some, for longer than forty years. Yet people continue to litter. Cigarette butts are the most commonly littered item in the world: over 4.5 trillion butts are tossed out car windows, thrown on sidewalks and streets, ground into the soil of hiking trails. Each takes from four to five hundred years to completely break down. We take for granted our hills and canyons, our lakes and streams, and the soil of our farmland. We have been reluctant to respond to the promise of a warmer earth. We roll our eyes at environmentalists. But reality is that we share a single environment with every other being on this planet. Our collective homes form one huge, interconnected home. Risk to one is, essentially, risk to all.

As residents of this common environment, we are vulnerable to nature's whims as well as to changes imposed by humanity. We have homes, rarely inviolate, but protected, sheltered, as best possible. Wild creatures are constricted to nests or dens only when they are newly born, giving birth or nursing. Once weaned, they explore trees and grasslands, hills and furrows and streams, expanding home outward. Knowing nothing of artificial boundaries imposed by humans until we enter their space and erect fences and buildings or draw lines on paper and state on this side of the line they are safe, on the other side, they may be shot.

My home changed when Jake left the hospital after six weeks in the newborn ICU. He came with an apnea monitor to alert us if his heart began beating too fast or slow, and a nasal cannula connected to a tank of oxygen almost as large as me. He was less than five pounds and slept in a sling to keep him from sliding down the angled mattress, raised to reduce regurgitation. He came with preemie-nippled bottles for his formula—he did not want to nurse—and medications to prevent his reflux and suppress his seizures. He also came home with significant brain damage, which we were told might or might not prevent him from developing like a normal child. I lost all trust in safety, in certainty. Women become pregnant, have babies, play peek-a-boo. Their babies don't die, they don't suffer brain damage. I scrutinized every burp, every flex of muscle: normal? a sign of developmental delay? Maybe he wasn't eating enough. Maybe we were offering too much visual stimulation, or not enough. Maybe we weren't giving him the right kind of movement, or enough Bach. I'd dance with him in the middle of the night, singing lullabies, every song I knew, desperate to soothe his wails, his arching back. My home changed in appearance and in attitude. The pillows and pictures and cozy places remained, but home itself became less of a refuge and more of a bivouac, completely unable to protect me from enemy attack.

4. muzzle

Snow melts back into the earth, new pups join the den. Sophie hunts, regurgitates her food for her new pups, sleeps nose to tail. Now a yearling, Yellow Eyes follows his father hunting mice, ground squirrels, pouncing, yipping, gripping. New scents, darting shapes lead him further from the pack. Yellow Eyes grows stronger, bolder. His fur has darkened at the shoulders, on his back, his forehead, the tip of his tail. Sleeping, he blends with the others, each one of their coats so subtly different they are like balls of heathered yarn. Days lengthen and nights contract. Sophie and her mate abandon the den. They travel half the day, their speed hampered by the ambling pups. Yellow Eyes passes his parents, leading the pack to their rendezvous site, a wide valley meadow bright with flowers bordered by sandstone and shale, windwhipped into smooth curves yet rough and coarse, forming the ridges of the mountainside. Copses of pine, lodgepole, and spruce are fat fingers spilling down from the top, meeting at the base of the mountain to create a tangled green moat. The leaves change, the air is crisp. The pups grow taller, stronger. Yellow Eyes tracks rabbits, geese. His father trots across the grass and sedge. Yellow Eyes follows. At the far edge, where grass meets trees, the two turn to face the pack. The alpha male lifts his chin and howls. The rest answer, Sophie's howl long and clean, the pups' howls full of barks and yips. Yellow Eyes' howl resounds. It slips like fog through the trees and echoes from the surrounding hillocks. It comes back to him and he sends it out again.

Tuffie and Duke are the first to greet me this early August day, barking and barreling at my car. Ranch dogs, they're both black and white border collie mixes, and it's not until the next evening I can, with sixty percent accuracy, tell which is which. Duke is younger and a bit wigglier, while Tuffie, a mature five, is always in front when we venture out. Duke is part Hanging Tree cowdog and Tuffie part Old English bulldog, but all I see is black and white fur, slender bodies with black noses, and awe of their master shining in their eyes.

Their tails are docked, and when I ask Jim why he tells me it's all about cleanliness, "so they don't get their tails all full of cow shit and stuff." The insufficient nubs wag something no longer there, the dogs untroubled by the absence. They're happy, and don't seem to care that I've got a bicycle on the roof of my car. Jim, I'm sure, is not so certain. He's a gentleman, though, and welcomes me to his home, this 1958 log cabin where he lives the six months of the year it's not snowed in. A horse corral, saddle shed, and a large garage-type structure rise from the nearby dirt and scrub grass. They nestle between tall pines that gird the cabin.

The ground outside is dusty with summer, the cabin windows open to catch a breeze. The kitchen is an el of the main room, where a loveseat faces a battered easy chair; a large dining table pushes up against the picture window. The hallway leads to two bedrooms and a bathroom where, unless you're flexible, it's easiest to just sit sideways on the toilet so you don't fall into the bathtub. Jim has utilized every inch to hold supplies: extra towels and blankets, hats and boots and books.

A pack mule brays as I toss my bag on the guest room bed. In the kitchen I unload the groceries I've brought and smile at his Keurig coffee machine. He gives me time to settle in while he moves the horses, and I take my notebook outside before dinner, sitting in one of his lawn chairs, the Tetons jutting skyward in front of me. I've come north again. I write, I absorb, I am astounded by the setting here, five miles up the valley from a lake caused by a 1925 landslide. The first homesteaders settled here in the 1890s, and this ranch has been in family hands since that time. They raise cattle, grazing them on Teton Wilderness land in the summer, and feeding them hay down below in a winter pasture during the bitter cold, snow-shrouded months of the year.

We cobble together an easy dinner, and I spend another hour sitting on a genuine buck rail fence, watching the valley just be, writing everything that comes to mind. Descriptions of trees, the swell of the land, the feel of the peeling bark on the fence rails. I head to bed not long after the orange and pink sunset fades and the sky turns darkly indigo. Rain splats on the metal roof as I drift off to sleep, and I awaken once to a pummeling patter, but my sleep is deep and I don't arise until after seven. I might have awakened in the night to hysterical barking, howling, but it's fuzzy, it might have been a dream. Jim lets me lounge the next day, Friday, reading with my coffee and sitting outside again most of the morning, writing, lost in thoughts of wide open spaces, sinking deeper into the land. Before lunch, we head out on his four wheeler to move electrical fence lines and ride through the cows, which all turn their heads to stare at us. The calves want to come visit until Duke barks and dashes around, sending them scrambling. Jim curses Duke, and Tuffie chases Duke until he catches him, pouncing on him, biting flank and ear and they tumble on the ground, a rolling ball of black and white.

The afternoon brings more four wheeling and fence moving, more down time, and a visit from two young women, one of whom has brought two horses for Jim to watch until she comes to get them Sunday morning. She works for the Forest Service and will be clearing trails out in the Teton Wilderness come

Sunday, when she'll use her horses to pack in gear. Friday night's dinner is relaxed and we talk about life and land, and just how much work it takes to carve one from the other.

Saturday I ride my bicycle from Landslide Lake through the tiny town of Kelly and into Jackson, then make a loop up through Wilson and Moose before pedaling back up the Gros Ventre River valley. The loop takes me on seven or eight miles of Grand Teton Park roads, where the land pushes back against mankind, frost heaves buckling the asphalt, mile after mile. In the afternoon, Jim lets me help him move electrical rope fences again, pasturing his outfitter friend's horses. I hold the spindle, let it unwind as Jim shoves metal posts in the ground, clips the rope, moves to the next. When we finish with the fence, Jim leaves to check on the cattle farther west, his two dogs running loops around his legs.

The day Jake turned one, he smiled for the first time. We'd had a baby portrait taken the month before, and nothing the photographer did could elicit a smile from him. Not a flashing light, not a squeaky toy, not his trilling nor his goofy laugh. But Jake was now less miserable than he'd been. He spent fewer hours crying. And when he smiled that very first smile, I was dumbstruck. Then giddy. Then nothing but tears. I was four months pregnant. I could see something on the horizon that looked more like normal than I'd dared hope.

Beau was born in early October, 1992. All eight pounds of him arrived healthy and in good spirits. At that time wolves were only visions in most westerner's imaginations, but details of their reintroduction were solidifying. Idaho Senator Jim McClure—recognizing that wolves were returning to his state whether people wanted them or not—and U.S. Fish and Wildlife's John Turner had been strategizing for the past few years, and finally succeeded in nudging Congress into funding an Environmental

Impact Statement on the reintroduction of wolves to Yellowstone and central Idaho. The first step was creation and review of a draft EIS: the plans, programs, and projected impacts. Then would come review, feedback, and revision, to produce a final EIS. The last step was the federal rule-making, which remained years away. When Jake shared that first smile, the draft EIS was underway. When Beau was born, open houses and formal hearings were being held throughout Wyoming, Idaho, and Montana, all to elicit comments and feedback about how we, as a nation, should restore wolves to their former homes.

I wasn't concerned about wolves. I had my own pack. One chubby, giggly, blond baby boy; one dark-haired, slender and solemn son; a husband who loved his children and was focused on creating a life filled with everything possible; and me. Alpha female. In her den, her rendezvous site. Holding it all together, because that's what one does.

"Jenny and Keith're comin' over for dinner, and Sabine's gonna cook an elk roast. They're comin' about six, Jenny's bringin' a watermelon she hauled back here from Missouri, says it's a real watermelon, a southern one. Whatever that means."

Jim's hosting a party, and I talk with his friends while he finishes his chores and cleans up for dinner. We're settled around the picnic table outside, everyone but Sabine and me in their Wranglers. Sabine, Jim's girlfriend, wears a pair of trendy jeans with embroidery on the pockets, and I'm wearing a t-shirt and skirt. It's my travel skirt: double sided, so you can wear it two separate days with two different looks. Right. Just perfect for the ranch.

"Pleased to meet you," Keith says, dipping his head so that for a moment I lose sight of his eyes beneath his cowboy hat. Maybe five foot ten, he ripples muscles and keeps his voice under control. And his smile.

"Have an appetizer?" Jenny is holding a plate out toward me, miniature round bundles of something, orange in the middle, stabbed by toothpicks. As I'm inspecting them she continues, "It's sweet potato wrapped in bacon, they're real good."

I take one, nibble, and of course she's right. I love sweet potatoes and who doesn't love bacon? We all laugh about bacon for a minute, and then I start asking questions. I'm curious about these people's lives, so very different from mine.

Keith's from St. Louis, where he owns an equestrian center that sits on almost eighty acres and can board a hundred horses. The forty horses he keeps in Wyoming are fit and healthy, well trained and to my admittedly uninformed eye, absolutely beautiful. Jim's been keeping half of them this past week while Keith was back east, and while moving them from pasture to pasture, I had time to admire them all, palominos and buckskins and bays.

I find Jenny the most fascinating of the group, a young woman in her late twenties who was raised in northern Wyoming with horses and dogs and a rifle, and who went to college to become a concert pianist.

"When I realized you have to be twice as good as the men if you want to perform, and I got tired of practicing eight hours a day, I changed my major to photography and digital media." Jenny's a bit peeved about the male-dominated music world not embracing her, and she's not about to let that happen in any other arena. After graduating, she joined her family's outfitting company, now in its fourth generation. Hunting elk is one of her favorite pastimes, and she's both a good cook and an excellent horse wrangler, so it made sense that she join the family business. She handles media, web management, and press. But that's not quite enough, so she raises and shows dogs, too, and is establishing a breeding business, selling puppies. She and Keith married six years ago, and now it's Keith who runs the family company, taking guests on pack trips, fishing trips, trail rides, hiking and backpacking trips, and of course, hunting trips.

Keith wears his hat low on his forehead, and a neatly barbered moustache. His shirt is tucked, his jeans clean and neat. He seems content to let Jenny sparkle while he plays the steady, sturdy role. As an outfitter he's taken people to his base camps hundreds of times, led them along trails, shown them where to most effectively fish and hunt, taught them to ride a horse. He's outdoors every day of his life, caring for his horses or teaching others about the wonders of the Teton Wilderness. I'm eager to hear his perspective on wolves. He must be thrilled to have such powerful, wild creatures back on the landscape. I ask him how many times he's seen a wolf.

"Maybe twice in these past five years," Keith responds. "They're nocturnal, and smart enough not to hang around where we are. Makes 'em hard to see. I've seen their destruction, though, and that's enough."

I swallow, realign my face.

"Wolves have learned to avoid humans, stay away from people. They've figured out about guns." The state of Wyoming issues wolf tags, licenses to kill wolves, for a mere eighteen dollars.

"They have six-eight pups a year, and travel in these huge packs of twenty or more, and they're just going to keep growing. We need to control them. They're getting out of hand." Keith believes there are many more wolves in Wyoming than the stated population suggests. But wolves are hard to find, and even harder to kill.

Each year Wyoming has authority to manage its wolves, the state sets a mortality quota for the wolf hunt. Once that number is reached, a wolf tag becomes worthless. In 2012, 4,492 tags were sold, and the mortality quota was fifty-two. Forty-two wolves were legally killed by hunters. The next year, 2,153 tags were sold, with a mortality quota of twenty-six. Only twenty-four were killed.

Keith suggests trapping as a more effective tool, that or poisoning. Wolves to him are varmints, and he'd just as soon have them all gone. He uses the word balance, but there's not much about the wolf that he finds justifiable and I don't know what he's placing on either side of his scales. He's matter-of-fact throughout this discussion, as if we're discussing what color to paint his barn or what kind of dog chow we prefer to buy. I struggle to remain neutral when he speaks of wolves that kill without eating their prey. Gordon Haber, wolf researcher in Alaska, points out that a smaller wolf pack often cannot eat an entire animal at the time it's killed. They'll eat the softer gut portions, and the carcass will take on a hollowed-out appearance. The wolves will return repeatedly to eat what they can, but when temperatures are well below freezing, the muscular parts of a killed animal will freeze hard as steel. The wolves must either wait for it to thaw, or abandon the carcass. I know this, but I keep quiet.

"They're the only animal that kills for sport, and they do it all the time. They'll kill an elk, and just leave it there, ripping it open and taking out the heart, leaving the rest there. Just for sport." Keith's eyes flash under the brim of his hat and his jawline tightens, though his voice remains smooth. I try not to lose myself in the hypocrisy of his statement. Isn't sport hunting what humans do, what Keith himself does for a living, guiding people to where they can best kill elk, deer, moose, bear, sheep, antelope, and mountain lions? Not only is his position untenable, this statement about tearing only the heart from an elk carcass seems impossible to prove. It can't have been captured on film. He hasn't witnessed it himself. This must be a rural myth making the rounds.

For Keith it's truth. He believes misinformation runs rampant, and that the real truth is exposed in a few key documentary films.

"Have you seen *Crying Wolf*?" he asks. "There's documentation in it about all of the lies the federal government and the wildlife departments are trying to pass off on us. There's no excuse for the decision to 'reintroduce' the wolf when it was coming back on its own. It's all part of a deeper agenda to make our nation the way the liberals want it.

"And any organization that promotes wolves is just in it to make money," he insists, lumping all environmental organizations with animal rights activists and pro-wolf groups. I wonder if Keith thinks the sportsmen's and hunting organizations are just in it to make money, too. I mention Ralph Maughan's statement about it not really being about the wolf at all, and he loves this.

"Nope, it's not about the wolf, it's a much bigger agenda they have. Have you heard of Y2Y, and Agenda 21? They're all out to change everything about the way we live."

Keith's big on stories and conspiracies. The Yellowstone to Yukon (Y2Y) initiative he distrusts is in alliance with the Spine of the Continent movement, working to create wildlife corridors to connect and protect wildlife. He's convinced that anyone who is pro-wolf is part of a conspiracy to rid the land of hunters, ranchers, and farmers, and make everyone move into cities so that the remaining land can all be returned to wilderness. Keith is certain that the wolves reintroduced in Yellowstone were brought in illegally, and are a sub-species of wolf far larger and more aggressive than the wolves that lived in the West a century ago, a belief well-embedded in hunting and ranching communities. He knows he can prove every one of his statements. The only time he offers anything positive about wolves is when he acknowledges that they're apex predators and that they didn't become that by being dumb.

"They're smart, sneaky, clever, and aggressive as hell." He rocks back on his heels and I imagine every fiber of muscle in his body tensing, ready to spring. I see a piece of Keith that wants to admire the wolf, but it's buried in so much myth, distortion, and hatred, that small speck is as likely to grow as a radish seedling soaked in ammonia.

I'm eight. I've already scared off one father, whose new wife is determined not to have my brother and me in her life. My father gave up parental rights, started a new family, stopped visiting. I call my new father Dad. He's adopted my brother and me. I proudly write my new last name in cursive on my third grade homework. I try so hard to please him I can barely see straight.

One day I say something he doesn't like, and he sends me to my room. I go—slamming my door behind me. Footfalls shake the house, and my door flies open. It slams back against the wall. Don't. You. Ever. Slam. That. Door.

He glares flames at me and I stare back, terrified.

Now come shut it the right way.

I creep to the door, and take the knob in my hand. I tug. It doesn't budge. I tug harder. Nothing. Wild eyed, I look at his tight face, the creases by his eyes, on his forehead.

I can't, I whisper.

Yes you can, he thunders.

A desperate jerk—not a millimeter of movement. I back away as he grasps the knob. One pull, another, then with a great yank the doorknob pops free of its hole in the wallboard.

He shuts the door.

I stay on my side, looking at the hole, the hole that is never, ever mentioned but neatly patched when it is time to sell the house.

My mother, a music professor, a pianist and actress, is busy creating a life despite her second imperfect marriage. I retreat into books, captured by fairy tale endings. I create a whole world inside where everyone is loved, always. I hide me. I'd lost my daddy, my footing. I'd gained a small, dark hole.

I know this space. I've explored its walls and edges. I know its roots, how it enlarges with time and circumstance, and how to shrink it so that I can fit into my armor. I treat it with compassion. It grows when I am belittled or ignored. It has a solid bottom, where I throw myself in the depths of despair. However, what encompasses it is bright, magical. Hopeful. Like Persephone, I have both meadow and underworld. In my meadow wildflowers blossom and grass is impossibly green. Serene, inspired, full of wildly dancing colors, what encircles that emptiness is brilliant light, happiness, bubbling laughter, transcendence.

My new dad is a handsome man. Dark-haired, tall, slender, a sparkle in his amber eyes. Narrow, sharp-edged cheekbones, a colorless scar on his temple, an uncompromising jaw. He'd fought in the Korean War, flies an airplane, sky dives, skis like Franz Klammer, and anchors the ski patrol, rescuing those stranded on the T-bar when power fails, strapping the injured into toboggans and towing them down moguled runs during blizzards. He sings, is an actor, performs in community theater. Knows Russian. Had graduated the Colorado School of Mines and owns a magical box filled with samples of all the rocks in the world. Is an engineer, can build anything. Can charm anyone, anytime, in an aloof, enthralling way, because everyone in his presence is intrigued and entranced, convinced that the mysterious distance can be travelled, his secret heart revealed.

He is bigger than me. The one who pays to feed, clothe, and house me. He likes angel food cake and Snoopy cartoons. He likes me well enough, when I obey and cause little fuss. But he doesn't take me seriously. My ideas are light, meaningless. His eyes slide past mine and onto my brother's, and spirited discussions ensue. Or they bore into mine, waiting for me to answer his rhetorical question, its circular nature presaging my inevitable failure.

I can't fight back. I can't question his decrees. I can't please. I want to be him, this powerful, athletic being who can do anything. He writes left-handed, small and slanted, and I, right-handed, work to make my printing just like his. I want to solve logic problems to impress him, tell a joke that makes him laugh. Bake peanut butter cookies because he likes them. He teaches me to pound nails and to stain siding, he teaches me to ski and to drive a manual transmission. To canoe and camp and string food up away from bears. But I am always uneasy, waiting for the next hole in the wall, waiting for his truth to be blurted out: I don't really like you—I'm only your dad because I have to be.

By the time I am a senior in high school, I wait tables three nights a week, am a class officer, drill team leader, actress, debater, yearbook editor, singer, pianist, cellist, tennis player, straight-A student, recipient of the Supreme Activity Award and none of this earns me what I desperately want, a daddy who adores me. One who hugs and teases and makes it clear that I am the cherry on top. Or the butter brickle pecan. Or at least wanted.

June, 2004. He stands four feet from me, his voice deep, his legs spread, arms folded across his chest. *I said I'll always take care of you.*

What does that mean?

I don't know how to ask that question. I am afraid of him. At forty-two, I am separated from Bob and trying to determine whether or not my current marriage can survive. I'm living with my children in a big demanding house. I need emotional support, I need money, I need someone to replace a light fixture and re-caulk a window.

I'm eight years old inside, and I can't ask.

He confers a one-shouldered hug after eating dinner with us, and then he's gone. He's offered nothing but words—superficial, disconnected, remote. I'm relieved he's gone, but the hole splits open. I have failed at daughterhood. Twice. And wifehood. What's left is parenthood, and though I've already proved to be a failure with my very first pregnancy, I am alone now with four children, so I focus on that.

It's 2012. Daniel is dark-haired, tall, slender. His amber eyes hide all truths, and he can charm anyone, anytime, in an aloof, enthralling way, and I am convinced that the mysterious distance can be travelled, the truth of his heart revealed. Two months into our marriage I realize exactly what I've done.

When Sabine brings the elk roast to the table our wolf conversation ends, and I accept a small jelly glass of wine to go with the succulent, rare meat. We pass salad and dressings and a vegetable-drenched pasta. Ranchers and outfitters take mealtime seriously, everyone's attention shifting to the food and away from talk. When the chewing abates conversation returns. Stories of stubborn cattle and temperamental horses exchanged and relived. The elk roast is better than any beef I've eaten. It's beyond delicious, as is the southern—genuine—watermelon that Jenny slices up for us and insists that we salt. My dad, who grew up in Atlanta, used to eat his with salt, seems to be a southern thing, and I try a bite that way. I try another, and Jenny convinces me I'll soon start needing it that way.

"It sneaks up on you," she says, her freckled cheeks lifting in a smile, "and before you know it you'll just crave it."

The fire is lit and we wait for the wood to burn down to embers for roasting our marshmallows so that we can squish them between graham crackers and chocolate. Jenny's warned us that at fourteen she took second place in a s'mores eating contest, downing fourteen of them. I'm glad she has her own box of gluten-free grahams so I don't have to fight her for supplies. She's the best marshmallow toaster of us all, each white cylinder puffing golden brown with crunchy edges and a warm, gooey middle. My first goes down quickly, and I ponder a second, the evening starting to work its way down into the low fifties, the sky beginning its transition to night. Stars are springing free, and aside from the crackle of burning wood and our gentle conversations, there's not a sound to be heard. I sit with my thoughts, letting them recede, letting the air move around me, trying to let every possible particle of this Wyoming ranch seep into who I am, who I want to be.

I am alone in my house. It's a quiet, May day. Children at school, Daniel at work. I open the book midway and find a poem, written in prose, by Mary Sojourner. Bones. *Leave the bones. They are my bones. They will never be yours. You have lost your place—perhaps beyond repatriation. You know. You do not want to know.* She speaks as a wolf. I press deeper into my corner of the couch. Bones.

I flip the pages of *Comeback Wolves* and encounter Rick Bass, who writes that he needs big wilderness as an antidote to his sins, a place to say "*Here I will finally devour nothing,* and I really need those wolves to make it." Another flip of page takes me to Pam Houston who, when she encountered a wolf on the Denali Highway in Alaska, saw the glint of his gold eyes and knew he belonged to no one but himself.

Comeback Wolves is a compilation of essays and poetry written by western writers during a time when individuals, communities, and states began considering how our existences might change as wolves gradually made their way back onto our landscapes. While I own a romantic streak about a mile wide and recognize the same in some of these writers, that shared romanticism is grounded in a love of landscape and wildness, realities that demand thought and pragmatism. Writers often complete copious amounts of research, and because research unearths facts regarding the past, writers become students of history. In studying the history of wolves on this continent and others, from the earliest myths and fables to what's occurred since the 1995 reintroduction, a big-picture view unfolds. It includes the hate, the fear, the respect, the science, and the distortions. The essays and poems in this collection are educated responses to the situation, though imagery and a bit of romance might bind the thoughts. Of the fifty offerings in the book, not a one concludes that eliminating wolves makes our world a better place.

Clarissa Pinkola Estes, one of the collection's contributors, is a Jungian analyst, author, and cultural anthropologist who grew up in sparsely populated northern Michigan. Estes believes that both women and wolves have been similarly mislabeled and marginalized for their indelicate appetites, while both desire only respect and opportunities to peacefully pursue their gifts. Though she speaks specifically of the feminine, of course the wild soul is important to the masculine as well. Estes views both wildlife and the wild soul as being endangered species in our culture, and she celebrates both. *Women Who Run with the Wolves* is filled with challenges to the female soul. Estes suggests women are healthiest and happiest when embracing their wild nature, understanding that what is outside in nature is also inside human nature. No wonder the soul-satisfaction of sitting or walking upon green valleys and riverbanks and mountainsides awash with aspen. Or running through wide-open meadows and hiking up dry canyon draws, singing to the sun and howling at a winter evening's star-flushed sky. Estes hooks the same place in me that is caught by the wild women in my cookbook. Truth resides in both: my truth, my need to rediscover this aspect of myself that became buried under a mountain of nice, respectful, and reticent, that was swallowed by an ink-black hole, that was shattered and scattered to the wind. Estes gives me a hint of where to begin with her list of General Wolf Rules for Life: Eat. Rest. Rove in between. Render Loyalty. Love the children. Cavil in moonlight. Tune your ears. Attend to the bones. Make love. Howl often.

My lifelong secret fantasy is to be a back-up singer for a band. A doo-wop girl, one who harmonizes as she moves and sways behind a microphone on a tall stand. I love to sing, would leap at any opportunity to back up a band, but that fantasy pales when compared to becoming a woman who runs with wolves. The thought is enthralling: it tugs at me. This is not a one-time event, not a doo-wop fantasy, but a new way of being. Like the wild women of my cookbook, I want to live less encumbered. I want to live from my soul. I want to know for my own being what the wolves innately know—that they are being what they're meant to be.

The embers, no longer needed to gild marshmallows, are revived with kindling, a log. Flames leap and dance. Jenny and Keith have left, and it's just Jim and Sabine and me, and hundreds of eyes, out there, hiding behind grass and tree.

"Did you hear the howling the other night?" Jim asks, looking at me across the fire pit.

"I wasn't sure," I say. "I was so deeply asleep, I didn't know if I heard it, or dreamt it."

My first night at the ranch, well past midnight and during my deep and welcome sleep, Tuffie and Duke howled. Not mournful or melancholic, it was blood curdling, histrionic. So it hadn't been a dream.

"They don't do that for elk or even coyotes," Jim says. "I think they heard a wolf. Or scented him. Had to be a wolf."

Jim's dogs sleep inside. Good ranch dogs don't come cheap,

and underneath all of the name-calling and complaints, Jim loves his dogs without reservation.

"They're out there. I'm lucky they don't bother us here."

Sabine's chair is pushed against Jim's, and she leans her head against his shoulder. "Yes, the wolves better leave us alone tonight."

I wouldn't mind hearing a howl drift across the valley, but it remains quiet, the only sound the crack and snap of burning wood.

Barks. Yips. Howls. *Ar-oooh.* The sound flies strong and wide. Faint echoes land like hawks in the trees, folding in heads, tucking wings. Disappearing into the dusk.

There are quick howls, long drawn out howls, and bark howls, the latter heard less often and beginning with a sound rarely made by wolves, the bark, then moving into a more typical crescendoing howl. We know little about the mind of a wolf, the reason behind his howl. But some howls seem straightforward. Wolves howl to call packmates home, or to be led home. Howls establish territory, let outsiders know to stay away. A howl at the conclusion of a hunt likely releases energy, celebrates victory. Other howls leave us wondering. Imagining. Scientists have listed ten different wolf vocalizations including the howl, growl, bark, yip, yap, squeal, chirp, and bark-howl—messages differing through the use of timing, intonation, repetition, rhythm. Appreciation, frustration, a release of tension. Playfulness, joy, the need to feel connected. Howls have been described as the glue holding together a pack. Bestselling author Jodi Picoult studied wolves for one of her projects. She visited Shaun Ellis where he tended captive wolves in a wildlife park in England. He describes howls as either defensive, locating, or rallying. She calls howls "wolf email."

Much remains to be understood about the communication

that exists in the howl of a wolf. John and Mary Theberge are Canadian wolf biologists and researchers who, after nearly fifty years studying wolves, are now focused on howling. They are recording wolves, comparing, assessing, hoping to gain greater understanding. They move among pine trees, early in the morning, microphones ready, to catch the howls that echo across valleys and float up to the sky. Open spaces grab low-pitched howls, and carry the sound for miles.

A wolf howl in deepest dark chills my bones. It resounds with my own yearning, my own desires, and floats them beyond my being. Barely audible echoes whisper *yes, I too, know.* In the following silence, I ache to hear another howl, its fragile reverberations. Sometimes a new howl travels across the sky. Sometimes I am left trying to hold that which is ethereal.

Wolves also communicate with tails, ears, teeth, eyes—their body language is elaborate and complex. We can imagine what a tail held upright, down, straight out, or sweeping side to side might mean. Bared teeth, ears laid back. Narrowed eyes. Other subtle signals are far beyond us. Wolves dance, bow, jump, rub shoulders, jostle one another. But it is the howling that captures us. I believe that sometimes, a howl releases steam or celebrates happiness or is simply an outer expression of an inner experience, be it pleasurable or deeply mournful. I might be right. I want to be right.

I search Jake's eyes for me, and find only blue. Worn denim blue, Levi's pulled on every day. Jeans that touch grass and hay, trough water, dog slobber, mud and dry dust and oiled leather saddles. A mountain lake reflecting cloudless sky. His eyes are beautiful. But in them I do not see his soul, for it takes two sets of eyes, engaged, for that.

At two, Jake cannot talk, cannot reach a hand out to touch. He hears, but cannot listen. He cannot walk, he cannot roll over.

He sometimes smiles. He feels discomfort, pain, and he cries. He can be inconsolable. I can hold him against my chest, rock from hip to hip, pat his back, sing, whisper every sweet word I know into his ears. And still he'll cry. The volume will increase, he'll stiffen his neck. Arch his back. Howl.

5. trot

*Yellow Eyes shifts his tail away from his nose, opens an eye. Half
an inch of powder rests on his coat. Moonlight shoots through
treetops and strikes the snowy ground. His father stirs, Sophie
too. Yellow Eyes moves from pup to pup, nudges them awake.
Snow flies as they shake, moonlight sparking the crystals into
a coruscating cloud. They stretch, stiff legs on fat paws. Sophie
leads. They trot, then lope, between trees and down a tunneling
draw. They ease the pace and separate, approaching the slope
where last week the elk bedded. The creek is frozen, willows
weighted, dripping snow. A solitary elk, its long neck extended,
nibbles dogwood shoots. Sophie switches her tail, she skirts left,
she looks to her mate. He splits right, and the younger wolves
arrange themselves between and behind. The elk's ears prick. She
lifts her head. Moonlight glistens off fur, and the cow elk sees her
stalkers. She jerks. Runs up along the creek. The wolves chase,
and Yellow Eyes gets the first bite. His teeth grip her flank, and
she stumbles. Still running, she turns her head, then kicks. He
thuds into a fallen log as Sophie and her mate sink their teeth
into the cow, one at her other flank, one at her neck. The elk staggers, and with a wild cry sinks to the ground, where her blood
seeps deep into the snow.*

*The wolves eat, the sun creeping upward in a brilliant sky. The air
above buzzes, thumps, vibrates. Sophie turns toward the hillside
where they'd slept. The others follow, trotting full-bellied, out of
the trees and across the meadow. Yellow Eyes looks back. A quick*

stab of pain grips his shoulder—he stumbles, limps. The others run past. He staggers, stops, falls on the snow.

He awakens still in the snow, at the far side of the meadow. Alone. He climbs to his feet and shakes. Something presses against his neck, resting between shoulders and ears. He stretches a leg forward, shifts body weight, walks. He moves into a trot. He lopes into the trees.

Sunday morning at the ranch. I'm the first one up, brewing a cup of coffee and curling on the loveseat to read, then write, then read again. Soon Sabine pops out with a cheery good morning, and Jim isn't far behind. The dogs head outside where sunlight pours over the world, and Louis whinnies out in the pasture.

Breakfast is hotcakes with Friday's blueberries, Saturday night's strawberries, and pure Vermont maple syrup. Jim and Sabine eat fried eggs alongside and jam beneath the fruit on their hotcakes, but I pass on both. Next time I'll know better. I do the dishes while the two of them prepare for the ride. Jim collects halters and Sabine's horse Louis from where we pastured him last night. Sabine throws chaps over her jodhpurs and collects Louis's blanket, saddle, and bridle from the trailer. Her black and white border collie mix, Tipsy, watches the activity, dancing in anticipation. I don long pants and my running shoes, not having thought to pack jeans and boots, and gather my unruly hair into a ponytail. I'm leaving today, and Jim's taking me out for a ride before I go.

He hands me a halter, and tells me to meet him in the corral where we'll collect our horses, then walk them over to the hitching post by the saddle shed. Waylon is my ride, the gentlest of his three. Jim will ride Tomahawk—Tommy. Waylon is sleek and black, patient as all get out. He lets me put the halter on him and walk him over to the saddle shed. Jim instructs me to curry and brush my horse before resting the saddle blanket on his back. Waylon's back is about my nose height, and hefting the saddle up proves awkward. I'm sure Jim is smiling as he holds the blanket steady and even. He shows me how to adjust the latigo, cinching the saddle snugly to the horse, and then we tighten the chest strap. When the saddle is secure I move on to the bridle, substituting it for the halter with such sleight of hand Waylon is barely aware until my fingers are in his mouth sliding in the bit. I mangle his ear while trying to slip the bridle home, and Waylon forgives me, the first of many forgivenesses.

Sabine gives me a short lesson while Jim saddles Tommy. I work to scoot forward on the saddle, open my thighs, drop my heels and flex my calves, keep my hips loose, and sit tall and proud. I recite all these instructions as I acclimate to the feel of the reins. I press in my heels, a subtle suggestion that Waylon move more energetically.

"It's like driving a car," she tells me, "you don't start with the steering wheel, first you have to push the gas. Sit up, feel his tummy with your heels and push left, right, left, right as he walks. Don't let him reach his head down to eat because he'll try, and when you need to bring him back do a gentle pull, release, pull, release. When his head is pulled back his neck is tight and he will be anxious, just remember to relax. And sit up. And once we get moving he will follow the horse in front of him, so you won't have to worry much, yes?"

Sabine's German accent colors each instruction, and her well-worn chaps are those of a true equestrian. She rides an English saddle, with a pert riding helmet and gloves, graceful and confident when she swings up on Louis. A woman with children in college and a rancher for a boyfriend, Sabine cooks a mean roast, and laughs from the belly. She regards everyone with a steady gaze. This woman is in harmony with her wild.

The early trail is shaded. A winding, rock-studded rivulet of water is nearly hidden by the thick green grass at its edges. We duck under pine and aspen branches and my stirruped feet swish through sagebrush, aspen shoots, and brush I can neither recognize nor name. I gently tug Waylon right or left to avoid squashing my knees against tree trunks as he navigates the narrow dirt trail, and soon we're atop a ridge and in the open, sage-covered Teton Wilderness. We're looking for cattle. Jim has a good sense of where his are, but he wants to know if they've been to a certain hillside, water trough, and salt lick, and our ride is an investigatory one. Louis is an outfitter's horse that Sabine is working with, a horse that needs some re-education and some healing, both physical and mental. Jim is known around the valley as a horse whisperer, and Sabine seems one, too. She coaches Louis to walk through the rivulets and creeks instead of jumping, as he wants to do. He approaches water as latent-aged boys do, something to either play with or to completely avoid. Louis will take a foreleg and splash the creek water violently, but will resist walking through it. When we stop by the water trough where the cows are not, he takes his long nose and sticks it into the water, jerking his head back and forth and splashing the water in two-foot arcs. Sabine speaks softly and repeats the skills she's asking him to develop, building his confidence with each limited risk taken.

Tetons jut up before us while cresting a hill, and I forget to drop my heels and press back my shoulders as I take in the pines and shrub oak, the rounded hills and the placidity of the day. The August sun is hot and I'm grateful for the hat Jim's lent me, its stampede string around my neck, its wide felt brim protecting my face from the scorching sun. We're about 7,500 feet above sea level, and it's creeping toward eighty degrees. My all-black clothing, chic in the city, is ridiculous here but still better than the sundress and skirts I packed for the ranch. The black yoga pants I'm wearing are patterned with brown dust, and while I'm grateful for its long sleeves, the black V-neck t-shirt I'm wearing is just plain hot.

We ride higher and higher, not much chatter, all of us absorbing the landscape, the gift of the horses' work, and the delight the three dogs display as they dart, chase, and splash through the cold water of East Miner's Creek. Jim is a cowboy through and through, an Iowa farm boy who moved to Wyoming at eighteen. Almost fifty years have passed since that move and he has never regretted it. He's worked this ranch for thirty years and is as comfortable on his horse as I am on my couch. He wears Wranglers—Levi's got too darn expensive—and a cowboy hat and boots, and his face, weather-worn and reddened, is creased with laugh lines. I watch him on Tommy, and they move fluidly, Jim's hips an extension of the horse's back. He rides away from us at times, looking for tracks, some indication that his cattle have moved through. Far from the cabin, after we've climbed hill after hill, we drop into a narrow valley where downed trees have rendered the trail impassable, their grayed, limbless bodies lying haphazardly as though tossed in a giant game of pick-up sticks. Jim scouts around for a way through, and calls to us when he succeeds. Louis, especially, is finicky about crossing obstacles.

Crocuses peep yellow and purple heads from soil only beginning to warm. My pack is about to multiply: I am again pregnant. With twins. Jake, almost five, has many labels and diagnoses: seizure disorder, vision impairment, and the one I most resist, mental retardation. How can we know his mental abilities when he can't communicate? The longest label describes his inability to move himself: severe spastic quadriplegia. Too much muscle tone throughout his body, his brain unable to control movement.

The red Snug Seat is more an enhanced car seat perched on long legs with wheels for feet. It holds Jake high above ground. It is why we moved to a flat, single story house tucked in the scrub oak and Russian olive trees of a rocky hillside. No entry stairs, a quiet bump of a threshold. Wide doorways, which I nick anyway. Jake sits in his chair, lets me buckle his chest and tuck his feet under Velcro straps, and rides the bus four mornings a week to the Utah School for the Deaf and Blind. He isn't deaf. He isn't blind. Not in the typical way. He is cortically blind, a medical and legal classification acknowledging that the musculature is fine, but the brain is not. What Jake sees is a mystery to us. And possibly, to him.

I push Jake in his chipper red seat out the door, down the driveway to where a stunted yellow bus waits. His lunch is in a backpack strapped to the chair. Lunch is a liquid concoction, formula, microlipids, protein powder, a special diet to help control his seizures. He is fed through a tube connected to a hole in his stomach. Jake disliked eating, and at two and a half, I'd conceded that a gastrostomy tube was the only way he could receive the nutrition he needed. The hole is held steady by a "button" to which we attach tubing for liquid meals, with a little cover that snaps neatly closed when not in use. Should the button somehow come out—it's held to the surface of his belly by a balloon underneath the skin—we have a catheter to insert, to keep the skin from immediately beginning to close.

The driver wheels Jake's chair into the cavern of the bus and Jake is gone. For four hours. Beau is in the family room, building dinosaurs with fat yellow and red and blue Legos. He decides they need a cave and empties the Lego tub, which he turns sideways and shoves between two lumps of dinosaur. I open a textbook. I'm studying social work, earning my master's degree. Bob's company finally agreed to insure our family through their healthcare plan, and I'd quit Nordstrom the year before. We've kept the nanny, the beta female, so that I can study.

I am carrying twins, again, but almost everything is different. These are girls. They are fraternal. There have been no concerns.

Except one. The babies are so eager to join us I'm on drugs to keep them in. I inject myself twice daily with Terbutaline. I wear a monitor that transmits information to an office miles away where a nurse checks the data, then calls me if I need to give myself another shot. And on Easter weekend I am hospitalized because the Terbutaline isn't enough. I am dosed with indocin, and then sent to the University Hospital, which has a newborn ICU, just in case my labor cannot be stopped. I live there for six weeks. In a room around the corner from where I stayed after I delivered Jake and Little Joe, far enough away that I can, almost always, suppress the memories. The threat of preterm labor ebbs and flows. The nanny takes over care of the pack. Bob brings Beau to visit, my classmates bring me schoolwork. Most days I lie in bed, reading, writing papers, eating. Twice my labor breaks through and I am wheeled to a delivery room where I am doped, once with magnesium sulfate, the other time, alcohol. Deep in the emptiness of hospital night I stare at the ropes of IV tubing, watching a bubble. I am convinced by my delirium that death is not a terrible option.

When my babies are thirty-five weeks along, I'm released. I again inject myself with medication. But fear has lifted. Thirty-five weekers are generally healthy enough to survive without intervention. When my girls are thirty-six weeks along, my doctor stops the injections, and I immediately go into labor. I am drugged to the gills, and deliver the babies in an operating room with two obstetricians, two pediatricians, four nurses, and Bob, dressed in white protective gear so that all I can see are his eyes, his bushy dark eyebrows. Jake's and Beau's little sisters are born that night. Healthy. One chubbier than the other.

When the silliness from the drugs wears off, I am tearful. We name the littler, bald one Caitlin. The louder one with more hair, we name Allegra.

We turn the horses homeward after reaching a meadow where the valley tapers and appears to end. We take an eastern route that involves less up and down. By my reckoning, it's been at least two hours since I planted my bottom in this saddle, and the water bottle I've stashed in Waylon's left flank saddlebag holds only droplets. As we cross a ridge the wind rushes over us, grabbing my slightly-too-large hat and tossing it on my back, the stampede string pressing into my neck. The breeze is invigorating and I trade potential sunburn for the feel of the wind in my hair. The hills are covered with sagebrush and not much else; we see few signs of life. However, the dogs are better hunters than we, and around the next bend Tuffie and Duke corner a ground squirrel, barking, yelping, and Tipsy comes to investigate. Jim calls them off and they move on to splash through the creek, wriggling and shaking as they exit and run, again, ahead of us all. We draw closer to home, and although I've loved the ride, my knees and thighs and butt are telling me they'd like to dismount, soon, please, and my parched lips and throat and growling tummy are reminding me to be better prepared next time.

Waylon steps carefully down the side of the hill just half a mile from home. I can see the cabin roof below, the corral, the buck rail fence ringing pastureland, and I think about the fact that at least one wolf pack lives nearby. I picture wolves running through this land under cover of night, marking territory, searching for prey, then returning higher uphill to home, bellies filled with ground squirrels, perhaps, because there doesn't seem to be much else around here besides these horses. Jim hasn't had problems with wolves, most likely because he's cautious and proactive and perhaps just far enough from the closest pack that they don't often travel to his ranch. I reflect on last night's conversations with Keith. I try to stay in a neutral space because I, myself, don't have to protect my dogs and livelihood from apex predators on a regular basis. However, as much as I love a good discussion, I'm perceptive enough to know when nothing I have to say, no matter how well documented or justified or even true, will be heard by the other person.

When my baby girls swelled my pack to six, in 1996, wolves in Idaho and Yellowstone were producing their first litters. The wolves brought in for the reintroduction were individuals collected from different packs, placed in the acclimation pens by social order: a dominant male and dominant female in each, along with a few other, more subservient wolves. The hope was that dominant wolves would choose to mate. It's fairly impossible to dart, tranquilize, and collect an entire pack, for the wolves scatter with the first dart. Having wolves from different packs also allowed for greater genetic diversity, key for sustained populations.

Isle Royale, approximately forty-five miles long by nine miles wide, is the largest island in northwestern Lake Superior. It's part of Michigan and one of 450 smaller islands of the Isle Royale National Park. In a romantic wildlife story, this long, narrow island that lies approximately fifteen miles from Canada was in 1949 connected to the Canadian province of Ontario by an ice bridge, over which a pair of wolves traveled. At that point moose were the only large mammals on the island, all of them having descended from a number of ancestors who swam over to the island from Minnesota in the early 1900s. Isle Royale has become the site of the longest-running wolf-moose study, now in its fifty-seventh year, due to its remoteness and resulting limited human effects on the environment. The study is at risk, though: scientists predict that the chance of future ice bridges forming is negligible due to the warming climate (the most recent ice bridge was in 1997). This means inbreeding, with its resultant genetic weaknesses and population declines. At present, a debate exists about whether or not we intervene to save the wolf population by either introducing new wolves to the island in what biologists call a genetic rescue, or by reintroducing wolves to the island only if the current population dies out. A third option, to do nothing at all, may be in alignment with the National Park Service's mission of not meddling, but some argue that it was our meddling which caused the problem in the first place. Philosophical arguments can be made for either intervening or not; relying upon pure science won't help anyone, least of all the wolves.

But the Yellowstone wolves, back in 1996, were reproducing with aplomb.

Pete Bengeyfield is a Montanan, a photographer who travels to Yellowstone every few weeks. He's made these trips ever since he moved to Dillon in 1984. Dillon, Montana, is home base for the Forest Service's Beaverhead National Forest, Pete's employer, and a town with one of the country's most beautiful settings. Encircled by mountains—the Pioneers to the west staggering in their beauty—Dillon's valley collects three fat rivers, and is a haven to its four thousand or so residents. But Pete cheerfully leaves home every few weeks to go hang out in Yellowstone.

"Back in the early days of the introduction, those wolves, it was like letting them loose at a smorgasbord. There were so many elk, the wolf packs grew really big. So those first few years, the photography was amazing. You could see wolves every day. That was a surprise. We didn't expect those wolves to be so visible."

One of his best photography days was spent by Mary Bay, west and south of Lamar Valley.

"It was spring, and the Mollie's wolf pack had killed an elk. And a grizzly found the carcass. Bison were around, and the wolves, and coyotes. And you could watch the dynamics, who would take over the carcass and defend it from the other species. The bison—apparently bison become excited by the smell of blood—would come in every once in a while and drive the grizzly and the wolves off the carcass, and just stand there— then eventually the bison would leave. But to watch that interplay, it was fascinating. Lots of good photographs."

Excitement was palpable. Wolves were new to us, killing prey and having pups. It stirs something primal, it connects us to the rhythm of the land.

The horses are back in the corral, and I sit on the back porch with Jim. I've downed an entire water bottle, am eating carrots. I find it easy to talk with Jim about wolves.

"They've got their place." Jim's words roll leisurely. "But there needs to be some control. There needs to be a balance. As a rule, ranchers are good stewards of the ground. They honor the earth. They make good decisions that are long-reaching, because they know they're going to be here on this land each day they wake up."

However, they also need to make a living, he says, which is not easy even without wolves. When you add livestock losses due to wolf and bear and lion predation, the rancher is often hard pressed to stay afloat. I ask about compensation, and Jim says the only problem there is you have to be able to prove the kill was made by a wolf. When the wolf takes the whole body, say a young calf, there's nothing to show, unless you get lucky enough to find tracks. If you can't prove a wolf did it, you're simply out of luck.

Same as if the cow died of disease, or was caught and stranded in a blizzard. There's no compensation package for those kinds of losses. But death by predators falls into a different category, one in which the government has a hand. This issue lies deep in western soil: for as far back as most ranchers can reach, the government has controlled—killed—predators for them. Wildlife Services—a program of the U.S. Department of Agriculture—spends millions of dollars every year killing coyotes, porcupines, squirrels, foxes, even birds, all in efforts to placate livestock operators. This process is entrenched, according to longtime Animal Damage Control trapper and wolf expert Carter Niemeyer, because what's important in ranch country is to keep doing what everyone's used to doing. We've always killed varmints for ranchers; we'll keep killing varmints for ranchers.

Jim tells me about a fellow rancher who lost his dog to what he believes was a wolf. The story raises a rancher's hackles. The man was out herding cattle and one moment his dog was with him, the next it wasn't. He whistled and called and hollered, all with no response. He finished moving his cattle, completed his work, hoping the dog would show up back home. After a long, sleepless night, he went back the next day to look again, fearing the worst. Exploring the hillside near where he'd last seen his dog, he soon found the body, torn and bloodied, long dead. Although the livestock compensation program includes the loss of personal pets, the fund refused the rancher's claim, stating that since the dog was found in what was technically the wilderness, the dog's loss was ineligible for compensation.

"These ranchers are honest as the day is long," Jim says, "and that kind of situation doesn't do much for their tolerance of wolves. The dog is a natural enemy of the wolf, just like the coyote, and the fox, and instinct drives the wolf to kill and eliminate the potential competition."

This same rancher has lost eleven head now to grizzlies and wolves, and is not likely to believe anyone who tells him wolves are necessary to the ecosystem.

Jim and I talk about solutions, and I tell him about the Blackfoot Challenge up in Montana, a community that combines efforts of agencies and landowners to solve issues like predation and potential losses. He's never heard of this kind of program, and is instantly enamored of it. He nods, the lines by his eyes crinkling—when people work together and talk about it, you can work things out. He's seen this time and again both in his ranching life and in the years he's spent working winters for the Park Service. The thought of agencies working together isn't something he's used to—neither is Keith—and I can see he's intrigued.

"Things have changed around here a lot, what with those conservationists buying up grazing permits and retiring the land. We used to have ten thousand cows here, and now we have at most six or seven hundred on the range. There're only three ranges left—Gros Ventre, Miner's, and Bier's Creek—and the ranch next to me, as well as the horse ranch down the valley, they don't have to make a living from it. Some's just a tax write-off. Those of us that have to make a living, well, we've got to be watching every fence and gate and cow, and there's not room for much loss. You can understand the tension."

Jim loves his land, his horses, the cattle, his dogs. He loves his work, his view of the Tetons. His life. Wolves are just one piece of it, and life is long. All things can eventually be worked out.

I haven't had cellular reception for days, here at the ranch. So I haven't called home.

I could have called Saturday morning on my bike ride, could have paused in Jackson, made the call. But I didn't want to. I feel bigger here, I reach down into earth and up into sky. And to call home and speak with Daniel will deflate me. It will connect me again with what I fear cannot be worked out.

After leaving Jim's ranch, I drive to the lookout above Landslide Lake. I sit on the grass, stare into what used to be a gentle valley, what is now a body of water broken by the tip-tops of pine trees. They were drowned almost a century ago. Sunlight bends and bounces off the flat surfaces and its heat slips under my skin. I breathe. A deep inhalation, an expansion. Breath sinks into lungs, spreads through abdomen, heart, into each limb, out to fingers, toes. If breath, *prana,* reaches each curving hill within me I am well. It touches dunes, creeks, buttes. Slides over plateaus. Stirs lakes. Finds caverns and whisks them free of that which a pack rat has stashed along the walls. Whips down slot canyons, uncovers star-bright skies, flashes power into a dormant volcano. Spies upon secret caches, blesses them with a gentle breeze. My inner landscape, cleansed and revived, draws closer to mirroring the solid grace that envelops me. I find another piece of myself here.

It's time to begin the long drive home. I rise, brush the earth from my skirt, breathe in one last lungful of the Gros Ventre Valley. I need to bring some home with me.

Speech cannot exist without breath.

6. fracture

He waits, resting. The old bull elk they killed two days ago has meat left on its bones, but Yellow Eyes is not hungry. Not for food. Leaves crunch under his paws. The hillside is covered with brush and grasses, now faded to palest wheat. Aspen leaves flutter yellow, the cottonwoods shed leaves mottled gold and brown. The scrubby pines alone remain green. The pack is fourteen strong. They begin arising from an afternoon nap. They stretch. Yawn. Yellow Eyes rubs his shoulder against Sophie. He presses his nose against his father's head. He nudges the four youngest pups. He steps away from them. He howls. They lift their heads, wail.

Yellow Eyes turns from the sandstone hillside toward the trees at the southern edge of the field. The others watch as his tail moves through the waving sedge. The dark tip disappears. Sophie howls again, and the others follow. The sound reaches Yellow Eyes. He lifts his head. His trot changes to a lope, and he moves through the trees in near silence. The river is on his left. He will follow it until he is done following it. Then he will find another guide. He runs until the sun drops below the mountains and the world glows gold.

The next morning he stalks a hare, flushes it from a bush. At the river he drinks. He follows a trail up a ridge. At the top he stands, sniffs the air. He smells elk, he smells coyote. He does not smell wolf. He howls, the call floating over the hanging valley below. Silence answers. He runs along the top of the ridge until it bends toward the valleys below. Yellow Eyes looks to his right, then to his left. He picks his way down the rocky cleft, toward a sea of trees that beckon him. He runs south.

The moment I land on the hard road surface I wail. *Shit-shit-shit.* I bang the heel of my right shoe against the asphalt, rotating it, the ball of my shoe still clipped to the pedal. Shit-shit-shit I'm done! I'm done, I give, I get the message, no more. No races, no more daylong rides. I hurt like hell, I can't move. Shit-shit-shit. Oh God, I hurt.

"Her cycling season is over." The words, the first I remember, come from a paramedic with dark blue cotton legs. They send a spurt of adrenaline into my system: oh, you don't know me. It's only August; my season is so not over.

Dualities.

I lie on my left side, unable to move my upper body. I let people help unclip shoes from pedals, remove my bike from beneath me. Daniel is there, hovering, had been a half mile behind me and missed seeing the crash, had rounded the corner to see me splayed on the ground. Someone helps me sit up and my left arm shrieks. Oh God, oh God. I lean forward, face over legs.

"I think I might throw up," I mumble.

"Here, we'll give you some Zofran, you're okay, let us get that on board, we'll get this IV going."

Two paramedics place an air splint around my left arm and an IV in my right. They shoot the anti-nausea medication into my vein as I sit, stupefied, wondering what the hell happened to my arm, my shoulder, my body. Then I am on a gurney, loaded into a shiny ambulance and whisked away, off to the emergency room, on to the end of the summer's cycling. Or maybe to the end of something else.

As we glide on the freeway I ask the attendant if he can please remove my heart rate monitor. It's unbearably tight around my chest, it hurts to breathe. I can't imagine why it's this bad. Last time it wasn't this bad. I'm fairly certain I've broken my left clavicle, but I don't know why my arm hurts so much. And my chest. Have I broken my elbow? I hurt like hell.

The emergency room is empty. The staff seem almost disappointed I'm not dripping blood and intubated. The x-ray technicians want me to lift my left arm; I moan. Stand here, twist that way, lift this, lean back. I glean their concerns are about shoulder and back, not arm, and soon a calm doctor tells me that my crash has broken ribs number two through six, fractured my scapula, and separated my shoulder. I stare as if he's speaking Swahili. Just the night before I'd been with friends watching a pro bike race in Salt Lake City, the course passing a corner of the University of Utah. We'd gathered at a small park, and watched the cyclists whip down a descent and make a right, passing us at speeds I would never, ever consider on a forty-five degree turn. I'd been wearing a sundress that exposed my collarbones, and someone had joked about how the left didn't match the right, as it didn't yet have a titanium plate holding the bone together. Yet. Ha-ha.

I'd expected the Swahili-speaking doctor to tell me my left clavicle was broken, not the scapula. Clavicle and ribs—I'd broken those three years earlier, and knew the process. Scapula, ribs, separated shoulder—no idea. I'm given some painkillers on top of the Zofran. Scapula, shoulder, ribs. Oh, that shitty gravel disguised as stable road surface. My arrogance. My bike, tasked with trying to bridge the two.

Diagnosis issued, we discuss insurance. They want to admit me, but my insurance won't pay for a hospital stay here. I climb into a second ambulance and am routed to the University Hospital, a teaching hospital. If my first emergency room visit had been anticlimactic, this second visit is anything but. Wheeled into a large room with a labeled disk of exam results on my gurney, the twenty people awaiting me perform as if I'd fallen off my bike moments before, am in cardiac arrest, and possibly have a brain injury to boot.

"Incoming trauma! Trauma code Quince, female, fifty-one years old, bike accident, move this tray, over here, one-two-three lift, move," as they swing me from gurney to exam table—they aren't about to let me, heaven forbid, walk—the neurologist takes over, look this way, eyes here, look there, can you see this light? Can you feel this, can you point your toes, does this hurt? My left arm is pulled from my side—ow—could you please warn me before you do things like that? I'm ignored. Five people are moving, five are talking, ten more are standing in their scrubs with arms folded or tucked in pockets, observing.

I'm admitted, they take more x-rays and a CT and shuttle me off to a room on the sixth floor where they can watch me begin to heal. There is nothing to stitch, no cut deep enough for even a Band-Aid. A few inches of road rash, a purple bruise by my hip, the serious hurt hidden within. Most of a day lost to emergency rooms. Then two more days lost to hospital life. Daniel brings me toiletries and updates from home, a friend brings magazines and chocolate. No one brings me what I truly want, a healed body.

Home. The scrapes lighten from angry to irritated, the deep ugly bruise on my left hip adds yellow to its purple and blue. I learn how to wash my hair and load the dishwasher with one arm. I try to sleep. I don't want my cycling season to be over. I'm crushed to miss the upcoming two-hundred-mile race I'd registered for. I feel like my bruise looks.

Eleven days after the accident I am able to walk half a mile. I can barely breathe by the end, but I walk. After, I finagle a ride from my daughter Cait, asking her to drive me to a nearby women's clothing boutique that has a wall full of cowboy boots.

I need cowboy boots. I try on three pair, with difficulty, since the left side of my upper body is useless and in low-grade agony. It isn't easy to pull on a boot with one arm. I choose a beautiful pair, pale earthy gray, embroidered with ivory loops and scrolls. I haven't worn cowboy boots since college, can't explain my need. Cait smiles as I pay. She drives me back home.

The next day I return to the hospital because my left lung is in a state of collapse. I'd visited my orthopedic surgeon that morning, posed for more x-rays, discussed whether or not to surgically repair the fracture in my scapula. We'd decided to let it heal naturally, and reassess later if necessary. Back home, giddy with relief that I didn't need to undergo surgery, I answered cheerfully when my phone rang.

"Susan, Dr. Kubiak here. I should have caught this while you were here, but your left lung is about fifty percent collapsed. I need you to go to the ER. I'll call over and let them know you're coming. Now is good."

Surgery—two tubes shoved through the side walls of my chest to drain the blood, the fluids, the air from my leaking lung. Four more days in the hospital; I contemplate death during darkest night. Then a wretched recovery. All a result of my bike sliding on a patch of well-camouflaged gravel, then hitting smooth asphalt and flipping, sending me violently to the ground. I have injured my core. The edge of my scapula, the meeting place of wings. Ribs—the cage protecting my heart. And now the punctured lung, what holds breath, life itself.

Life halts. Hours of nothingness slink by. I read meaningless fiction once I give up the narcotics that nauseate and incapacitate me and instead take Tylenol, ibuprofen, naproxen. Each evening I prepare a bed on the couch or the chaise, molding pillows into shapes to support my broken spots, and set out pills to take at midnight, at three, at five. I sleep in fits and starts, in pain. I spend hours staring into the dark, tears threatening, exhausted but unable to sleep for more than an hour or two at a time.

The day of the crash, Daniel had said, you don't know what it's like to see someone you love lying there on the ground, broken. And he'd cooked, run errands, ordered pizza and handed out lunch money. But he can't actually tell me what it was like to see me lying there on the ground, broken. And he barely touches me—doesn't want to hurt me—offering me neither physical support, nor a big, safe space for the emotional healing I need. He doesn't know what to do with me. I tell him I am touchable, I won't break. My scars are ugly and I want him to ask to see them, I want him to soothe them, I want him to help me make them better. All things he doesn't know how to do. And he doesn't know he doesn't know.

Little by little, I heal. Each day moves me closer to something approaching normal. I tick off my follow-up appointments, my releases from the trauma department's care, the orthopedist's care. I gain a physical therapist who touches me with concern and compassion, setting free the tears I've held. At six weeks post-crash, she is the first person to touch me, my skin, my scars, my broken places. I am one lonely wolf tired of licking her own wounds. I don't want to be so alone. I want my pack. I restart my own psychotherapy, digging deeper into why I am in the situation I'm in, what made me choose it, why I remain in it. What I need to do to find my voice again.

In the mornings I wake up wounded. Scratches mar my belly, my back. A shoulder. I battle myself as I sleep, clawing my skin.

I stare at my cowboy boots. Somewhere out there, there are others like me, with their own quirky needs and desires. These boots make me happy. They're proof I honor my inner wolf. Someday soon I'll put them on and revel in my howling, love-filled, authentic *life*. And in that life, someone will ask to see my scars. Will touch them with love. Will let me see and touch his own.

In the 1800s wolves still ranged throughout the northern and western United States. Their prey: deer, elk, caribou, moose, bison. These ungulates—herbivores all—eat grass, young plants, saplings, willows. Such flora flourish in riparian areas, the rich bedrocks of ecosystems. Rivers, streams, even creeks and marshes. Here soil is fertile; water brings life. Herbivores collect in riparian areas, attracted by not only the water, but by young growth, shoots and stalks, tender, easily masticated and digested. However, herbivores with wolves in pursuit rarely lingered at the edge of a stream. Constantly wary, they nibbled, moved along, ate, moved farther downstream. Not all willow was eaten, enough aspen sprouts survived to become trees. Riverbanks remained intact. When wolves were culled from the land, herbivores relaxed. They slowed. They stayed longer in each spot, they ate a willow bush to the ground. They chewed and tugged at a sapling until it came unrooted, then started on the next. They ate the grass that lined and crept down the riverbanks' slopes.

Today, wolves return to these riparian landscapes, and challenge both herbivores and scavengers. Wolves have the potential to return balance. Recent research shows the wolf's presence to ignite a trophic—feeding—cascade. The wolf, by threatening and killing the ungulate, permits greater willow and aspen growth, which draws more beaver and small mammals, which attracts more songbirds and frogs and on down to an assemblage of helpful insects. Riverbanks themselves benefit when elk are kept anxious and moving, since the shrubs and scrub at their edges have greater opportunity to grow and mature, their roots stabilizing the soil.

Wolves also trim coyote populations by directly killing them, or decreasing their access to prey. Fewer coyotes means more rabbits and small rodents in an environment. Which means more food for foxes, owls, hawks.

And since wolves can't usually consume an entire, large ungulate carcass in one sitting, they provide carrion for eagles, falcons, ravens, grizzly bears, and foxes. Grizzlies eat whitebark pine seeds, which are becoming increasingly sparse due to warming climates and the resulting increased number of destructive pine bark beetles. When wolves are in grizzly country, the grizzlies have more dietary options. They feed both on wolf kills, and on berries, which are more abundant, since elk are less often mowing young bushes down. When we ignored Aldo Leopold's precaution of intelligent tinkering—to save all the parts—and extirpated all of the country's wolves, we operated without full understanding of the wolf's purpose. Doug Smith suggests that the return of the wolf is like a pebble at the top of a mountain. As it rolls it gathers speed, bumps into others, sending them spinning and turning. They bounce and bang, thunder downhill, and suddenly a single pebble has generated an avalanche.

The wolf, who performs a vital function in the ecosystem, is guided by its own nature. The wolf simply is. He never tries to be what he is not. His nature dictates behavior, attitude, demeanor. He will learn from his pack, and will take on the role his pack and temperament accord. However, whether an alpha female or an omega at the bottom of the social scale, each wolf remains, at heart, a wolf. We humans have greater breadth in our range of possibilities, limited as it is by our inability to sprout wings or fins. But we too are guided by what our nature dictates. Discovering strengths, passions and limits, learning to celebrate who we are, is a process Gerard Manley Hopkins called selving, a self-enactment, an inevitable self-expression. A line from his poem "As kingfishers catch fire" is my guide along this journey: "What I do is me: for that I came." I need to think like the wolf. Focus on what I do best, be who I'm meant to be, honor that authenticity.

Knowing why we came takes time. It begs an internal assessment, a soul-searching. This is human work, we are the only animal capable of such examination. Choosing to do so is like signing up for a never-ending graduate course where exams and assignments appear regularly and the grades are all self-assigned. It requires accepting truth, grieving and healing wounds, embracing the parts of human nature that are both wild and self-reliant, wolf-like. Fanged, hungry. Untamed. Wounded. Mended without benefit of splint or surgery.

As a top predator, the wolf roams and dens where it chooses. Territorial disputes erupt with other packs or individual marauders, but a wolf has little to fear from other animals. She may steer clear of a grizzly bear, but she also knows she can outrun one. The human mind, as well, roams and dens where it chooses. It will hide in denial to evade pain, or will cycle through petty worries to avoid confronting more significant concerns. It dodges threats and wounds, wraps itself in comforting fantasies. Taming these wolf-like aspects of our mind is part of our work, part of what deepens and enriches us. Accepting that we have a wildness to our nature is good, but letting it take over the mechanisms of our mind is not. I ache to be wild and brave and howl. But I'm most likely to get there by addressing wounds and potential harm, rather than by trying to outrun it all.

I've been expending tremendous effort to be who I can no longer be. Someone who was effective in an earlier life, who behaved in ways that kept her safe. Who said yes when she ached to say no, who made everyone else more important than herself. What would happen if I let that go? Looking behind my words, actions, and masks is akin to flaying my own skin, exposing what is messy and unappealing. I am protective, passive. I do not speak. I suppress my truth. I repress my woundedness. Pain roars. But exposure to light reveals truth.

What I do is me, for that I came. Daniel doesn't want the true me. He wants someone who lives on the surface of life, who doesn't need deep emotional connection. I cannot be her. I am trying to fit in a box, my arms up and askew, knees to chest, one foot twisted inward to fit inside the edge. Miserable, growing sore spots and stretching joints beyond their limits, knowing aches and blisters will result. Don't explain, don't defend, my soul whispers. Speak your truth. Maybe when you landed on the ground and shouted I'm done, it wasn't about your cycling season. Unfold yourself from that self-imposed box, clear your throat, throw out a howl. *Now.*

We claim to have killed wolves to keep us safe. In truth, I become safe when I learn to control that which is within me. It is by accepting, understanding, and learning to control my base nature that I am freed to fully participate in the world around me, understanding that greater purposes than my own exist. When I recognize myself in the wild beast, I see how my own urges and desires may create harm. I learn that control is a form of wisdom. Freud's *Civilization and Its Discontents* describes human nature as being instinctually endowed with a powerful desire for aggressiveness, and suggests that any neighbor presents as a temptation to satisfy that aggression, inciting behavior from theft to humiliation to murder.

Human work includes acknowledging the beast within, celebrating the positive aspects of this wildness, and taming the harmful, a concept Herman Hesse explored in his classic novel *Steppenwolf.* Hesse examines this duality of nature and declares it is not exclusive to humans. Harry Haller, the protagonist, explains himself as having two souls within, the soul of a man and the soul of a wolf, who clash and battle and occasionally move together in unity. Haller undertakes a pilgrimage toward harmony, to either overcome the wolf, or to renounce mankind. But Hesse goes further, noting that wolves, too, are not simple creatures, but creatures of manifold complexity. Research, driven by man's curiosity, has determined that many of the world's creatures share this complexity, from dolphins to chimpanzees to wolves. We are not the only beings possessing both intelligence and natures teeming with dualities. It seems man is not really so different from wolf.

A significant distinction, however, lies in our ability to explore our complexities and our wounds. Digging deep within exposes scars, begins to heal them. Of course, this process is hardly a pleasant one. Self-analysis can feel like walking a gangplank blindfolded, no idea where the next step will lead: solid ground, or a trembling board, or a fall into salty water ringed with sharks. And even healed wounds rarely disappear. My vulnerabilities travel with me. I will always react to healthy twins with a twinge of hurt. All men possess the potential to destroy my confidence. I am often naïve and gullible, giving my trust too easily. It is difficult to accept these still tender places.

Because the complexity of the human psyche builds on past experience, even small traumas affect us, especially those experienced when we're young and our immature minds develop defense mechanisms to help us survive. But, to the frequent detriment of lives and relationships, often these mechanisms and their negative side effects remain long after the trauma is past. Common defense mechanisms include projection—attributing our own negative beliefs, feelings, or attitudes to others—and denial, the refusal to accept information in conflict with our beliefs. Another frequently used tool is displacement, which amounts to kicking the dog when we're upset with our spouse and can often result in scapegoating: when it's difficult, unacceptable, or dangerous to direct anger at the true target, those feelings are redirected toward another target. Sometimes, it would seem, onto wolves, who have become the recipients of astonishing vitriol in the rural West.

Of course, scapegoating is just one way wolves are vilified and detesting wolves is not a sure symptom of unresolved child-hood trauma. Shakespeare wrote, "in time we hate that which we often fear." Barry Lopez suggests humans have a fear of the beast—an irrational, insatiable creature—and that we also fear the beast within ourselves: we fear our own nature. Internal fears are often projected onto things outside ourselves. The wolf, powerful and large-toothed, absorbs many fear-based projections, and in turn suffers our hatred, poisons, and bullets.

William Makepeace Thackeray may have been close to the truth when he said, "People hate as they love, unreasonably." Not everyone who hates wolves is irrational. Proponents of wolves aren't all brilliant and emotionally stable. But those who acknowledge their own wild nature, the fears and angers and furor within, are more likely to be receptive to wildness without.

A man who was once wounded and angry himself, Doug Peacock suggests one of our society's maladies is an antagonis-tic alienation, found primarily in white males, that presents as hostility toward people of other races, wild animals, and wild land. Peacock contrasts this in *Walking It Off*—his book about returning from the Vietnam War—with the attitudes of indig-enous peoples, who relate to the land and its inhabitants in ways that are both symbiotic and sustainable. Peacock spent decades walking the land, working to regain his humanity. He has strug-gled with alienation and anger, even vitriol. But he also knows that to live a life filled with such is to miss the point. And that the best, and easiest, way to regain health is to connect with something greater than oneself. The wild, the unpretentious, the genuine: nature. Doug believes, as do many others, that changing an individual life today requires reconnecting spiritually and metaphorically with the land, with wildness.

And it's okay if some of us need a therapist, too.

Bob and I worked with a therapist when Jake was three, Beau was almost two, and the girls weren't even a thought. In the newborn ICU a nurse had told us, *Lots of divorces begin right here.* Bob and I would be different. Whenever Jake developed a symptom, doctors spoke to us in numbers. There's a ninety percent chance this won't happen. Only about fifteen percent develop that complication. A good ninety-five percent don't need further surgery. Jake was always, always, in the smaller group, the less fortunate. We started to laugh about it. And we were absolutely not going to join the group whose marriages fell apart because of a child with special needs.

We learned it was better to talk than not, and that we were extremely different. We shared values, goals, some activities. But Bob loved to socialize, to party, to go and do. I loved to retreat within, to talk with just a few people at a time, to stay and be. We compromised. We were married for life.

And then we decided to have one more baby. Which turned out to be two.

Once the twin girls were mobile, our family developed a divide, a fissure. Bob and the three younger children would go do. Jake and I would stay and be. Bob took them to the pool, to movies, to barbeques. I prepared Jake's formula, kept his medications organized, rotated boxes of syringes, diapers, tubes, skin care creams, bed liners. I did laundry. I read and wrote. I held Jake on my lap and breathed with him.

Wolves, in 1998, had spread throughout Yellowstone—and outside its borders into Grand Teton National Park, Montana, and Wyoming—and a large portion of central Idaho. Packs were thriving, protecting territories, producing pups, keeping prey on its proverbial toes. The original thirty-one wolves released in Yellowstone—fourteen in 1995, and seventeen in 1996—had increased to 112, in ten packs. Idaho's wolf population—which began with fifteen released in 1995, and twenty more brought in the following year—had climbed to approximately 121 in twelve different packs. In the first few years, Doug Smith knew each wolf intimately, could recognize it by its appearance and its behaviors. Wolves are highly individualistic, which made theories difficult to substantiate. It was becoming clear to Doug that his research projects were going to be complex—that wolves were unlikely to offer irrefutable facts, but more likely to "lure us on a long and crooked journey of constant learning."

Jake mellowed. He settled into himself, became fairly predictable. He liked a dry diaper, to have his position changed frequently, to be held. His primary complaint was sitting in his wheelchair. The Snug Seat, long outgrown, had been traded for a Quickie, a true wheelchair. But Jake's spasticity, his high muscle tone, was drawing one hip higher than the other, curving his spine. His scoliosis caused pain in a rigid seat. The next step was a custom molded seat system. He sat in a bean bag chair filled with special pellets, from which all of the air was then sucked out. Jake's impression became a mold for his new seat, which would finally fit his unique curve of hip, ribs, pelvis.

The structure of his new seat cradled him, it fit. And it would be perfect until he outgrew it. Then, a new mold would have to be made, a new form created.

In the film *Never Cry Wolf*, the old Inuit's face is lined, so wrinkled and worn he looks a hundred years old. A fur-lined hood frames his face. His body, his hands and feet are bundled to seal his skin from the frigid air. He speaks little English, but wishes to assist the young American, Farley Mowat, who asks him questions about wolves. But do they eat caribou? Chase humans? Eat mice?

The Inuit stares into Mowat's eyes. He pauses, then lifts his head, lets it fall. He speaks a single word. *Sometimes.*

Nunamiut Eskimos have never known life without *amaguk*—wolf. They observe how the wolf participates within an environment, and what it does in the context of the larger universe, never attempting to explain the wolf as a singular concept. *Amaguk* is part of the landscape and part of the experience. From observing wolves, the Eskimos learn to track prey, and predict prey behavior. They don't, however, expect a wolf to behave predictably. They know that the wolf will sometimes do things because she is young, or old, or because the temperature shifts, or because her pups are close by. Nunamiuts value the wolf for what he teaches, and admire his skill. What the Nunamiut, the Inuit, and other Arctic populations don't feel about the wolf is fear.

Wolves are elusive predators that are, at times, surprisingly unpredictable. They usually hide from humans but sometimes approach them, staring, curious. They won't always kill an exposed and vulnerable elk calf. They will sometimes kill twenty sheep and then leave without eating more than one, or any at all. (Doug Peacock will tell you that a self-respecting wolf will kill any sheep it can: sheep—stolid, bleating, moving only when others do, releasing a constant stream of feces—are just meant to die.) Wolves are intelligent, and capable of making decisions based on assessments. Just because they usually behave in a given way doesn't mean they always do. This capriciousness is part of their intrigue, their charisma. Their complexity.

Wildlife biologist David Mech's wolf-moose research on Isle Royale has shown the unpredictable nature of wolves, documenting cases where a wolf pack will ignore a moose, or walk away from a stare-down. A pack of wolves on the hunt may surround a moose, looking ready to kill their prey, when one wolf will suddenly start nipping at the other wolves, calling them off, leaving the moose, curiously, unharmed. One of Mech's studies documented 160 moose sighted from the air that were close enough to wolves to be hunted: thirty percent escaped unscathed, almost twenty percent were ignored. Almost a quarter held their ground and were left alone, four percent were attacked. And just over twenty percent were encircled by wolves, but then not attacked.

Barry Lopez tells stories of the Alaskan Nunamiut who have been watching wolves for years, decades, and lifetimes. While they study wolves differently than biologists do, the Nunamiut, too, observed wolves that, at times, behaved in unexpected or never before seen ways.

One day Justus Mekiana, one of the older Nunamiut men, saw a wolf following a grizzly bear around all day, at a distance of about twenty yards. He took his eye from the spotting scope to say, "That's a new one, I haven't seen that before." Someone mentioned a family of wolves that had howled every day for two weeks during the denning season. Mekiana said he had never known wolves to do that, in forty years of watching them, but added: "I wonder if wolves change their behavior over time, you know, different in some ways from thirty years ago?" If he is correct, then the implications for wildlife biology are staggering. It means that social animals evolve, that what you learn today may not apply tomorrow, that in striving to create a generalized static animal you have lost the real, dynamic animal.

Max Scheler, who died in 1928, was a German philosopher whose life spanned the decades Americans were killing the nation's wolves. Scheler suggested that animals are born with a specific set of instincts that limit their behavioral options. Because an animal must immediately upon birth survive in its environment, these instincts guide all behavior, forcing the animal into dependence upon its role in that environment. In contrast, humankind is physically free from both the organic world and the environment, providing a foundation for its flexibility—a Darwinian concept—or free will. Our ability to master multiple environments, to exploit this flexibility, becomes an argument for our superiority, justifying our right to determine how and where animals, as lesser beings, will live. But confronted by an animal with what appears to be its own free will, its own idiosyncrasies, I rethink that stance. Maybe I'm not superior after all. The wolf has a wide range of behaviors and is less predictable than many other wild animals. She learns, changes habits, evolves, neglects to follow established patterns. She makes choices. Is cooperative and playful. Wild. Perhaps to learn from wolves is an intended piece of my own evolution.

As enchanting as the Amorak fable—the story of how wolves saved the caribou population—is, it's true that wolves don't always select the weak, the ill, the old. At times wolves luck out and kill a large, healthy cow or bull elk, a strong caribou. Even a healthy bison. But such animals can injure or even kill a wolf with their kicks, leading wolves to more often choose the young, injured, or feeble. However, as Nunamiut Justus Mekiana proffered, it's possible that what we studied and learned twenty years ago may change before the next decade ends.

Indeed, similar to David Mech's findings and the Nunamiut's understanding, biologist Rolf Peterson, fifty years into his study of wolves, found the longer the period of study, the less possible it is to take data and bundle it into a concise representation of what a wolf is and how a wolf behaves. Though his studies are scientific, the interactions he observes and evaluates aren't necessarily predictable, repeatable, and generalizable.

Biologists continue to study wolves, wanting to understand pack structure, social norms, predatory patterns, behaviors, how and why and when they howl. They want to say wolves will do this, wolves won't do that. They search for these understandings in part from the human desire for predictability and control. In terms of data on reproduction, stature, genetics, answers are easy to find, and usually, to quantify. Just like with humans. But when it comes to certain predictability and real understanding, biologists—and I—might have to be satisfied to know that wolves are creatures a lot like us. They follow particular patterns. They chase elk, they will eat ground squirrels and mice, they shy away from humans, they kill bison calves. *Sometimes*.

A fractured wolf pack operates poorly. David Mech's research shows that when both alphas are killed, young pups will likely die of starvation, while yearlings will disperse, usually mating with other stragglers or joining another intact pack. With the death of an alpha male, the subordinate males begin jostling for power. Without the oppression of the alpha male, more males will mate, and more new pups will be born in spring. Hunting and social skills aren't taught as competently. Young wolves, having not fully incorporated the way of the hunt, are ineffective. They then search out cattle or sheep, easier targets. They stray far from home. They're shot for killing domestic animals, or they starve.

Consequences can be just as dramatic when the alpha female dies, especially if the death occurs during breeding season. Although a surviving alpha male will often keep breeding controlled by choosing a new mate from within the pack, a willing partner isn't always available.

When 06, the alpha female of the Lamar Canyon pack, was killed, her pack was splintered too severely to heal. Wolf packs are nomadic in winter, following prey. The pack had left the park and was miles from Lamar Canyon when 06 was shot and killed in December. The pack's alpha male, 755, was mateless when breeding season arrived in February. Every female in his pack was his daughter. Each refused to mate with him. 755 left the pack and returned to Lamar Valley, where a female from the Mollie's pack mated with him. Soon 755's daughters and the rest of his pack returned to the valley. They attacked the new female, who, pregnant, dragged herself off to die in the trees. The alpha male left the pack in search of another mate, but his daughters refused to travel with him. The Lamar Canyon pack had fallen apart.

My pack, in our Salt Lake City home, was still functional. The fissure separated us at times, but it was navigable. Four on one side, two on the other, all of us able to leap across it and rejoin. Jake wheeled.

7. absence

Yellow Eyes runs. A deer jumps ahead, its white bottom flashing beneath its tail. A doe. She leaps, bounds, darts between trees. He is a dozen yards behind. Twigs crack. Leaves explode. He gains a foot, another. Breath spurts from the doe's moist nostrils. Her ears press against her neck. He is another yard closer. She plunges down a ravine, through a creek, up the other side, losing more of her lead. Sleek and smooth, Yellow Eyes runs until the doe nears collapse and turns to look back, slapping a lodgepole pine with her shoulder. She lurches, off balance. Rights herself, then bounds again. Yellow Eyes is within feet, a foot, and he draws alongside nearest her neck, avoiding those rear legs. He launches, teeth spread wide, and crunches through skin, cartilage, muscle. She flounders, staggers. He holds tight, twists his head back and forth, blood pouring over his throat and chest. She falls to the ground, and he falls with her.

Each day he follows scents of pine, oak, river, elk. A mountain lion, a coyote. Rabbits. No wolf. He walks. Trots. Alone. He sleeps at night, naps after hunting. By day, he travels. The air dries out, the ground hardens. The trees thin. And still he heads south.

I've checked the weather forecast—it's going to be damn cold in Missoula. It's already late October, but weeks of indoor recovery from my bicycling accident robbed me of our Indian summer, and I am not yet ready to embrace winter. Thick wool socks and mittens lie in my bag, and I have a seven-hour drive to resign myself to putting them on.

Clark Kent has nothing on Seth Wilson. I'd met Seth briefly on our June trip to Missoula. Strong cheekbones, a shock of dark hair, glasses. His canvas shirt and rugged Carhartts were just the western version of Kent's suit and tie. Seth works for the Blackfoot Challenge, a private non-profit, organized to conserve and enhance both natural resources and the rural way of life. As the organization's wildlife coordinator, Seth lives and breathes coexistence: people, livestock, and predators. He knows he's saving animals one at a time, a laborious undertaking, but his group steadily inches forward. Nestled in a large valley northeast of Missoula, the watershed is home to approximately 7,500 people living in seven small communities, about forty working calf-cow operations, and ten- to twelve thousand cattle. It encompasses a million and a half acres of land. In June, I'd asked if I could visit in autumn, to work with his range rider, to meet a few ranchers, to see how real people were making peace with wolves. We'd penciled in an early September date, which changed to later in the month. Then to the first of October, and eventually to the final week of that month, when it turned bitter cold and snow began to fall.

I've packed attire that will allow me to blend into the watershed. Jeans. Long underwear. Down jacket. I want to be taken seriously, and decide the best way to achieve this is with enough layers to keep me warm, thick-soled boots, and an attitude of acceptance. Montana folk don't complain about the weather. I won't either. I pack snacks and fill a messenger bag with my laptop, journal, digital recorder and enough charging cords to power a small town. I have water, Diet Cokes and carrots in my cooler, a fleece blanket and gloves in the passenger seat, and a traffic report that terrifies me.

I had planned to drive my Mini Cooper from Salt Lake to Missoula. When Seth and I talked on the phone the morning I was leaving, he warned me to check the weather forecast and Department of Transportation maps. Monida Pass, at the border of Idaho and Wyoming, is treacherous when blizzards rage, and it looked like it was going to be that kind of day. Crap.

"Do you have four-wheel drive?" he asked.

No.

"Front-wheel drive?"

Yes, I think, no, I'm sure it must be.

"If you can't make it, have to spend the night somewhere along the way, just let me know. We can reschedule things, don't worry," Seth said.

Each word sped my pulse, and my hands trembled. After we disconnected I checked out the Idaho road conditions on the DOT website, which posted blizzard conditions at the pass. *Crap.* My car is not a snow car. I'd be driving a car without snow tires, a car that weighs less than a buffalo, over a pass the Idaho DOT described as snow packed, windblown, wicked. My car was loaded, though, and I was determined to get to Missoula that day. It was Monday, and I had to be home Thursday evening, to catch a plane Friday to New York. There wasn't time to be a wimp.

I walk into the living room where Daniel sits. I tuck my hands into my back pockets to still them.

"I just got off the phone with Seth. I guess that big storm is in Idaho, and the pass is terrible. Monida Pass—have you ever driven that? It's I-15, just before you get into Montana."

"No, I don't know that." He types on his laptop, feet propped on an ottoman.

"Well, I guess it's really raging there—I'm nervous about it," I say. Daniel has a big truck parked in his company's warehouse, and his all-wheel-drive sedan sits outside our house. I don't want to ask for either, but I'd like him to offer some concern, some empathy, encouragement even. Something to help me deal with the fear squeezing my throat.

"You know," Daniel says, "they just delivered the windows this morning to that house they're building across the street, and they've already got three installed. They're fast."

I look at him. He looks out the window at the new house.

I ball my fists, feel sweat on my palms. I'm shaking inside. He can't show me that he cares. It's as though there is a great big abyss where his heart should be. Maybe an abyss, maybe an abscess. I can't care anymore. I can't try anymore. I walk away.

During the first two hours of my drive, the weather is calm but I am not. I cannot believe him, I don't understand, my marriage is over—the words recycle through my head again and again. My stomach knots. I knew he had difficulty with emotions, but he'd always been a gentleman, considerate, protective. Concerned. But this morning it was obvious he didn't give a flying fuck about my wellbeing. And then I just walk away, unable to speak. This is my pattern. I am shocked into silence, then can neither defend myself nor even express my confusion. I lose my voice.

I drive on through Pocatello, through Idaho Falls, on to Dubois, where I stop for gas and the restroom. Frozen wind shoves me across the parking lot. The pass looms ahead. It's not visible, but the map tells me it is thirty miles and seventeen hundred feet of elevation in front of me.

Back on the highway, the wind, now carrying snow, blasts the car. As long as I can see the gray-black road surface in two lines for my tires I'll be okay. Swirls of white blow viciously, forming ridges and drifts, but the road remains clear. Until it fills with snow. Packed by tires, melted by tire friction and instantly frozen by the frigid air. Ice. I loosen my grip on the wheel and stab the stereo off. I ease off the gas. I become a little white bump of a road hazard. Semis whir past me, and I feel the draft tow then repulse my car. Near the top of the pass I slide, panicking for a split second before I lift my foot from the gas and let the car catch itself. No going over the edge for me. I take in a huge lungful of air and slowly let it out. Shit.

My marriage is so over.

Monida Pass summits 6,800 feet above sea level, anticlimactically. No alpine vista greets you, no Swiss chalet of a restaurant beckons. If there is even a sign telling me I am there, I can't see it for the snow dashing and storming around me. Forget Daniel, forget this blizzard, forget the perilous roads, I am going to Missoula and I am damn well getting there by this evening.

On the phone earlier Seth had apologized for a scheduling conflict that meant I'd be sharing him with others. An NPR team would be meeting up with us for some of the experiences. Not a problem, I'd said. Who knew what excitement these NPR guys might add to my trip. We'd all gather tomorrow afternoon, but I'd have Seth to myself in the morning. If I reached Missoula.

I pass a sign for Dell, which gives me hope. Dell is in Montana. The mountains now have trees, the hills round gently, and soon I'm in a pretty place I can enjoy when I dare take my eyes off the road. Eventually I hit Interstate 90 and am able to listen to the stereo again, so I play a recording of Jack London's *White Fang*, a story of wolves, and of men. I'm getting myself in the spirit. Only an hour away from Missoula and my hotel room. I'm every bit as tough as I need to be, and apparently, I'm ready to be single, too. Daniel can have his windows, his avoidance, his denial. Eight hours of driving, 525 miles away. I don't miss him one bit.

Clark Kent is waiting for me in the lobby the next morning, and after a quick breakfast in the Doubletree's restaurant where I pay ten dollars for oatmeal—wanting to write on the bill, *this is Montana, not Manhattan*—Seth and I take off in his sturdy Subaru for the watershed, half an hour away. Yesterday's storm didn't travel this far north, and it's clear and colder than hell. Nine degrees, maybe. I've layered up, adding a good twenty percent to my body size, yet fear I'm unprepared. Seth has an extra coat and gloves, which he offers. I hope not to need them. I grew up in Utah, and I think of myself as hardy. But in Montana I'm just a visitor from the city, from a state nowhere near as rough and challenging as this here country. A crack stretches its way across the Subaru's windshield, and scuffmarks ghost the inside of the passenger door, the glove box. A side pocket by Seth's door is filled with maps, a crushed aluminum can, a beef jerky wrapper, empty plastic bags. There must be a roll of duct tape somewhere in the back, a sleeping bag, lantern, freeze-dried food.

"David Brooks said there can be no unity without empathy. Empathy is crucial." Seth's words are firm as we discuss the concept of community-based conservation. He lists other groups that function as his does, noting that they're usually based in watersheds or drainages. "Riparian habitats are extremely productive, and that's where you'll find your ranches, your farms, where people make a living from the land. And we have to meet people where they are, work with them, have empathy for their positions. You know, being an environmentalist means being a walking contradiction." He laughs, a twist of a smile tugging his cheek, and admits he is no better than most of us at living, every minute of every day, how he believes to be best for the environment. "We're not always welcomed, for that very fact. These people live what we don't have to."

We pass through Milltown, a tiny community whose main street is lined with empty houses. Logging is a dying industry in these parts. One more casualty of limited resources. Growing trees takes much longer than felling them. I look through picture windows into empty rooms, house after house. The town behind us, we enter a winding canyon that soon opens up into the watershed.

"Somewhere around eighty percent of all species that are listed as threatened or endangered depend on private land for their history, and their lives. We need to work with those land-owners, support them, help them take care of what they have. Look, over there, a herd of elk." Seth points to the right and I see forty or fifty elk bulked together in a field. A small, scrubby hillock protects their flank. Regal, most weighing between five and eight hundred pounds, elk are sculpted creatures. Cow elk watch us, turning their heads, bodies sleek and stationary. Bull elk, their antlers three feet above their heads, a good five feet across, stare.

"Here's a situation. Some ranchers allow private hunting on their property, and some don't. Elk figure it out. They know they are safe right there, because that field's owner doesn't allow hunting. The problem comes when those elk wander into the fields next door, and start eating all the alfalfa another rancher is growing. Elk are not a rancher's best friend."

We pass the herd, round a corner. The landscape is tinged white, frost thick on everything from grass to wooden fence posts to barns. I wonder how much of the day I'll spend shiver-ing out in those fields. Maybe some nice ranchers will invite us into their kitchens.

"It's like an iceberg," Seth says, and I nod, hugging my arms. "All of our work has gone on under the water. Building relation-ships, hosting forums, listening." Oh, a metaphor. "Ninety per-cent of the work we do is with willing landowners. We've been working on all of this for years. And those six or seven years spent doing bear work, before the wolves showed up, has helped us grapple with the wolf issue—we'd already built a founda-tion. The beauty and the magic of the Blackfoot is that we've built trust, we've broken down barriers, they understand we're not here to force our values on them. And this is what leads to changes in practice. We've come to realize if it isn't voluntary, long term, it isn't going to work. Things move at a snail's pace, but they move."

The valley widens further, and fields line the road. Set back are ranch houses, big barns, hulking machines at rest by fences and outbuildings. A sign cloaked by pines announces the Paws Up, a Luxury Ranch and Resort, and we pass a small eatery named Cully's. Seth tells me we'll probably grab lunch there. I ask him how the Challenge has convinced area residents to work together on issues.

"Basically there are three ways to deal with it. One is to go to the coffee shop—like Cully's over there—and complain. That doesn't do any good. Then there's the political way, enacting laws or filing a lawsuit—one side will always lose. The third way is to sit down together. It may take a little longer, but the resolution will be a hell of a lot better for everyone involved. We work hard to help people understand the third way, and it's caught on. It's working really well here, almost seems like some of these guys are proud of figuring this out.

"My grandpa once told me, if you're not sitting down with people you disagree with, you're not accomplishing much in life."

Our first stop is to meet a rancher, Denny Iverson. I'm prepared for anything but the fit, guileless man who comes out to greet us, preceded by two wiry, playful dogs, one of which spits a pinecone at my feet.

"Don't be throwin' that for him, he'll never stop," Denny says. He wears jeans and a snug sweatshirt over a collared shirt, dirt smudges on thighs, shoulders, knees. Either he threw on yesterday's clothes or he's been hard at work already today. His light hair, tinged red, bespeaks his Norwegian roots. I throw the pinecone anyway, and it comes back, wet, at my feet. Denny picks it up and sends it sailing fast and hard. We stand in the sunny but frigid dirt yard between his house and barn, and I shiver so hard I shake. Denny suggests maybe we could go sit in the bunkhouse. A structure that looks like an elongated storage shed with only a few small windows and one off-center door, it boasts an old Formica kitchen table with metal chairs, a kitchenette, and boxes piled against every wall. Heat, too, it has heat. He offers us coffee, and we plunk down around the table. I ask, and he tells the story of how he came to be here in Montana.

"My dad's family immigrated to Minnesota, and two of his uncles came out here to eastern Montana, where they homesteaded. My dad visited as a young boy, and came away saying, one day I'm going there. So when I was a junior in high school and he was fifty-five, he up and moved the family here, knowing nothing about ranching, and bought this ranch here in the Blackfoot, wanting to eventually find land out in eastern Montana. Within a year we were so broke we couldn't leave.

"One way my dad was different from the other ranchers, is that he came from Minnesota, where he learned to trust and respect agency folk. He came out west, where the rancher-agency relationship is adversarial, and my dad was this peacemaker, saying, what do we need to do to make things work. He earned the respect of the BLM people, other agency folk, and made enough friends in the area who supported he and my mom, kept their spirits up." Denny's forearms rest on the table. His gaze is clear. I don't know why I'd expected gruff and taciturn.

"I went to college in Bozeman. I'd saved money from working on another ranch for a couple years, helping out on ours when I wasn't working for pay somewhere else. Had a summer job thinning trees. Then in 1991, my brother and I bought the ranch here from my parents, which basically means we inherited debt, and then bought this piece here next to us. Needed more land to run the cattle we want to. Things'd changed by then, of course, because now we were competing with recreational interests for the land, which sent prices soaring. Ranching doesn't pay nearly as well as, say, a dude ranch, yet we have to pay the same price for the land. Anyway, it's not a business you get rich in. My wife, she works for a dentist in Missoula, and helps run this place too. It's not about money, or none of us would ever be doing it."

Seth isn't getting rich doing his work, either, and neither am I. But we're all passionate about the work we do, it's who we are. It's why we came.

"So, then, how do you feel about wolves? About the fact that they're here, something your dad never had to deal with?" I ask.

"Those damn wolves, well, we'd just as soon they weren't on the landscape, but they are." He swings his head slowly from side to side as he looks at the table, then back up at me. "They're here, and they're here to stay, so let's find ways to help us stay in business, is the way I look at it. See, the people who I sell beef to, want wolves. They want elk, they want fish in the rivers. The public wants this. So for me to argue, say it's wrong, well, that's not going to help me sell my beef."

I ask if there's anything positive about the wolves being back.

A thoughtful pause. "Well, I'd say the wolf has some purpose out there on the landscape for us. As beef producers, those damn elk can get in the way, eat what we grow to feed the cattle, so yes, if they keep those elk herds thinned, that is a benefit for us." Relaxed, self-assured, Denny is treasurer of the Blackfoot Challenge and not one bit uncomfortable answering the questions I throw at him. Even when I ask him about changes in the environment due to that factious term, global warming.

"I'm a rancher—hell yes I've got climate change," he says matter-of-factly. "I've been working this land for over forty years, and things've changed. We're kidding ourselves to say they haven't. You don't need to create friction where there isn't any, but there's also no excuse for avoiding the obvious."

We leave the bunkhouse, and walk across the frozen dirt to the fence of his calving yard. "Damn eagles," he says. "They get in here, flap their wings to get the cow all flustered, keep her away, they can kill a damn calf. Damn eagles."

Damn Bob. He is retreating, abandoning me. Parenting our brood is exhausting, and I didn't sign up to do this alone. He may still be physically present, but the Bob I married has disappeared. He drinks every night. He's distant, he slips into inebriation, or he's on a rampage. The dot-com bubble burst almost three years ago. Bob is a casualty. No longer a financial analyst, he's lost. Searching for what's next. Angry. I hold a vision of something different in both head and heart, and am vulnerable. Friends become oases, offering escape from the bleak, arid marriage Bob and I share. I want to fix us, but my encouraging words and self-help books don't improve anything. I want him to work his way through this, be a functioning part of the family again. I finally realize I cannot fix it.

Jake is twelve, Beau eleven, Allegra and Cait, seven. It's December, 2003.

Wolves, in late 2003, were so well-established that Idaho had almost 450, and Yellowstone, close to 180. Tourists flocked to Yellowstone by the thousands to catch glimpses of these legendary canines. The state of Idaho was negotiating with U.S. Fish and Wildlife on a plan to manage its own wolves—the federal government and the Nez Perce tribe had been managing the wolves since the beginning of the introduction. Wolf populations in Montana and Wyoming were growing. Wolves were having little problem finding homes.

Bob and I, however, can no longer afford our house on the hill, and need to sell.

"I want to find our next house, move out," I tell him one evening. "I'll take the kids. You can stay here, until this house sells. And work on yourself. Figure it out. You're not okay. And I can't live like this anymore."

"Like what, what do you mean?"

"What I've been saying, Bob. The drinking, your anger. I need you to be okay. You're not."

"I'm fine. This isn't anger, this is passion," he yells.

"You need to fix yourself. And then we'll talk."

The talk, seven months later, after therapy sessions, both separate and together, is brief.

We're on the back deck of our house, which hasn't yet sold. I've brought the kids over. Jake is inside, the other three are playing down by the pool. Bob's feet are propped on the railing. He's smoking, something he'd only ever done socially or in times of stress, had given up half a dozen years before.

"I think we need to divorce. That's what you want." He looks out toward trees, not at me.

"Bob, what about another therapist? Can't we try harder, work this out?"

"What, and have you blast me again? No thanks." He drags air through the cigarette. The end flares red. Goes black.

My shoulders sag and I blink back tears. My chest feels hollow. Deep breath. I'm full of air, nothing but air. I don't speak. I've used all my words.

Seth and I are headed to the livestock compost site. A half dozen miles from Denny's, we park in a graveled parking lot with a gate at the far end. Beyond the gate are huge mounds of what looks to be wood chips and dirt, some six feet high, some ten or twelve. We're here to meet Barry Lewis with the Montana Department of Transportation, the guy who hauls animal carcasses around and covers them with mulch. Eric Graham, the

Blackfoot Challenge's range rider, is meeting us here, too; he has a dead heifer in the back of his truck.

Ranch and farm animals die of disease, illness, weather-related challenges, during birthing, by accident. And wildlife die of these same causes, too—on private property, and when struck by vehicles on the road. Although the smaller animals are easy to dispose of—a farmer might bury his dead dog—big steers can weigh twelve hundred pounds, and that much dead weight is more than many ranchers can easily deal with. Hiring someone to remove the body can cost hundreds of dollars, an expense not easily absorbed. In the past, such carcasses were often left where they fell, or dragged to what's called a bonepile, on the ranch or farm, to decompose. Dead animals, however, attract predators, and with grizzlies and wolves back on the landscape, watershed inhabitants found that these dead cows, sheep, and horses invited trouble. The Blackfoot Challenge, after discussing possible solutions with residents, established the carcass removal program to eliminate this enticement and provide free removal for watershed residents. They'll come pick up a dead cow, or a deer carcass lying in a field, and deliver it to Barry.

Tall, slender, with a mustache longer than my bangs and a shiny silver buckle as big as my hand on the belt cinching his Wranglers, Barry opens the gate and lets us in. Cement half-walls delineate stalls where individual carcasses are placed, then covered with compost to speed decomposition. There are four or five stalls for domestic animals, a separate grouping of stalls for wild animals, and different compost piles for each. We watch as Barry hops in his front end loader and scoops the heifer from the back of Eric's truck, then drives it to a stall on the domestic side. He plops it into the six-foot by eight-foot space, then drives his loader to the domestic compost pile, where he fills the bucket with compost, returning to dump it on top of the carcass, twice. In a few weeks, he'll stir the contents of the stall, then repeat, and eventually what's left in the stall will be added to the huge pile of domestic compost.

A truck pulls into the lot, and two men dressed in Carhartts and jackets, one bearded, the other not, join us. Nathan Rott, the NPR reporter, and David Gilkey, the photographer. I'm curious why a photographer is assigned for a radio piece. The internet, of course. Sound alone is no longer the draw it once was. The six of us stand in a circle, talking. A seven-inch section of hoof on the ground between us captures my eye. I back up, stepping on a bleached and decomposing hipbone, and swallow hard. It's just a bone. Or two.

The DOT shares the cost of this operation with the Blackfoot Challenge, utilizing the domestic compost generated for high-way roadside ditches. Domestic and wild animals are segregated because of Chronic Wasting Disease—a contagious, neurologi-cal malady affecting some deer, elk, and moose—the fear be-ing that its presence might taint the compost. Ten months into 2013, they had already handled 450 wild animal carcasses and 400 domestic. The larger bones of domestic animals don't com-post, Barry tells us, but everything else does. Most every land-owner in the watershed takes advantage of the carcass removal program, and the number of livestock predations by wolves and grizzlies here has dropped to almost nothing: so far this year, with those 850 animals safely composted away, there's not been a single livestock predation in the valley.

After we're back in the car and heading to lunch, Seth tells me there is one landowner who refuses to take advantage of the program, a woman in her late seventies or so who manages her ranch by herself, her husband having died a few years back. I ask why she doesn't participate, since it apparently benefits ranchers without costing them a penny.

"She says when one of her animals dies, it's like losing a

member of her family. They're not just stock, they are a piece of her life. So she has a bonepile, and she takes her animals there when they die, where they can decompose and stay with her land, remain a piece of it." He glances over at me. "She honors them by keeping them."

I cannot fault her for that.

Cully's is doing a fairly good lunch business today, most of the tables around us occupied by men wearing hats. Aside from the waitress, I'm the only woman. The three of us order today's soup, which is some kind of a prime rib stew our waitress recommends, and when it arrives Seth and Denny each crumble four or five packs of Saltines into their bowls and dig in. The table behind Seth is directly in my line of sight, and I watch the seven young men there while trying to not. Four wear cowboy hats, all weathered and bent edged, the others wear ball caps. They all wear flannel shirts and sweatshirts or vests, and when I later ask Seth about the group he tells me they were having a "shipping lunch." I'm visiting the watershed during shipping week, when the ranches round up the calves they're selling, load them onto trucks, and send them away. Every ranch requires extra hands for the event, and will often treat the crew to lunch when it's done, or while they're waiting for the empty trucks to show up. Most ranchers in the area sell their calves off each fall: the calves go to feed lots where they'll be bulked up before eventually giving up their lives for those who eat burgers and steaks and prime rib stew. The Mannix ranch keeps their calves, feeding their cattle year round, selling the highest quality grass-fed beef around, but in this watershed, their operation is atypical.

After lunch, the NPR guys and I drive with Eric out to the Mannix's ranch, where we listen for wolves using Eric's telemetry antenna. Not a peep. The wolves are far away. Eric guides us along a trail, looking for wolf sign or scat, and we see a few paw prints but nothing else. We cross a field, approaching a small herd of cows, trying to move without scaring them away, but fail. They trample away from us, re-collecting in a corner, lowing and moaning. Strawberry blond, bearded David takes picture after picture, and Nathan holds his big padded boom microphone toward the cattle to catch the lowing. I reconsider prime beef stew.

Seth drives me back into Missoula as the sun is dropping behind the mountains, and we have dinner at a restaurant by a bend in the Clark Fork River, Scotty's Table. Seth orders a burger made of grass-fed beef from Mannix's ranch, and I order mussels. We muse about people, carnivores, motivations and desires, wolves, and what it is that makes a fulfilling life. We solve no issues and have no epiphanies, but enjoy a beer, a glass of wine.

In my hotel room I stretch my left side, my shoulder. Eleven weeks past my accident, the two scars from the chest tubes are angry purple. They twist my skin, are ugly. But they're healing. The ribs have knit, the scapula is mending. The bump where clavicle meets scapula just protrudes, doesn't hurt. My shoulder is regaining strength, some flexibility. In my jammies and thick socks I curl in a chair. My journal is open, pen in hand. I write. I write about everything that's missing in my life, all the holes, the voids. There is more out there, somewhere. There is wildness and passion and life. I want to be out there. *I want out.*

Rolling Stone Ranch is our destination the next morning, where I meet Jim Stone, the current chair of the Challenge's Board of Directors. Jim's a few inches shy of six feet tall, and his back is straighter than a little boy trying to make the height cut-off for the roller coaster. Mustached and sun burnished, he crackles with energy. His eyes are in constant motion, his fingers, toes, and limbs not far behind. There are dirt smudges on his sweatshirt and on his Carhartts, the bottoms of which could tell a few stories about where they've been. A fellow rancher, Bob Roland, joins us, as does Liz Bradley, representing Montana's Department of Fish, Wildlife and Parks. Liz and I renew our acquaintance from our meeting last June, and we all talk about the twelve packs of wolves near the Blackfoot. The ranchers sometimes hear them, and almost never see them. But they are continually revising their ranching practices because of them.

Jim is showing off his fladry machine, a rolling gadget on a four wheeler that will let out a length of rope fencing decorated with small red plastic flags. Wolves are off-put by the rippling plastic flags and will steer clear of them. Jim's invention eases the work of putting up and taking down the moveable "fence" as cattle move from one grazing site to another. The use of fladry made its way to the West from Europe, where it was used to manage wolves, and the origin of the word itself is likely German, from the word *flattern*, to flutter. Fluttering flags apparently aid ranchers throughout wolf country on multiple continents.

These ranchers are like big kids, excited to show off their toys. Jim's barn is a stable for vehicles—four wheelers, tractors, a truck—with a large wooden workbench, around which we gather. His corgi mix runs between our legs, her brown coat smooth, her truncated legs moving like pistons as she races around the space. She would be no match for a wolf. Luckily, Jim's land lies in the flat of the valley, which sees little wolf activity. Bob Roland lives east of here, at the base of Ovando Mountain, where wolves more often visit.

"It's a riot to get on the wolf tracks in the snow, it's like a family circus playground. Here, there, two hundred yards that a way, and then back. It's more fun than you can imagine trying to figure out where they were going." Bob is a tall, slightly gawky fellow who reminds me of Gilligan or Barney Fife—the nicest, sweetest guy around.

Jim chimes in with, "You don't send a young son out fixing fence all alone anymore." He continues, "Management has changed since wolves are back around. We do things differently. We ride through our cattle more often, and the Challenge has given us a few tools to work with. But it's when FW&P's hands are tied that problems occur. Doesn't do a darn bit of good when they can't act on information. New problems always crop up—we continually need a bigger toolbox."

I ask Bob if he sees wolves as a big problem. "Well, it's like waiting for the other shoe to drop . . . you don't know when it's going to come. Something's bound to happen, and you're always on guard for it."

Jim sees the wolf issue as one that has potential to tear apart the relationships ranchers have built between themselves in the Blackfoot. It's taken a long time to get these self-admittedly stubborn folk to talk to each other, let alone trust each other, and they've come a long way. "It used to be we'd lob rocks at each other overhand, and now we lob our rocks underhand." The Challenge holds people together, but because wolves are affecting some ranchers more than others, he fears what they've created could be destroyed. Not every ranch is visited by wolves, not every ranch has to protect itself in the same ways, so not every ranch is able to reap equally the benefits of belonging to the Challenge. Or willing to agree on how best to handle wolf activity.

"It's way more complicated than 'those damn ranchers hate wolves,'" Jim says, crossing his arms against his chest and leaning back on the heels of his boots, his shoulders against a metal cabinet.

"It's never just one tool that will solve it," Liz adds. "Being willing to try new things is huge, sharing information, talking, communicating. Like I trust Bob here, what he tells me, because we've built that over time. If he tells me we have a problem, we'll work on it, to the extent that we can."

"A total change in culture is needed before our nation has an understanding of what ranchers deal with. Not just about wolves. Organizations like the Challenge help connect those dots, but everything affects something else, and we're stuck here trying to make choices, while still trying to earn a living," Jim says. "You used to just go swath a field, but now I have to think about if I do it too early it'll impact the birds nesting, if I do it too late the red-tailed hawk won't find anything to eat . . . the more we know the harder it is to do anything."

"And the biggest problem," Bob adds with a laugh, "is that most of us just don't like other people all that much. That's why we're ranchers."

For lunch we go to Trixie's—Seth, the NPR guys Nate and David, Jim Stone, Eric the range rider, and me. Decked with antlers and neon beer signs, the gray paneling on the walls is older than most everyone at our table. The bar was once owned by Trixie McCormick, a trick pony rider in the 1940s who went into the saloon business after retiring from the rodeo, and pictures of cute-as-a-button Trixie adorn the walls that aren't covered with those antlers and beer signs. The menu is surprisingly extensive. A few of the men play a quick game of pool while they wait for their food. I chat with Nate, who grew up in Missoula and earned a journalism degree from the University of Montana, and who also spent time working for a salmon fishing operation in Alaska and solving problems at McMurdo Station in Antarctica. He's lanky and lean with a square jaw and a radio voice, smooth and deep enough to warm honey, and he's all of twenty-seven years old. Nate is working on a story about the wolf controversy, and has already compiled enough hours of interviews to keep NPR on air for a solid day or two, and has plans for many more such hours. He's trying to decide how to frame it all, knowing that without tension there is no story. Wolves? He has plenty of tension to work with. And irony, too. He's interviewed a woman who shot and killed a wolf and has it stuffed and mounted in her Gardiner home, a woman who told him, *people just don't understand: wolves are killers.*

Here in the Blackfoot, folk are relatively calm about wolves, but we all see the Challenge as a solution, not a place of tension and extremes. Nate will show the extremes, the craziness, the anger and frustration, and show the Blackfoot watershed modeling coexistence—that peace is, perhaps, possible.

I eat my bowl of Italian wedding soup and watch the beer truck driver wheel in load after load of beer cases. Trixie's sits right outside tiny Ovando, on the highway, and evidently does a darn good business keeping ranchers and tourists lubricated. Seth stops to speak with a rancher, then shakes hands and exchanges greetings with another half dozen men before we leave.

Bob and I had been married fifteen years when the fissures in our family finally broke us apart. When we separated, all four children came with me. Bob would pick them up for the weekend, then bring them back. The first weekend, I packed all of Jake's food, medicine, diapers, extra clothes, bed liners, the stuffed animal he slept with. His feeding pump, which fed him, slowly, throughout the night. The tall wheeled pole it hung on. The car seat.

The next weekend was different.

"I can't take Jake," he said. "It's too difficult, I can't do it."

The cleft had pulled our family apart, and now we were splitting in even more ways. Jake and me. All four children and me. Bob and the youngest three.

I knew Bob, and knew why he couldn't do it. It hampered

him, spread him too thin. It kept him from being as mobile as he wanted to be.

I would probably just stay home, anyway. I let it be.

The Manley's ranch is our next stop; its brand, 17. Tracy Manley's great-grandfather homesteaded this property back in 1883 with his two brothers, and eventually sold off the neighboring parcels, keeping just parcel 17, thus the brand. One of those brothers was hung for being a horse thief, but Tracy lives on the right side of the law. His three dogs circle us, two border collies and an Australian shepherd, all desperate to keep us together. The German hat Tracy wears has earflaps and ties, somehow at odds with his navy sweatshirt, worn canvas jacket, jeans and kilted leather boots. His hair is thick and white, as is his mustache. He doesn't have much of anything nice to say about wolves.

"The first time, wolves came down here and killed nine calves, only ate one of them. Then two years later, they killed three of my calves. One was killed within a hundred fifty yards of my door." He doesn't believe wolf biologists' claims about packs having just one breeding pair. "There's a pack up on the hill nearby that has fifteen pups. Yep." And more damningly, "We didn't need to spend all those millions of dollars to bring them back—they were never really gone."

Regardless of whether any of this is true, Tracy Manley is a rancher whose livelihood has been affected by wolves. He is one of a very small percentage of Americans who actually has to deal with wolves, on his property, regularly. He doesn't like them, but there's no vitriol. It's just a problem he's confronted with, a situation about which he's remarkably calm. He shows us the electrified fence protecting his calving yard, ready to zap interlopers with five hundred volts. The fence does an excellent job of keeping his new calves protected. Tracy says it's not as easy as you'd think to track and trap a wolf, because he's tried. And behind that stoic face and accepting manner, I believe I catch in his eye a glimpse of respect for that wild creature, the wolf.

What I don't catch sight of, anywhere, is a wolf.

8. range

Snow blankets the high hills. Yellow Eyes leaves wide paw prints on the white land. As the trail descends, snow thins, is eventually frozen mud. It thaws by day, freezes again each night. His prints linger a day, two, then disappear. The land relaxes, widens. Hills and trees edge the plain. He smells death, follows it to a coyote carcass, little more than bones and fur. He sniffs, moves east. Elk, close. Land stretches before him, nothing larger than a hillock to hide behind. He follows the scent. He's had little but rabbits and squirrels the past two weeks. His nose quivers. Yellow Eyes lopes across the hard soil, through elk droppings, gaining speed. Dark bumps scatter on the horizon. He runs. He nears the elk herd and searches for limps, awkward movement. A small body.

Hours later, he lies by his kill, sated. He's over three hundred miles from his pack. A new year is about to begin. Yellow Eyes, within days, will be written about, described, discussed by people across the nation. He has entered a state that hasn't had a wolf on its land in a hundred years. A naming contest in the Oregon school system will decree that, as of January 4, 2012, Yellow Eyes, officially wolf OR7, will be known as Journey.

Eric and I pass through a gate, then stand back as a ranch hand opens another, and lets us into the corral. The five calves move away from us, one more awkwardly than the others. He's the one we're here to see. Black as pitch, he is two years old and stocky. His right rear leg has a peculiar bump on it, though, and he not only limps, but seems bothered by it. I watch as Eric and the rancher cut him from the other black bodies and move him to a place where we can all look at the leg. Eric is here to inspect it, help decide if the injury is a result of a wolf bite. Dan Pocha, the rancher, is the most dapper one I've met, a teal blue bandana around his neck and not a dirt smudge to be seen. He wears a red fleece vest over a long-sleeved windowpane plaid navy shirt, a dark gray wool hat, and neatly pressed jeans over brown leather boots. Metal-rimmed glasses frame hazel eyes, his cheekbones and nose are reddened by cold, and the slightest stubble on his face matches exactly his salt and pepper hair. His tooled leather belt with conches and rivets is held fast by an ornate buckle.

After spending two days with Seth in the watershed, I'd been turned over to Eric Graham, the Challenge's range rider. My romantic vision of a range rider—sexy, slouchy, undaunted—evaporated when I met Eric. He drives a U.S. Fish and Wildlife truck—a substantial crack running through its windshield—that's fully earned the name utility vehicle. He is just completing his first winter as a range rider, and though engaging, is a far cry from that seasoned man on the horse I'd dreamt up.

Watching Eric bend down to look at the calf's leg and listening to his exchange with Dan, however, convinces me that he's the right man for this job, despite his steed. Dan had come across a photograph of a wolf bite and its after-effects on the leg of a calf, and thought it looked an awful lot like the wound on his own calf. Eric can't do much about the injury, but he'll pass word along to Liz Bradley, who will decide if it's something she'll investigate further. Eric is in his late thirties, a husband and father, a wildlife technician who changes jobs with the season, the study, the funding flow. He's worked primarily on grizzly bear studies, most recently a DNA study collecting grizzly hair for analysis. However, he finds the range riding job extremely satisfying for the same reasons Seth does: the relationship-building that leads to trust, friendship, and resolution of difficulty or stress.

"Gosh, Dan, that sure does look strange, doesn't it? And he's favoring it something mighty. Let me get a little closer."

Eric squats low as the calf turns its head and eyes him. Eric gets a good look at the leg, which appears withered in comparison to the other hind leg, and boasts that strange lump. No open wound is visible, and Dan thinks the bite might have occurred weeks ago.

"I'm going to have to do something, this guy just can't move along with the others. It's going to be a problem."

"I can see that, he's obviously not too happy, not moving as well." Eric nods, standing back up. We walk back to the truck, Dan closing the corral gate behind us. Eric's dark hair flops over his brow, and he's got his own stubble roughening his jaw. His Carhartts are worn, and he looks every inch the Montana man he is, sturdy, down to earth, unflappable.

"Do you want to show me where those dead deer are now? Do you want to drive your own truck, or come with us?"

Dan says he will lead, and climbs in his big red truck, which is clean and without cracks in its windshield—an exception to the standard vehicle in the Blackfoot watershed. We jump in the utility truck and follow Dan to one of his fields, across the highway, where two deer carcasses lie. Montana FW&P is concerned about Bluetongue disease, a virus moving through the watershed's deer population, and Eric plans to grab a lung tissue sample, if possible, to send for analysis. The first body we reach is too far gone for a lung sample, but has a nice rack of antlers, which Eric hacks off for Dan. Eric offers to take the carcasses to the compost site, and Dan says sure. He helps Eric swing the first one up into the bed of the pickup. The second carcass is also too long dead for a lung sample, and joins the first. As the men start to exchange goodbyes, Eric broaches the serious topic, this season's calves.

"So how'd you do on shipping, with your weights?"

"Weights were up, except for the cattle that were up in the mountains, up closer to the wolves. You know, we figured they were light, about forty or fifty pounds lighter." Dan and Eric are standing by the truck, the deer carcasses just inches from their backs. "People are asking, how come they're so thin up there? They're thin boned, lighter, not as broad across." Dan leans against the truck, arms folded across his chest. The ends of his bandanna flap in the breeze.

Eric says, "I just got to thinking, I don't see them springing for new wolf or grizzly collars anytime soon, to see what's going on up there, so it's one thing, you saying they're coming home light, but if we could document that, get some numbers on paper to back it up. Especially with people now talking about indirect losses, recognizing that."

"Yeah, see that's where, like I was telling you, it's not the dead loss that's the big contributor, it's the loss of pounds, the few more open cows, that's what adds up," Dan says.

They're talking about the stress on cows from marauding wolves. Cattle move more, eat less, and are more likely, if female, to not become pregnant, remaining "open." In a calf-and-cow operation like Dan's, an open cow is lost money.

Dan's neither angry nor resigned, he's just matter of fact. He wants to run his ranch efficiently, carefully, and well enough so that he can eventually hand it over to the next generation. Selling calves that are forty pounds light isn't going to help him.

The talk turns to hunting, where the elk are, how many deer have been moving through the valley. Dan tells a story of a man who shot a deer on his property. "I ran into a few guys who'd shot a few bucks, and I was asking them questions, like I always do before I chew 'em out, and one of 'em told me his wife had cancer, and he really needed the meat for his family, and I didn't have the heart to tell him he couldn't shoot over here, that he needed permission to be hunting, that it was archery only over on this side of the road. Told him he'd better hurry and get that thing gutted out and loaded up before he got caught."

"So you didn't tell him it was you he needed permission from?" Eric laughs, eliciting a chuckle from Dan.

"No, I just thought, he needs this meat, get him out of here. He just needed some food for the table, his wife going through chemo and all. I felt bad for him."

I didn't wake up one morning determined to save wolves. I grew up in landscapes without them. I only knew the fairy tales, the myths. Big teeth. Voracious appetites. But then a friend raised the issue of their protected status, that western states were eager to see wolves lose that status. I read a book. Another. A local conservancy organization sponsored a documentary called *True Wolf*, about a Montana couple who raised a wolf from pup to adulthood, then traveled the country with him, educating schoolchildren about wolves. I began researching what town dwellers, hunters, ranchers, conservationists had to say. I traveled to wolf country.

I learned about farmers and ranchers who lost sheep and calves and beloved pets. As someone from a non-hunting family who abhors guns, I developed great respect for the hunter who dresses his animal, and freezes the venison and elk steaks to eat throughout the year. I empathized with the rancher who follows his or her parents' footsteps and knows no other life. I considered my own experiences, living in cities and towns, and tempered my assessment of those who live in closer proximity to wildness.

Like a swing state in a tight presidential election, I found myself courted and fed information to sway me first to the plight of the wolf, then to the ranchers' and hunters' hardships. Hunters' facts dispute those of conservationists, and even those of government agencies. Feelings are intense, stories escalate, taking leaps into sensationalism. I kept returning to the science. Scientific inquiry at times infers and suggests, based upon study and observation. But it remains science. Data. Not stories, not exaggeration, not apocalyptic thoughts based on fear.

Most Americans will never encounter a wolf. We see photographs of them, films, television programs. But only a small percentage will ever see one in captivity. Fewer than that will see one through a scope or binoculars, and only a relative handful will see one with a naked eye. Hardly anyone will have a wolf step foot on his or her property, let alone catch the wolf in the act. A miniscule percentage will lose a pet or animal to a wolf, and even fewer still will be harassed or physically touched by a wolf. Yet the number who care about wolves, who want a voice in their management, is huge.

Pete Bengeyfield, the photographer who also works for the Forest Service, saw a wolf on a grazing allotment in the Beaverhead Forest outside Dillon, a hundred miles from Yellowstone, and he gave an inner cheer. He likes wolves, believes they belong on the landscape. He lives in a state imbrued with the controversy, and groups its participants in three categories.

"You get the people who think wolves are devil incarnate, and should be exterminated. On the other end of the spectrum you get the people who are spiritually entwined with the wolf—they hear the wolf howl and they think it's the meeting of nature and man, all that stuff—that's like the wolf watchers. In the middle are the scientific types. I think most of those folk look at wolves as just another animal that should be there, has a very definite role in the ecosystem, just another animal trying to make a living out there. They have a more dispassionate view of the wolves. That's the camp I'm in. Most of the photographers out in Yellowstone are in that camp as well.

"That first group, they're tough. I think for most of them, wolves are a surrogate for anti-government sentiments. It's a cultural thing—it's the Tea Party, these people who think the government has just shoved wolves down their throats. Early on, when the reintroduction was in the initial stages, I thought most of the resistance around here would come from ranchers, and I could understand their point of view, don't agree with it, but I think they have an argument. But really, the resistance mostly comes from hunters. They don't want those wolves killing what they want to kill. And I don't have much patience with that at all."

Kirk Robinson is an activist. He runs Western Wildlife Conservancy out of a Salt Lake City office. He believes we should manage wildlife on an ecological model, rather than on an agricultural model that favors one or a few species at the expense of others. In the West, the favored animals are typically deer, elk, cows. Kirk is frustrated when native carnivores—wolves, mountain lions, bears, wolverines, even coyotes—are effectively held responsible for perceived declines in game herds, and for livestock losses suffered by ranchers who graze their animals on public lands. The continual cries to "control" those carnivores is a kind of subterfuge, he says, to shift attention from the real causes of what problems might exist: herbivore habitat destruction, and ranchers who neglect to employ good animal husbandry to protect their herds and flocks.

He decries Utah's Mule Deer Protection Act as an example of a program that's scientifically misguided, as well as unethical: a bounty is given for dead coyotes, though there is no science to prove that fewer coyotes correlates with increased mule deer populations. The legislature set aside five hundred thousand dollars per year: at fifty dollars per coyote, that's ten thousand coyotes. Total coyote population in the state isn't measured, but Kirk estimates it could be well over one hundred thousand. If left alone, the coyote population will rise and fall with the ecosystem's carrying capacity. If there's not enough food, populations will decrease. When more prey is available, they will rebound. Death by gunshot, especially of a small segment of a population, has little effect on long-term populations. Wildlife Services trappers have a saying: if you kill one coyote, two will come to its funeral.

Bob Ferris, a conservation biologist with Cascadia Wildlands, agrees. For twenty years he has argued that "predators generally do not drive down prey populations in the absence of other—usually more important—habitat issues." Most biologists know this. However, explaining the complexities of the issue is made more difficult by a public perception that dead predators means more deer, elk, and sheep. Compounding this, says Ferris, is the fact that

> . . . fish and wildlife commissions are too heavily influenced by livestock interests mistakenly echoing the same call for control. And the climb out of this pit of predator prejudice is further hampered because it is all happening within regulatory settings and agency cultures—particularly in the West—that have historically treated predators as unwanted and undeserving of much in the way of consideration and thought.

Kirk defends wildlife, specifically carnivores, via letters, essays, public gatherings, and participation in legislative processes. And occasionally, melodrama.

"I'm planning a demonstration at the state capitol next month. We're going to have people dressed in wolf costumes, and others holding fake guns, pointing at them, pretending to shoot and kill them. We've got to show people how serious this is."

I think this might be a bit much. However, Utah is the state that just proposed a bill to make transporting and releasing threatened or endangered species into Utah a third degree felony. And over the last five years, the Utah legislature has committed 1.3 million dollars to a lobbying group to protect our state from wolves. Perhaps a little melodrama is appropriate.

Bethany Cotton isn't an activist, but she, too, defends native carnivores. A Colorado-based attorney with WildEarth Guardians, she describes the organization's two different approaches to wildlife work.

"The first is about endangered species and their habitats, ensuring they are protected, that they aren't allowed to become extinct. The second is an ethical framework, based on each species having an inherent right to exist and thrive in its native environment. That means confronting cruelty, and addressing what has no place—especially on public lands—such as trapping, contest hunting and offering bounties, and hunting carnivores just for sport and not for the meat. These actions are scientifically unsound; they create disturbances in the ecosystems. And they are morally unsound, undermining our respect of wildlife and wilderness. Part of this second part is reining in Wildlife Services, exposing the facts of what they do on public lands with public money: they shoot, do aerial shooting, and poison, to appease a tiny segment of our population, ignoring the rest of us. Ignoring what ethical behavior demands."

Bethany had never seen a wolf in the wild until last fall, when she traveled to Yellowstone. Enthusiasm lifts her voice as she tells the story.

"There was a carcass with a grizzly bear on it, about nine hundred feet from the road, and then some wolves showed up, and they were interacting with the bear, and then a mom grizzly with three cubs came to the carcass, too, and there were five bears, five wolves, all basically playing there with that carcass.

It was unreal. The next day, hundreds of people were watching. The entire road was lined with cars, and people were just sitting on the side of the road, from before dawn to after dark. Because it was a once in a lifetime experience, to get to see this. Nobody was afraid—one of the wolves came down to drink from the river, he was maybe three hundred feet away, and there was just excitement. Hundreds of people. Watching these wild animals doing what wild animals do."

Bethany's work with WildEarth Guardians focuses on protecting endangered and threatened species for legal and ethical reasons, but she acknowledges that perhaps the best part of her work is allowing ordinary people experiences like hers in Yellowstone. Wolves and bears—a scene impossible to view twenty-five years ago, and even now unlikely to be seen outside of a protected area like Yellowstone. An intangible, difficult to quantify in legal arguments. However, she admits that the legal battles have little to do with actual wolves, and more to do with powerful entities working to retain control of resources.

"If it were just about wolves, it'd be easy," Bob Brister, of Utah's WildEarth Guardians office, tells me. "But it's not. It's about myths, and politics, and fairy tales. How long did it take for blacks to receive the right to vote? Women? Social change takes time. Decades, sometimes more than a lifetime. I'm patient. You can't expect these things to change quickly, it just doesn't happen. It takes time."

Significant change takes a Martin Luther King. A Rosa Parks. And millions of people listening and rethinking positions. Bob works in the same ways Kirk does—educating, empowering, involving, making small movements—but he probably wouldn't dress in a wolf suit, or aim a pretend shotgun at someone who did. Bob believes we, as a society, will eventually realize that wildlife—and the lands on which they live—must be protected from many kinds of human harm. He has faith that this social change is unfolding. He may be right. But it's possible the truth is closer to what Max Planck stated, that we must wait for the old generation to die out, and let the next generation take the new path. Bob is patient, Kirk wants to stir the pot, and everyone who works for or with conservation agencies understands that no matter what, it ain't going to come easy.

On the edge of Dan Pocha's field in the Blackfoot Watershed, Eric and I climb back in the truck and head westward, to his next task, which is to collect a camera and a dead calf out on another rancher's property, the Mannix's. On the way, he grabs a pamphlet from his side door and offers it to me to look through. "It's kind of a gross little book, but it might show you something. I use it, helps me figure out what's going on sometimes." It's published by a government office in Alberta, a predation guide, showing photographs of kills, linking predators to their victims. Wolves use teeth, bears use claws, things like that. It is gross. I'm perusing it half-heartedly when he explains his conversations with Dan.

"I don't want to just talk about bears and wolves with these ranchers out here. Because that strikes deep feelings, they're touchy subjects, hard things to talk about. So I like to make a point of talking about other stuff, too. So hey, those are nice binoculars there, or maybe about deer hunting, or what their kids are up to. Let 'em know I'm not only about the wolves, I care about other things. See, I ride the fence on a lot of this stuff.

"I just fell into this work—it wasn't about I love grizzly bears, or I love wolves. My major was Resource Conservation, with a minor in wildlife, and I didn't go on for the master's because I was married, starting to have a family, needed to focus on those things first. So I don't have an agenda. I think it's a good thing. If they see me as a big pro-wolf guy, they're not going to want to work with me. As it is, a rancher says to me, those fucking wolves, I'm going to go kill them, I say okay, that's your business, go for it. I'm not here to tell them what to do."

We pull up behind David Mannix, who happened to be driving ahead of us, and just stopped to open the gate to the pasture we need to access. Eric hops out to tell David what his plan is. Mannix's white cowboy hat is the most beat-up, misshapen, dirty, mangled cowboy hat I've ever seen. He's wearing a zip-front leather vest, stained to within an inch of its life, and a heavy denim shirt underneath. He's hauling a bull around in his trailer, going to release it in a nearby pasture.

Once through the gate, Eric drives us over to the calf, which is no small thing, although surely it was bigger a month back. Its body is still relatively intact, but it's obviously shrunken as fluids have released and dried.

"I don't know what's with this calf," Eric says, shaking his head. "Nothing wants to eat it, except the birds." He's untying the wire holding a camera to the T-post, wiping bird crap off the top and edges of the camera. He's going to load the carcass in the truck bed, and I offer to help.

"No, there's really nothing you can do. If I was you, I'd sit in the truck."

Perhaps I'll miss an opportunity to get decomposition slime on me, and I try to decide how I feel about missing the experience. I think I feel okay. When Eric jumps back in, I ask him how he came to have a camera on a dead calf.

"Well, it was after a community meeting one night. Mannix mentions he's got a calf just died, and I knew Seth'd been wanting to try setting a camera up on a carcass, see if we could catch a grizzly getting on it, and this seemed the perfect opportunity. Mannix says sure, and I have a camera in my truck, so I go pick up a T-post from him, then head out to the pasture. Of course it's about eleven p.m. by then, and I'm out there in the dark, thinking man, this is stupid, there could be a grizzly over in the brush, and here I am trying to rig this camera here in the dark." Eric laughs.

"Then, it'd also come up at the meeting that there was a dead deer up by the creek, and they were wondering about Blue-tongue, so I thought I'd go get a sample from that—I had a lung sample from the calf, too—then haul the deer to the compost site. Well, on the way to the compost site I stopped at the game range out by Two Creek to do some telemetry, listen for wolves, which by then was about 12:30, and by the time I'd dropped off the deer carcass I'd convinced myself that the lung samples needed to get to Missoula right away, rather than sit around until the next evening when someone was headed out of the watershed. So I drove down into Missoula and dropped those samples off at two a.m." He laughs again. "See, I had a lesson to learn. When I started it was like, here you go Eric, here's this little map showing where the twelve wolf packs are. I have this huge country to cover, and the only thing to do is work off old information, what happened in the past, where wolves used to be, what they'd done. And I feel like I've gotta be the expert, the guy who saves the cow from the wolf. But nobody knows what the wolves are thinking. Nobody knows where they are at any given moment, or what they're planning to do next. Where do I start? I was working seventy-five hour weeks—getting paid for forty—emailing, training, doing paperwork, running errands here and there. The first year of this job is miserable. It's not all trapping grizzlies and seeing wolves. My job is part ranch hand, helping out. Helping Liz, the ranchers, Seth. I had to learn not to let it run me crazy. There's a bunkhouse out at the game range, I spend two nights a week up here, and two nights down in Missoula, and don't get me wrong, this is a good job. I go into town, see guys mowing lawns for a living. I love my job."

Eric tells me about spending nights in a colleague's cabin up by Marcum Mountain, not far from where we are, where he leaves the door open at night and listens to the cows. And the wolves. Landowners have given him permission to be on their properties up there, and he'll motorbike around during the day, looking for scat and sign, checking on cows. But at night, he's off, and it's a different world.

"It's awesome. I like to stay up late, by a fire, just look at the stars and think about life. One night the wolves just lit up howling—it was so cool." Goose bumps prickle my skin.

"I'm a little hesitant about my howl," he says. "Most people are, you know, but another time I howled, and they howled back at me." His eyes shine.

Our conversation wanders into the gift of being away, immersed in wild country—even if it's shared with cattle—not so much to be without things, but to be aware of what exists when we're not surrounded by human creations, tools, gadgets, devices, distractions. Eric likes to camp, to look at those stars when their power isn't diluted by ambient light.

"And then there's the Bob. I spent some time there with friends, we hiked it end to end, took our time, doing ten mile days, just being in this awesome place." He's talking about the Bob Marshall Wilderness, over fifteen hundred square miles, a piece of land just north and east of here that stretches all the way to Glacier National Park. "There are these huge trees, huge, the kind that get harvested everywhere else, and man, it's just awesome, the Bob. To walk into a landscape and know it just is what it is—I can't go in there and act like I know what's best for it. Just does something to you."

The four children and I move to a different Salt Lake neighborhood after Bob and I separate. Cait and Allegra are in third grade, and Beau is in sixth. We are establishing new patterns without their dad, and I drive them to school each morning. Sometimes the early sky is tinged pink, the bottom of each cloud, coral. I tease Cait that I've ordered this for her, had it shipped in from far, far away—like a line in our favorite movie, *Cinderella Story*—all the way from Norwegia.

Jake rides the bus each day to a school for children with disabilities. When he's unhappy he moans, cries, yells. When he's happy, his face splits into a crooked grin and he laughs like Buddha. In between, he's calm, he's patient. I still try to catch his eyes with mine, to hold them, to look inside. I cannot.

Three hundred miles north of us, wolf populations in late 2004 are holding steady across Idaho and Yellowstone. Outside of the park, Montana has about 150, and Wyoming, ninety. All three states have been working on management plans for their wolf populations, and U.S. Fish and Wildlife Service finally agrees to hand day-to-day wolf management over to both Idaho and Montana once the new year begins. Wyoming is told to come up with a better plan. On the whole, wolf populations across the area are stable and healthy.

Bob, however, is not. In November of 2004, he lands in the hospital with pancreatitis. He leaves a week later, diagnosed with alcohol and drug addiction. He'd hit rock bottom during the five months after the children and I moved out. But after his release from the hospital, he stabilizes. He quits smoking. He signs the divorce papers. He goes to AA. He tells me he doesn't miss the alcohol that much, but he does miss the drugs. Drugs I hadn't even known he was using. The counselor at the hospital had suggested I might have a diagnosis, too: codependent. I don't like this. Not one bit. I explore to see if it fits.

A dozen years ago, tiger researcher Sergei Sokolov was attacked and mauled by a tiger in Primorye, a mountainous, forested region of Far Eastern Russia. The three years of recovery and rehabilitation afforded Sokolov much time for reflection. He says that he feels only gratitude toward the tiger, for the ordeal has made him stronger. Not physically, but spiritually. I am not as generous as Sokolov—I do not feel gratitude for my baby's death, nor for Jake's disabilities or Bob's difficulties, nor for the end of my marriage. But I do have gratitude for my journey, for the strength I've gained over these years. It's fire, after all, that forges the strongest steel.

And so it may be with wolf work. The documentary *Crying Wolf* claims that the wolf reintroduction elevates animals over man, and shows footage of ranchers catastrophizing, *the wolves have eaten everything*. Many people involved with the recovering wolf population have been persecuted or vilified, like the wolves themselves. Doug Smith chooses not to live in Gardiner, Montana—the town closest to his office—but instead commutes eighty miles each way, to avoid Gardiner residents who are vocal in their hatred of everything associated with wolves. Wildlife biologist Carter Niemeyer, who trapped wolves for the federal government before coordinating the Idaho wolf recovery efforts, has been harassed, accused of dishonesty, and alienated for his evenhanded approach to working with wolves, all of which helped him clarify his position and goals. Gaining support isn't easy, but the process offers opportunity for growth and increased compassion. Seth Wilson, by involving people on both sides of the fence, has witnessed the positive results of working together to achieve peaceful coexistence.

There is a spiritual component of wolf work, too. Aldo Leopold was one of the first to document his evolving belief that perhaps we had been wrong to kill all of the wolves back in the early 1900s. Leopold worked for the U.S. Forest Service from 1909 to 1924, when managing forests meant killing wolves on sight. One day, he watched a wolf in her dying moments, and he was struck with the understanding that the wolf has a place and a purpose in the land. He was stunned, shamed, into reconsidering his ideology. He began valuing the presence of wolves on the landscape. Despite today's virulent wolf-haters, many in America are coming around to Leopold's position—one person, one group, one small valley or watershed at a time.

Except, perhaps, for Idaho. This state, notorious for its collection of white supremacists, is also a haven for those with a far-right political bent. Idaho fought the 1995 wolf reintroduction, prohibiting its Department of Fish and Game from participating in the reintroduction, and in wolf management or control. (U.S. Fish and Wildlife partnered with the Nez Perce tribe of central Idaho to manage the wolves in the state. Today, management is a partnership between the tribe, USF&W, and the state.) And Idaho—individual citizens, groups, and its government—continues to fight against wolves. In late 2013, a chapter of Idaho for Wildlife sponsored the Salmon Youth Predator Derby, a two-day coyote and wolf hunting event geared towards children of ten through fourteen, but open to adults, too. The Idaho for Wildlife motto includes the call "to fight against all legal and legislative attempts by the animal rights and anti-gun organizations who are attempting to take away our rights and freedoms under the constitution of the United States of America." Of course, the wording of the second amendment, which states that "a well-regulated Militia being necessary to the security of a free state, the right of the people to keep and bear Arms shall not be infringed," leaves the passage open to interpretation. It's possible that what these Idahoans for Wildlife are fighting to protect is a right not intentionally given. Was the intention a well-armed militia, or a state filled with well-armed citizens operating under all their unique and conflicting desires and needs? It's possible our founders meant the former, but the Idaho for Wildlife motto suggests the rights of each individual are of greater importance than the right of the whole. *My right to go kill a coyote or wolf is greater than the government's right to maintain order.* Idaho for Wildlife has determined that "wildlife" includes only the animals they wish it to.

Idaho allowed Salmon's derby. And then the next month hired and sent a hunter to kill two packs of wolves in a designated wilderness area to bolster elk numbers, since Idaho's hunters like to shoot their elk there. Nine wolves were killed by the hired hunter before a lawsuit—rejected by the first judge—in an appellate court convinced the Idaho Department of Fish and Game to rescind the kill order. In January of 2014, Idaho's governor, C.L. "Butch" Otter, proposed a two-million-dollar tax-payer-financed fund to kill wolves in order to bring the state's wolf population from approximately 680 to 150, the minimum mandated by the federal government. More tax money, litigation, and political obstructionism have been devoted to reintroducing wolves than to any other endangered species effort. But this ongoing fight obscures the real struggles.

In *Lasso the Wind,* Timothy Egan calls the controversy over wolves a phony debate: the real issue is what the West should be like and who should control it. Traditions root deeply in the West, where ranchers and hunters often operate just as their fathers and grandfathers did, usually on the same land. Change unleashes fear, which can cause heels to dig in deeper, even when science explains the benefit of the change. In Idaho, it appears the desire is to have everything just like it used to be—and to be governed by ignorance and shortsightedness.

From scientists and wildlife organizations to landowners, ranchers, farmers, and hunters to city dwellers and lobbyists, everyone involved in the wolf controversy during the past sixty years have been part of a social movement. It is both political and personal, and it has stirred emotions as has no other wildlife issue, and has been tangled up in so much political muck that it's miraculous a small population of wolves was ever brought into the northern Rockies and released into the wild. In a political maneuver engineered by Montana Senator Jon

Tester, the gray wolf, placed on the Endangered Species List in 1977, was delisted in 2011 in a land mass sitting predominantly in Montana, Wyoming, and Idaho but reaching into Washington, Oregon, and Utah as well. Outside of this single exception, endangered species determinations have always been made by scientists, not politicians. But in this case, fear and misinformation supplanted science in the decision-making process, a reminder that it's not really about the wolf. It's about people, and the values and feelings generated by a belief in the big bad wolf, or by a connection with something deeper than our human selves.

Even so, we have more decisions to make that will affect the status of the wolf as a species, wolf populations across states, individual wolf packs, and individual wolves. As wolf populations increase in regions across the country, federal protections will be removed and states will enact management plans to control wolf numbers, primarily with hunting licenses. Politicians will propose bills and pass laws, and it's in the ecosystem's best interest if they are guided by science. Wolves pay the price for our inability to protect what's wild and beautiful and possibly fleeting, to exist side by side in peace.

On a lackluster January day in 2014, a week after a judge ruled against those who objected to the state of Idaho hiring a hunter to kill two packs of wolves deep in the Frank Church Wilderness, following a month in which Idaho hunters from ten years of age and up were encouraged to shoot and kill as many wolves as they could, during a year of constant negative news for wolf supporters, Kirk Robinson sent an email to encourage his fellow conservationists. He suggested they look past Idaho and toward the hope of greater federal protection for gray wolves, and not get bogged down in negativity. He ended with an Edward Abbey quote:

One final paragraph of advice: do not burn yourselves out. Be as I am—a reluctant enthusiast....a part-time crusader, a half-hearted fanatic. Save the other half of yourselves and your lives for pleasure and adventure. It is not enough to fight for the land; it is even more important to enjoy it. While you can. While it's still here. So get out there and hunt and fish and mess around with your friends, ramble out yonder and explore the forests, climb the mountains, bag the peaks, run the rivers, breathe deep of that yet sweet and lucid air, sit quietly for a while and contemplate the precious stillness, the lovely, mysterious, and awesome space. Enjoy yourselves, keep your brain in your head and your head firmly attached to the body, the body active and alive, and I promise you this much; I promise you this one sweet victory over our enemies, over those desk-bound men and women with their hearts in a safe deposit box, and their eyes hypnotized by desk calculators. I promise you this: You will outlive the bastards.

Abbey isn't talking about life expectancy; Abbey is talking about life *lived.* He's right.

After reading Kirk's email, I take my snowshoes and clump up a canyon where the air is calm, no human voice is heard, and rabbit and moose tracks crisscross in the snow. Clouds hang heavy and not a ray of sunshine breaks through, but I can breathe, I hear the chatter of a far off bird, and I am in a place I love. I howl.

It's quiet in Eric's truck, aside from the wind moaning against the windows, the metal-on-metal rattles as we bump over cracks in the road. Eric has unloaded the carcasses at the compost site. He's checked in with his wife to see where his daughter's music concert is, where he'll meet them once he's back in Missoula. The sun has dropped, and dark is settling in pockets and spreading across fields and meadows. I ask where he thinks the valley will be twenty, thirty years down the road, and he tells me about the ranchers who send their kids to college, and hope they'll one day come back. Go get educated, get experience, follow your heart, then come back home. Of course this doesn't always happen. Some folks don't have children to pass the ranch along to. Take Norma, the older woman who chooses not to utilize the carcass removal program.

"She's running her cattle, cutting hay, of course she hires help, but she's still running the ranch, it's her family. She has no kids, and she's looking for someone to take over, carry it on, and just hasn't found the right folks yet. You know, we've had lots of conversations over time, so I can ask her things like this, she's okay talking about death and stuff. So I ask her, how do you see this place in the future? She says, just as it is."

Eric's vision of the Blackfoot Watershed, thirty years from now, matches Norma's, with ranches remaining in the family, or transferring to new owners with the same mindset as the old. A community of folk who make their living from the land. He delivers me to Scotty's Table, knowing he's missing the beginning of his daughter's concert, resigned to how things go when you're a range rider. I ask for a table for one, and settle against the cushioned banquette. I twist to slip my notebook out of my backpack, and feel the tug in my left side where the tubes were, where the scars are now healing. I order a glass of wine and the warm lentil salad—goat cheese, radishes, snap peas and lentils over spinach—and uncap my pen. It isn't easy to adjust, to be open to new ideas. I once believed I'd have happy twin boys running around my backyard. I thought I'd be married to Bob forever. I didn't expect any of the challenges that entered my life. But I'm learning to adapt.

These ranchers here didn't expect to contend with wolves. But they're figuring out how to do it, tightening their bonds with one another as they do so. They sat down across the table from people they disagreed with, and listened. They compromised, and became creative. Having wolves back is a political process, but it's personal, too. To ranchers and range riders, to photographers, and to everyone who spends any amount of time out in the wild, watching a wolf be a wolf.

9. nature

Days begin to stretch. Dusk leans toward night, dawn breaks mo-ments earlier each morning. Scraggly trees and pine stands cover much of Journey's new home. Mineral veins stain rock faces in shallow gorges. The land teems with tranquil lakes, flashing riv-ers, fleeing deer. Coyotes and jackrabbits dart between brush and shrub, and one day, in the far distance, a mountain lion crosses the ridge, silhouetted against a darkening sky. Ravens lead Journey to kills. He makes many of his own. Each mile he travels drives him to the next. He roves ten miles east, seven miles west. Twenty-five miles due south. She is somewhere. To the west, and east again. He finds food. Water. He sleeps. Naps. Each day, Journey wakes, walks on, searching.

We board the plane in the dark, stars high in the onyx sky above Salt Lake. It is still dark when we deplane, but this city's glow burns upward, brighter than the hint of daybreak tinting the ocean. Cait and I take the next taxi in line, and I say, *Soho, please.*

We drop our bags at the boutique hotel. The lobby is smaller than my living room, the luggage storeroom, a broom closet. Cait and I walk down to the corner for a bagel, some fruit, coffee. It's barely six a.m. A grocer sweeps his sidewalk. Store-fronts are gated and padlocked. We have until early afternoon to explore this corner of New York, but more than anything, we crave sleep. More coffee. Cait wants to visit bookstores, and she searches her phone for one between where we are, and NYU. The Strand is closest, and it opens at 9:30. We dawdle as long as we can, then finally leave the deli and head toward Greenwich Village.

The Strand is just blocks from NYU, where our campus tour begins at two. Cait knows she wants to leave home for college, knows she is interested in psychology, and isn't sure if she could live in Manhattan. But the draw is powerful. The city's energy increases with each block we pass. We window shop. I see a bike store, stop to take a picture. Cait and I walk side by side, parting for strollers, fast-walkers, shopping-bag laden women. Being with Cait is easy. We talk, not of deep dark secrets, but of moving through the world in ways that matter. Of listening to hearts, of painful journeys, of joy.

"This has been the hardest year of my life, Mom."

"I know, hon." I hug her to me.

She's wearing a boot on her right foot, a fat, black, padded walking boot. It's protecting the stress fracture in her fibula. It had happened while I was in Montana, just three days ago. She'd landed on someone else's foot after spiking the volleyball, and crumpled to the floor. Playoffs are next week, then the state tournament.

"And the leg is just a little thing."

"I know that, too."

"I can't wait to just be somewhere new, where there's no history, where everyone just accepts you."

"Where there's no Mia, no Tawny."

"Right," she says. "I just never thought anyone could be so mean. So awful."

"Oh, hon, girls can be so cruel. It's hard to comprehend. Little fights, squalls, I get it. But to be blatantly cruel, to go out of their way to hurt people, it just floors me."

"Yeah. Me too."

"You know the nature versus nurture discussion?"

"Sure," she says. She looks at me, squints.

"Having children, especially you and Allegra, has enlightened me. You all arrive the way you are. Unique, with your own temperaments and passions. But it's nurture that lets your nature blossom, that develops empathy. If we're well-nurtured, we nurture others. We accept responsibility. We don't place blame, pick scapegoats."

"Is that what I am to them, a scapegoat?"

"I'm not sure, hon. But as angry as I am with those girls, I also feel empathy. Until they figure this out, they won't have true friendships. Or real peace."

We pass red brick buildings with black awnings. There are thirteen signs—triangular, round, octagonal, rectangular—on every street corner, telling everyone where and how to go. Cait is silent for another half block.

"I wish I could just be done. I can't wait until next year."

"Me too," I say.

In *Grizzly Years,* Doug Peacock tells the Myth of the Mother Bear. A woman marries a bear and their children become the ancestors of all people. As kin, both bears and people are part animal and part human. The Bear Husband, a divinity, dies for the good of the people, and his flesh provides sacramental food. The Bear Sons, also divine, are intermediaries of the hunt and teach men that success in hunting depends not so much on power but humility.

We know that early humans hunted, fashioning arrowheads and spears to kill creatures so that they could eat. The hunt is man's primordial myth, the marrow of innumerable stories and fables. Many believe the desire—or need—to hunt is innate, inseparable from who we are. Perhaps it clings to some genetic strains; I know it's been wiped out in my family. None of us hunt, not even two generations back, and only a few even fish. But eons ago, we killed to eat, and many still do, filling freezers with meat to feed their families. Many children are taught to shoot while they're in grade school, and hunting with dad or an uncle or grandpa is a family tradition. It's a rite, and to many, a right. Regardless of the benefits of wildlife to non-hunters, game and predator populations on most public lands are managed by state wildlife agencies who work to please hunters, because, as Liz Bradley acknowledged, hunters pay the bills. Most of these agencies have been holding hands with state legislators and hunters since their inceptions, especially in the wild west where the de facto law of the land is set—and maintained—by whoever got there first.

Hunting and fishing licenses bring in approximately thirty-six million dollars annually to Idaho's Department of Fish and Game. In Wyoming, forty million, and in Montana, forty-eight million. These numbers jump by ten to almost twenty million dollars per state when federal excise tax from sales of hunting and fishing equipment is added. My annual bicycling, snowshoeing, and hiking permits, because such things don't exist, contribute absolutely nothing, and this means I have no voice in the management of the wildlife that are so important to me.

In addition to permit fees, state wildlife agency budgets are supported by organizations that advocate for big game hunting, such as the Boone and Crockett Club founded by Theodore Roosevelt in 1887, and the Congressional Sportsmen's Foundation (CSF), which boasts of over twenty years making policy advances for sportsmen. The Rocky Mountain Elk Foundation has over two hundred thousand members in five hundred chapters across the nation, and uses part of its annual revenues of fifty-four million dollars to argue against wolf protection in judicial actions. Sportsmen for Fish and Wildlife is a non-profit wildlife conservation organization working to preserve and increase populations of wildlife throughout North America, which in 2010 created a spin-off political action organization, Big Game Forever. Big Game Forever—based in Utah, which has no wolves—is committed to removing the gray wolf from the endangered species list, and in its first three years accepted almost a million dollars in private and Utah state funds to fuel lobbying efforts. Big game hunting is big business. The CSF states that hunters and anglers are a seventy-six billion dollar economic force, a statistic providing a megaphone for hunting and fishing voices. I can't howl anywhere near that loud. Few can.

However, one recent study reframes this issue. By considering total funding for wildlife conservation and management—not just license and excise tax fees that go directly into state wildlife agency coffers—the picture radically shifts. Approximately ninety-four percent of total wildlife conservation and management funding comes from the non-hunting public, through federal sources (Forest Service, National Park System, BLM, Fish and Wildlife, National Wildlife Refuge System, Wildlife Services, and specific hunting-related funding acts), and non-profit sources (Nature Conservancy, Land Trusts, Wildlife Conservation Society, World Wildlife Fund, and six other similar organizations). The study, completed by Mark Smith and Donald Molde, suggests the perception that hunters fund wildlife management misrepresents reality, and is used to both manipulate public opinion and influence policy. Non-hunters need a voice as loud as their spending.

While hunting organizations continue to influence wildlife management, some individual hunters have their own big voices. The virulence, unsurprisingly, has gone viral. Finding websites and photographs that demonize and denigrate wolves is as easy as finding celebrity gossip. Bill Hoppe, who legally shot and killed a collared Yellowstone wolf, says he made a mistake in letting a friend take a picture of him with the dead wolf, for within hours that photograph circled the globe. Hate mail found its way to Bill and his wife, messages of outrage, enmity, and anger. Messages of support filled his inbox as well, because of course there is a larger story. Bill is a Gardiner, Montana resident, a man who raises cattle and runs a business outfitting hunters. In April of 2013 he, curiously, decided to buy and start raising sheep. Within ten days, wolves attacked and killed thirteen of his sheep, and Hoppe applied for and was given two shoot-on-sight permits for wolves returning to his property. Montana FW&P's agent had determined that the wolves responsible for killing Hoppe's sheep had approached from the east, and were not Yellowstone wolves.

Hoppe allegedly left the sheep carcasses out on his bone-epile—a practice known to draw predators to a location—and began to take his rifle with him as he moved through his property at dawn and at dusk, looking for a wolf to shoot. Within a week he found one, killing the Yellowstone wolf, which had likely been enticed by the smell of the dead sheep. Hoppe insists he did everything by the book, just the way Montana FW&P instructed. But it certainly appears that Hoppe didn't care where his victim came from. He was out to kill a wolf.

One Minnesota blogger suggests the blood lust to put some wolf pelts up on our rec room walls is palpable, and a bit scary. Bloody pictures decorate the web, men standing with dead wolves, holding American flags. A YouTube video shows a man torturing a trapped wolf. There are pictures of dead wolves, heads propped on chopping blocks, hanging from trees, lined up on snow or walkways.

Much of the anger is about elk populations. Many elk hunters believe that the presence of wolves on a landscape reduces elk numbers dramatically. A direct correlation between the addition of wolves and a reduction in elk exists, but the exact effect is difficult to determine and document with certainty. An elk death cannot be attributed to wolves just because wolves are in the area. Idaho Fish and Game studies and manages elk in twenty-nine distinct zones, analyzing population patterns, predation, weather, habitat, and herd movement. Their latest study separates deaths into predation by wolves, cougars, legal harvest (hunting), and other. Six of the management zones have significant wolf predation of elk cows and calves, and in the remaining twenty-three zones, humans and sometimes even cougars kill a higher percent of elk than wolves do. Overall, six of the management areas are below elk population objectives, and it is clearly attributable to the presence of wolves. On the other hand, a Montana FW&P study of elk populations in the Bitterroot Valley is finding that less than five percent of elk calf kills are attributable to wolves, while cougars are responsible for thirty percent. Unfortunately, the perception that wolves kill too many elk can lead to aggressive predator control, which often backfires as packs lose their structure and begin to over-breed.

Doug Smith points out that in the thousands of years leading up to the late 1800s, wolves and elk lived together across the northern Rockies, the populations balanced by the carrying capacity of the land. Wolves didn't decimate elk herds, nor did they overrun the land. In fact, while wolves were absent from the park, the Yellowstone elk herd grew to a record population in 1994 due to low natural predation pressure. Hunters and outfitters became accustomed to picking from the thousands of elk that migrated out of the park each winter, and management practices outside the park actually allowed for increased hunting due to the size of the herd. Biologists knew the herd was larger than benefitted the ecosystem. When the park's bear and cougar populations increased and wolves were reintroduced, the elk population naturally decreased. The park service considers this a success: fewer elk equates to greater balance, and a more natural, healthy, biodiverse ecosystem.

Wolves do kill elk. But across the board far more elk, deer, and caribou are killed by weather-related issues, illness, malnutrition, and humans, even when wolves are in the area. A biologist working in an Alaskan wildlife refuge says that to make hunters in Alaska happy, to increase caribou numbers, what's really needed is a big fire. That, more than anything humans can do, will increase game populations. Wolves certainly have an effect on caribou numbers, but an increase in available food is the only factor that will increase caribou populations. The Idaho Fish and Game study concurs, acknowledging that extensive fires in particular regions created excellent conditions for elk, peaking ten to forty years following the fires, and slowly declining after that. Our tight reins on fire control have a greater effect on game populations than the wolves we've brought back onto the land. If burgeoning elk and caribou populations is our greatest goal, then we should pray for a big fire.

Bookshelves at the Strand tower over our heads, packed tightly. Cait heads to the fantasy section, while I wander through aisles of fiction. I buy Cait three books. For Daniel's son Max, I buy a magnet: Keep Calm and Eat Bacon. He's sixteen.

We have time, so we stop at the NYU bookstore. We buy Cait an NYU hoodie, gray with purple, then walk to campus. Its buildings are distinguished from the rest of the city by banners, flapping in the wind, affixed high on each facade. I'd never visited the NYU campus, and I'm smitten. A tree canopy protects the square where students hike backpacks on their shoulders and lounge on benches. Buildings are squeezed, most of them built when craftsmen carved wood and stone. Wildness here is limited to unmown grass. The largest critter, a red squirrel.

Manhattan's landscape is metal and steel and glass, mountains of architecture everywhere I turn. I love the idea of Cait here, and it seems absolutely ludicrous. She loves water, lakes, the ocean, has just discovered the red rocks of Moab. She advocates for wolves, loves the rugged West, is much like her mother.

Early conservationist and wildlife guardian William Hornaday realized a century ago that humans hold the potential to devastate wildlife populations. A taxidermist who helped save the American buffalo population from near extinction, Hornaday advocated for wildlife protection laws, national parks, and wildlife refuges. In *Our Vanishing Wildlife,* Hornaday argues that humans can quickly exterminate any given wildlife population, regardless its volume, as evidenced by the extinction of the Steller's sea cow, the passenger pigeon, the great auk. Today, his warning echoes over lynx, sea lions, sage grouse.

Hornaday recognized a value inherent in the very existence of wildlife. He saw that people who were not hunters found enjoyment in animals, and he argued that non-hunters and hunters shared equally in any ownership rights of wild animals. Hornaday spoke to the part of us that sees animals as more than meat—as fuel for thoughts and dreams and deeper connection with life. Born in the mid-1800s, Hornaday was just over fifty when he became president of the newly formed American Bison Society in 1905. He spent the rest of his life working to protect wild creatures from human arrogance and destructiveness. He educated, and suggested we form respectful relationships with the creatures sharing the land with us. Hunting, for Hornaday, was but one way to interact with a wild animal—an obviously limited way, killing one of the participants as it does.

Proficient, open-minded hunters acknowledge and respect Hornaday's concerns, and are willing to share the landscape with predators. I have a friend who falls into this category, a man who, given the opportunity, would spend most of his waking hours tracking critters and creatures out in the wild.

The first time I met Brad Tolliver I was greeted by Georgia, his black Labrador, as she wiggled her butt and tail then rested in Brad's truck camper while we humans ate dinner. Brad is a hydrologist by educational degree, a forester by training, and a hunter at heart. A Midwesterner now living in the true west, Brad grew up with shotguns and hunting dogs and trucks, and these three continue to lay claim to his soul, regardless of his love for sandy beaches and soaring green forests and city nightlife. He views his job as a forester, in part, as ensuring that different folk all have opportunities to make use of our nationally managed land. Mixed use, multi-use, multiple use—all terms tossed about in conversation about federal land. The National Forest Management Act of 1976 mandates that the Forest Service provide for "multiple use and sustained yield of the products and services obtained therefrom…and, in particular, include coordination of outdoor recreation, range, timber, watershed, wildlife and fish, and wilderness." No small task, considering the breadth and range of each individual component. Outdoor recreation alone includes hiking, backpacking, skiing, snowmobiling, snowshoeing, trail running, and mountain biking, many of which are in conflict with each other. Wilderness, range, timber and watershed can all exist on the same piece of land. Brad's job isn't simple.

But when it comes to wolves, he doesn't have to think twice. His job is to manage the habitat, not the wildlife. The only time he really reflects on wolves is when he's hunting big game and realizes there aren't as many visible as there used to be. Wolves on the landscape have taught all prey animals to be more cautious.

Brad sees contention as rooted in differing values.

"It's all about what people assign importance to. They look

at things in nature and instead of just accepting them for what they are, they label them good or bad. Take for instance a fire, which many will describe as a catastrophe. They'll say so many acres were destroyed by fire—well, those acres weren't destroyed, an acre is a unit of land measure, those acres are still there. And the fire actually unleashes new growth—fires are extremely important. Although individual animals may die in a fire, those fires create open spaces where grasses have room to grow. Aspen, the lodgepole pines all start growing again. This brings in songbirds, hares, small mammals and deer, elk. Then the predators come in strong, because prey is so plentiful. The animal cycle follows the vegetation cycle. And when the forest matures, the songbirds and hares and grass eaters like elk thin out, and more animals like lynx and fishers, wolverines, certain owls, they start to repopulate. And then it's time for fires to start occurring more frequently—we're beginning to see that these past few years, we're now in that part of the cycle."

Brad reframes roaring fires and hillsides of blackened tree trunks into events that are not only acceptable, but predictable and necessary.

"It's all well-choreographed. It's this masterwork that plays out on a grand scale, over and over again in a hundred- to hundred-fifty-year cycle. A fire resets the play. It's only a catastrophe when someone puts his or her values on it, which is what we tend to do."

He views wolves as creatures in a healthy ecosystem—like fire, they have a role to play.

"The wolf is only an animal. It's not a catastrophe either. Unless your values are that you want to hunt and kill an elk, and you don't want that increased competition, and you resent it. Other hunters have values that allow them to see nature as a work of art, a spiritual place. I'm not religious in the aspect of following a particular teaching, but I'm aware of this spiritual center, and when I do things like hunt, it puts me more in touch with that center. I feel small out there—I'm more aware of how large the world is, how old the world is, how many lifetimes these huge trees have stood through, what a small part of it all I am."

"I feel more spiritually connected in those places, too," I say. I imagine this connection would intensify if I were tracking an animal, searching for scent, sign, movement, behavior patterns of other creatures. I'd have to think like a predator. I ask Brad if he finds anything negative about having wolves back on the landscape.

"One thing does make me sad—this is a value, a selfish human value—when wolves are around you don't get to see as many elk. It's fun to see elk, it's special. I remember walking up a road, working a detail in Idaho, and seeing a herd of seventy or so elk just standing there, looking at me. They're big animals, it takes a lot of energy for them to run or even walk, so they're not going to move unless they feel threatened. Outside of hunting season, they generally feel safe enough around humans that they won't expend that energy. But when wolves are on the landscape, they are always being hunted, so elk're just not very visible. This makes me sad, but I try not to let my values here get in the way, don't let myself get too caught up in that. It's just nature, just part of the plan.

"And death is death. If you take the judgment out of it, it's not pretty, it's not ugly, it's just death. To me what's more important is there's a respect for life, for the animal's place in nature. If you're shooting just to kill, or killing and letting it lay, that respect is missing. It's like a rancher killing a wolf that's killed his sheep—if there's no hatred in it, just an acceptance, a respect, then I don't have a hard time with that at all."

I ask about trophy hunting, having my own misgivings about the practice, and Brad gives me something new to consider.

"Trophy hunting, well, it gets back to rarity. You know, you're walking on the beach, there's all kind of pebbles and seashells you might pick up. Once in a while you find the perfect seashell: shape, colors, something makes you want to stick it in your pocket and take it home. Usually because it's somehow different from all the others, it's more rare. For me, with elk hunting, you don't see a lot that are big, massive, antlered—you remember them. Of the maybe thirty elk I've shot, the big one, I saved the head and had it mounted, had it up on the wall of my house for a while. Hunting isn't always just reduced to sticking meat in the freezer. Sometimes you're trying to push yourself, physically, mentally, go for the rare one. There's no sure thing when you're out hunting, but you can make it tougher by going after something special, testing your skills. And that's often a peak experience.

"Now 'trophy' trophy hunting, on the other hand, that's harder for me to understand. You know, the fifty-thousand-dollar guided hunts, the hunters' work done for them, just so they can point to this special zebra they shot in Africa, a bear they were guided to, some animal they shot from a plane—I don't understand how someone truly enjoys that."

"And a wolf—do you see yourself ever hunting a wolf?" I ask.

"For me, no. I do enjoy the meat of what I hunt, and people don't eat canine meat, or I don't know anyone who does. So I can see me doing it if someone created a reason, say, we need a museum subject, to teach kids, will you go kill a wolf for us, Brad? Then, sure. But I'd have to have a real reason. A good one."

Brad is a thoughtful man fulfilled by sports, hunting, nature, his dogs, and Thomas Merton's *No Man is an Island*. So when I ask whether he has any other thoughts he'd like to share, I'm not surprised he gives me something else to chew on.

"Hunting, like many things in this world, can be seen as an indicator of our society as a whole. We used to be a lot more rural. A lot more people hunted, a lot more people knew where their food came from, hunting was part of life. Now so much of our population is urban, so much doesn't understand the cycle of life, the web of nature, from earth to sky to water, animals, how it all comes together. A lot of people judge hunting as bad. It's not wrong, those opinions are based on their knowledge systems. But the negative judgments about hunting are an indicator of how much we've lost an understanding of where we came from. At some level, people are more connected with human spirit these days—who we are and why we are—but our spiritual consciousness as a nation is that we see us, and then there's everything else, instead of seeing us as part of everything else. People can't look at a tree and see the same divinely connected thing as we are. We see it maybe as divinely *created*, but not divinely connected in the same way that we are. When you're in nature, and hunting is a part of that, you see that divine connection more. It surrounds you, it's harder to deny."

Brad won't typically hunt the hunters—the predators—though many hunters receive a thrill from killing them. But we're learning there are consequences. It's possible that we are tweaking nature more than we realize. A recent article in *Biological Conservation* journal reports that hunting of apex predators—wolves, mountain lions, bears—can change the way those predators influence their environments. By hunting them, we change predator to prey, teaching it to look over its shoulder, shifting its behaviors and effects upon its environment. It's not only about the number of predators we keep, but also about understanding and supporting the roles those predators play in their ecosystems. It might not matter as much how many we kill as where we kill them. Balance is crucial for restoring and preserving healthy ecosystems, and nature is best balanced when we limit our tinkering.

Fewer of today's hunters have been schooled by past generations. Many are now armchair warriors and shoppers. They park their pickups off the side of the road, get out their guns and scopes, and wait for a deer to approach. Some stand outside the borders of Yellowstone in the fall and wait for elk to cross the border, then shoot. I see them parked on shoulders as I ride up my canyon roads in the fall. They glass hillsides, guns in the crooks of their arms. I wonder, each year, if I should be wearing orange. My friend's husband, an experienced hunter, was shot and killed as he was heading down the mountain at the close of a muzzle-loading deer hunt. Shot by an out-of-state hunter who mistook him for a deer. I may want to reclaim my wild self, but I do not want to be mistaken for a wild animal.

I am not alone in observing that hunting integrity has waned over the last century. Barry Lopez suggests men often turn to hunting in attempts to become grounded again in nature, or to dislodge the sense of impotence bestowed by our modern world. He suggests, however, that the "modern hunter pays lip service to the ethics of the warrior hunter—respect for the animal, a taboo against waste, pride taken in highly developed skills like tracking—but his actions betray him." Hunting, a powerful form of connection with the cycle of life, is most honorable when grounded in respect and humility.

Utah requires no license to shoot a coyote. The state offers a fifty-dollar bounty for each coyote killed, if a hunter registers beforehand. There are few instructions given, no guideline providing information about the physical differences between a coyote, a dog, a wolf. There is no warning posted that wolves could possibly be in the state. In late December, 2014, a hunter in the Tushar Mountains, in south central Utah, shot and killed a wolf, stating he thought it was a coyote. The wolf was Echo, the female collared in Wyoming, sighted at the north rim of the

Grand Canyon a few months earlier, nicknamed by an elementary school student in a national contest.

My friend Greg's dad taught him to hunt, and Greg has taught his own children. He hunts deer in the northern Utah mountains each fall. Greg talks about the planning, the search, the glassing, the thrill of the hunt. Of walking in the woods, of waiting. Of looking for a sign. He follows trails, he hunts the deer down. And, he says, that's why they call it hunting, not shopping.

Jake isn't peeing. His pattern is to wait until his bladder is stretched fat, then release it all, a huge flow. He soaks himself thoroughly, even when I double-diaper him. I place bed-liners, those hospital blue "chucks," under him on the bed, and on his wheelchair. And do a lot of laundry. But he hasn't peed all day, not since last night. It's Saturday, a holiday weekend, Presidents' Day. I search through my drawers and shelves of supplies. I have a catheter pack, leftover from last summer's surgery, when Jake had had a Baclofen pump placed in his abdomen. The pump released a muscle relaxant directly into his spinal column, regularly, and it was miraculous. Jake's muscles were relaxed, more than they'd ever been. His legs flopped, instead of arching off the bed. He had to be more comfortable.

But not right now. There must be a pint of pee in his bladder. He isn't complaining, isn't crying, not even grimacing. I pull on gloves and open the pack. I can do this. I've watched nurses, it's fairly straightforward. Only one place to go. I clean him. I open the pack of KY.

Lots of lubricant. I smear it on the catheter, on Jake's penis. I lay the open end of the catheter on an unfolded diaper, on top of a chuck. I warn him it will be a pinch of pain, then over. I take a strong breath and press the catheter gently into Jake's urethra. A hitch—he jerks. Smooth, it glides. Urine flows into the bag.

Jake doesn't pee again that day. The next morning I cath him again. By Sunday afternoon, when he still can't pee on his own, I call his pediatrician.

"Sounds like you should take him up to Primary. I'm not sure what's going on."

Primary Children's Medical Center is familiar. We've spent days here. Sometimes weeks. Each stay was unique, yet the visits piled upon each other like layers of sediment. His early weeks were spent here recovering from surgery that placed a temporary reservoir in his brain, to release excess spinal fluid and reduce his hydrocephalus. When he was a year old, Jake had a permanent shunt placed in his brain. He had a gastrostomy tube surgically placed, and surgery to release his hip muscles. We had an atypical, peaceful stay, when he started on the Ketogenic diet—for seizure control—and had to simply be monitored. Just six months ago we were here for the Baclofen pump insertion, when his abdomen was sliced open like a melon. We come for clinic visits every few months, meeting with the dietician, pediatrician, neurologist, ophthalmologist, psychologist. I know the imaging lab, the cafeteria, and how to navigate back stairways. And now I know the emergency department.

The surgeon who finally visits me in our small assessment room is the third doctor we see.

"His white blood count is elevated. There's infection. Let me look at his belly."

He lifts Jake's shirt, slides his pants down to hipbones. He presses against Jake's abdomen, on both sides of the scar, near his belly button. It doesn't look angry. It doesn't look like infection is raging under the skin.

"We'll have to remove the Baclofen pump. We'll admit Jake, get him on the schedule."

"It was just put in last summer," I protest. "It's helped him, it's been wonderful." How can this be? "Does it have to be that?"

"I'm afraid so," he nods.

A surgeon removes the device. Eighteen hours post-surgery, Jake's abdomen is impossibly swollen, his stitched wound millimeters from rupture. He cries, he screams, and no one knows the cause of the swelling or his pain, or what to do. He is rushed to the ICU. His surgeon worries that Jake's bowel has been perforated, which could kill him. The ICU attending asks me our plan—did we wish to intervene, operate if necessary, fix this—or let him go if it comes to that.

Jake is fifteen. My first child. Grace embodied. He is all that remains of that early dream of two healthy little boys, identical, who argue and yip and squeal and grow into young men, happy, intelligent, handsome. Loving.

When Jake was only days old, his brother dead, his prognosis questionable, I had asked of God, of the universe, three things. That Jake be able to use his intellect, to enjoy the tremendous thrill of its workings. That he be able to rejoice in our incredible, astonishing natural world. That he be able to give and receive love.

Though he'd never been able to speak or walk or hug anyone, after his first few miserable years Jake had learned to smile, and to chuckle. He couldn't make eye contact, but he smiled. He developed a great big belly laugh that shook his body. His eyes moved to one side, his right cheek lifted as he broke into a lopsided grin, and he laughed. At what, I don't know. I liked to think it was in response to jokes, comments, sly observations, invisibly whispered by Little Joe into Jake's ear. Of my three requests I received this: Jake's sighs, as he softened into my lap, my arms around his crooked body, seemed to indicate he wanted to be there. That he liked being held. That in his own way, he received and returned my love.

Bob and I tell the physician we are willing to let him go. No operation. Let his body do what it needs to do. Let nature take its course.

A nurse administers painkillers. Jake quiets. We leave the cacophony of the ICU and return to our room with the bright window and fish on the wall. Jake sleeps. His vital signs are steady. Over the next hour his tummy deflates, a centimeter, another. The stitches relax. His heart beats steadily. A few hours later, his abdomen is soft, and almost back to normal size. He wakes, throws his eyes around the room. Then he sighs. Closes his eyes, and goes back to sleep.

Jake's abdomen had nearly burst, but within a few weeks it was almost as if it hadn't happened. He ate, slept, moaned when he was unhappy, engaged in body-shaking belly laughs when the mood struck. March of 2006 eased into April, and our routines resumed.

Meanwhile, eleven years after the reintroduction began, Yellowstone wolves moved into spring with 118 wolves in thirteen packs. Only thirty-two percent of the previous year's pups had survived, whereas the average pup survival rate is greater than sixty percent. Disease is blamed for the unusual number of pup mortalities. However, Wyoming's wolf count showed 134 wolves, Montana had 256, and Idaho, 512. Survival, overall, seemed a certainty.

We brunch in Soho on Sunday, where Cait has me surreptitiously take a photo of a film star I've never heard of who's sitting at the table behind me. Sunday brunch, in Manhattan, is a thing. The concierge at our hotel had asked, the night before, where we planned to brunch. He made a few suggestions, gave us a few menus. In the morning Cait had chosen Peel's, and we walked the few blocks, waited for twenty minutes. Then were given the ideal table, just feet away from a movie star. Oatmeal is only eight dollars. I order biscuits and eggs.

Times Square is next, where we snap a photo with a six-foot-tall, pale green Statue of Liberty who harasses us for money. We shop. Cait clomps in and out of stores. She's searching for the perfect souvenirs for her sister and brother, and the one friend she has left at school. Beau gets a shot glass for his collection. Allegra gets one, too. Cait buys herself some NYC boxer shorts. In the afternoon we go to the theatre, *Romeo and Juliet*, Cait's choice. Orlando Bloom, shirtless, even from the thirtieth row, is profound. Cait gleams.

We fly back to Salt Lake on a Monday morning. She is a hedonist, taking a day off school. I catch up on work, whirling through papers, orders, emails. NYU remains high on Cait's list, but she's also thinking about schools in San Diego, and her sister Allegra is looking at schools in the Northwest. I want them to find schools that offer opportunities to explore who they truly are, that engage their passions. They are both hunting, eliminating schools that don't fit, searching for signs a school might be the right one for them.

"I've been seeing a counselor," Bob says.

We're sitting with Jake at his school's spring program. Jake has just turned sixteen—it's been an entire year since the Baclofen pump was removed.

"And how's that?" I ask.

"It's been good. I really like her."

Bob's been sober for three and a half years now. He's working as a recruiter, and seems steady. On weekends, he takes the three kids to his house on the hill by Millcreek Canyon. He attends AA.

"A few months back, we were talking about, well, sexuality. I told her I wasn't sure if I was attracted to women, or to men."

I stare at him, then adjust the blanket on Jake's lap, forcing the muscles in my face to relax.

"So," he continues, "she said, well, maybe you should just see who comes along. Who comes into your life. A man. Or maybe a woman."

"And?" I rest my hand on Jake's leg.

"His name is Tom. We've been seeing each other a couple months now. I really like him."

"Oh," I nod, blinking. Bob's been seeing a man. Named Tom. I smile. "Wow. That's good."

An hour later, when I am alone, the pieces click. His misery and anger, his denial, the drugs and alcohol, my frustrations. I am lighter, my guilt over the divorce halved. My entire marriage wasn't what I thought it had been. Maybe I am halved, too.

10. scars

Summer sun sears the land. It splits soil open; cracks reach down into what lies below. Lethargy drips. Journey sleeps while the heat pours over hills, treetops, shimmering lakes. He lies beneath trees, runs on shaded trails. He moves uphill. The air cools. He splashes through a creek, catches sight of a white bottom. Leaps, is quickly on the deer's trail. They crash through undergrowth. Jump the creek. The deer has spikes, velvet brown. A yearling. Journey presses, his nose nearing the young buck's churning hooves. Suddenly the forest fills with deer, five, six, charging him, their chests broad, three times his size. Journey spins, tucks his haunches and flees. The pounding hooves soon fall back and Journey begins to walk, sniffing the trail. No deer. No prey. He trots on through a creekside ravine, the ground under his paws cool and moist. He heads up, wanders the mountainside and tucks in under a rock ledge to rest until dusk.

Leaving home at eight o'clock Wednesday morning I had a full tank of gas and little apprehension. I'd stuffed my duffle bag with warm clothing, two pairs of boots, four jackets, two pairs of gloves, mittens, a blanket, some hand warmers, digital recorder, phone, laptop, three different chargers, and directions that would take me through roads that the Montana Department of Transportation showed as dotted yellow—scattered snow and ice—for a stretch, but otherwise dry and fine all the way to Gardiner, my destination. I'd visited Gardiner five months prior, in June, and remembered little except that it's a typical western tourist town with casual restaurants and motels, outfitters offering river running and hunting, souvenir stores on every corner. I'd chosen my motel from a website showing photos of dark green siding and rust-red concrete steps fronting small suites with renovated kitchenettes and travertine showers. I'd received both discounts available: winter rates, and the longer-than-three-nights offer. Solitude, quiet, a good night's sleep. Time away from home and marriage. There were over five hundred miles between home and Gardiner, though, and I stuck the motel, like a reward, in the back of my mind.

The car, on loan, was a sturdy Subaru and full of road-trip necessities: my cooler of carrots, clementines, apples, and cans of Diet Coke on the floor of the passenger seat; my coat, gloves, handbag and wool scarf directly behind me; a canvas bag with licorice and pretzels wedged behind my seat; a collection of compact discs on the passenger seat. I'd brought two Jack London books, a Coldplay album, and a lecture on decision making to listen to. My plan was to drive quickly, stopping for gas and bathroom breaks only when imperative. I should be in Gardiner by 4:30. Maybe 5:00. Time to eat dinner, relax, and prepare myself to hang out with the Yellowstone Wolf Project winter study team for a few days.

I tucked a CD in the drive—*The Call of the Wild*. I listened to Peter Coyote read words penned by Jack London 110 years ago, the story of a wolf-dog hybrid of tremendous strength and, at the end, an inability to deny his wild nature. Interstate 15 was dry and fast, and I sipped coffee from my thermal mug until it was gone.

In Idaho Falls I exited Interstate 15 and turned onto Highway 20, a road that was a straighter shot but was also showing those broken-yellow-line, snowy, icy roads on the DOT map. Not for a while, though, and with any luck the plows would be out. The Subaru's tires whirred away on dry pavement, and I settled in. I opened a Diet Coke and dug into the carrots. Licorice: two reds then a black. I had a huge two-pound mixed bag and would need to pace myself.

Rexburg, Idaho, came and went, and soon I was approaching Ashton, where suddenly the backside of the Tetons jut from a flat nothingness to unimaginable heights: five peaks, knobby and bumpy, like wet sand squeezed through a superhuman fist. It took effort to focus on the road before me. I love those mountains; they exert a magnetic pull over me. I imagine my soul lined with things and places and people in miniature replicas: the Tetons, my children, a mountain lake, a green-eyed boy I once loved, a book called *The History of Love*, heart-shaped anythings, dark purple tulips. I meet them again in real life and am smitten once more, a circuit made complete.

Warmth lingered in my chest as I passed through Ashton and neared the next mountain range, which stole my view of the Tetons. A light rain began to fall and I could see, far ahead, a fog bank hanging low. I entered the Targhee National Forest. The road ascended until my car was solidly embraced by a mist that began dissolving into small pieces. Rain. Sleet. Then snow. The road climbed and turned, suddenly slippery, treacherous. Grateful for the Subaru—knowing my Mini Cooper would have failed miserably—I drove cautiously, uncomfortable with the ruts and snowpack and unpredictable behavior of the snow beneath my tires. Muscles tightened and slowly pulled shoulders toward ears; every five minutes or so I'd take a deep breath, release it, and send my shoulders back down. Relax. You can do this. I'd grown up in snow country, learning to drive in a mountainside neighborhood perched seven thousand feet above sea level. My older brother, while driving me to school one January day, did a three-sixty on the icy freeway, not hitting a thing but scaring the bejesus out of me. We lived in a land of steep, narrow roads that frightened me on both the uphill and the downhill. Once I'd skidded off the road into a ditch, and another time I'd slid down an iced city street and slammed into a parked car. Since moving off the hillside of our city eight years ago, though, I'd spent less time driving in serious snow and had lost some confidence. Just keep driving.

It was my sixth trip of the year without Daniel. Last April, I had driven to Jackson Hole for a weekend escape, taking snowshoes and a journal. In June I went to Yellowstone and Montana, and in August I'd spent the long weekend at the ranch. Last month, Missoula. Three weeks ago, New York with Cait. I'd been married just over a year, and I was heartbroken. Our lives functioned smoothly enough, but I'd struggled to foster and create intimacy between the two of us, and I'd failed. We'd been working with a therapist since last May, but the chasm between us remained, my heart and soul lonelier than if we'd never married. It was as if vibrant purple mixed with stunningly brilliant yellow, and produced mud brown. I'd been single for eight years and had grown accustomed to plentiful air, my own energy, a sense of peace, emotional honesty. I craved solitude, a break from the frustration of living with someone unable to share his deeper self. I'd have that this trip. I had it already, as long as my tires stayed firmly on the road beneath me.

I breathed. Snow fell. Windshield wipers flushed wet flakes. I held the steering wheel loosely, trusting the car, breathing away my tension. Somewhere between Island Park and West Yellowstone, I rounded a wide, sweeping bend and saw flashing lights ahead, the world white and gray and sunless. I braked. An orange diamond-shaped sign on the right, tow truck ahead. A burly man in an orange vest trudging along the edge of the road. I came to a stop behind a big white pickup. Off in the left-hand ditch a semi-trailer truck rested, its cab off the road, the wheels of its hind end resting on the snow-covered asphalt, and its middle parts angling between the two. Men in orange vests and hats were hooking a tow truck to the rear of the semi, and more were milling in the snow. I used the down time to check in with Daniel, letting him know where I was in my journey. I wrote in my journal, five sentences. I was too agitated to write. I watched the drama. I wondered if the tow truck employees were on an adrenaline high, or if this was routine and they were bored. They'd hook up the semi, tow it back a bit, then reposition everything and do it again. The wheels of the semi's cab regained purchase on the snowy road. Whew. It had been thirty-five minutes since I'd stopped, and the storm was worsening. Roadblock removed, the white pickup in front of me roared off. I became the lead car on the white road in the white world, the pickup's white dust soon gone. A gold SUV and two semis lined up in my rearview mirror as I drove over the snow-packed road. At West Yellowstone, I pulled over. It looked like a ghost town. Nothing had been plowed, anywhere, and snow was piled eight to ten inches high along sidewalks, parking lots, and business entrances. Five vehicles passed me. An ancient Chevy Blazer fishtailed as it made a left turn at the blinking stoplight. I took a deep breath, sent it out loudly. Pulled back onto the highway.

I veered left ten miles out of West Yellowstone, taking Route 287. The trucks before and behind me continued straight, and Robert Frost and I were alone, diverging left toward Ennis. I'd chosen the 287 route because hours earlier, the Montana DOT map had indicated it was less snowy and icy than the one everyone else was taking. Immediately the road surface improved, showing dry spots and lightly dusted surfaces. From jaw to toes my muscles relaxed. I'd survived the worst. Then the snow appeared. As the road curved and rose, it packed on the asphalt and swirled down with gusts of wind.

Alone on the road, no idea where I was, I regretted the decisions I'd made about my route, sitting home in calm, dry Salt

Lake City, looking at the Montana DOT website, choosing roads based on broken yellow lines. I knew only that 287 would eventually reach Ennis, where I would turn right. I crept on at thirty-five miles per hour and tried not to strangle the steering wheel.

Hillsides rose around me, drenched with pines black in the flat light, every other detail a shade of gray. I was in a diorama, colorless, a scene from my grandfather's old photographs. At the next curve in the road, a lake appeared on my left, a deep shade of gunmetal gray, wind-whipped, flashes of white froth in the chop. It spread from just below the road across to a distant hillside, where a slender, snowy white bank separated the sea of black conifers from the gray water. A half-mile later I passed a sign that read "The Lake That Tilted." Then a dam. The road gradually descended and another small lake appeared, this one speckled with treetops that poked through the dark water. I'd passed Hebgen Lake, where in 1959 an earthquake dropped the shelf on which the lake rested, tilting it northward, overflowing the dam, and creating, downstream, Earthquake Lake, treetops rising from its depths. Ah, another landslide. I passed a sign with a fishing tackle logo carved into the wood: I'd take up fishing just to spend time here. Stunning in a blizzard, the land must be breathtaking on a late spring day. With dry roads.

The road settled as I came off the mountain and drove through the Madison Valley, where large homes hunkered here and there, ranches, ranchettes, cattle sprinkled around—each cow with one black side, the other pure white with wind-driven snow—tall wheat-colored grasses blustered by the storm. Wind swept snow onto the roads, swirls blinding, beguiling. The pavement was dry, the snow near moistureless. Not vast, the valley was large enough to luxuriate in, small enough to feel held, safely, in the palm of some giant hand. In Ennis, where I stopped for gas, a terrible squealing sound issued from underneath my car as I turned to park. So much snow and ice coated the wheel wells that the tires barely had room to move. Bitter wind whipped my hair, my entire self, as I walked the thirty feet to the store, shocking my car-coddled body. Imagine life here on a horse. After confirming my route with the clerk, a customer at the counter mentioned he'd come from Livingston that morning and it was wicked there. The road from Bozeman to Livingston, Interstate 90, was snow-packed, wind-blown, rutted. Nasty.

Couldn't wait.

Life after trauma. I was divorced. Bob was gay. I'd decided to let Jake die, but he hadn't.

I started riding my bicycle.

I ran a small business from home, wrote when I could. I nurtured, guided, fed, and drove my four children, and for the past half dozen years, had found few opportunities to connect with the core of me, which wanted to sing and jump and be wildly joyful. The bike forged the connection. It took me up to places green and wild, it provided swoops of exhilaration on my way back down. My heart sang with each deer sighting and lazy hawk circle. Stress, contention, pressure, all melted as I pedaled, my heart raced, breath grew short. Up meant mountains, hillsides, brilliant skies and water—reservoirs, creeks, streams— quiet, the minimization of artificial noise, peace. Riding early in the morning while my children slept energized me. Beginning each day with a full soul enabled me to better parent my boys, then fifteen and fourteen, and my girls, ten. I started to ride every day. I was in recovery.

Naturalist and author Doug Peacock had returned from Vietnam traumatized. A Green Beret medic, he'd killed, and watched others be killed. Saved lives and failed to save lives. He spent his first few years back in America wandering in wilderness. Finding connection with grizzly bears, solitude, the stark honesty of nature. He began, slowly, to heal.

I, too, need to heal. I need mountains, canyons, creeks, fledgling owls and stodgy moose. I need the coyote's howls and the chattering of squirrels, and all the nuts and plants and smaller prey that feed these creatures. I want my hillsides green, I want the wildlife abundant and healthy. I want the thrill of seeing it all, being part of it, connecting with the wild natural world. When I round a corner and come face to face with a doe, I feel instantly grounded to something personal and genuine, bonding me more deeply with the land.

I need that bond. And I need that mountain to be healthy and whole, its ecosystems complete and complex. The wolf is a part of the natural environment—or should be. A century ago it roamed the mountains and valleys that surround my home, retreating to hillside caves and selecting prey from the elk and other smaller mammals that lived alongside it. The wolf, with the elk and deer, moose and beaver and bear, the mountain lion and raccoon and coyote, was a dynamic participant in the ecosystem of the mountains and ranges, keeping ungulates on the move and leaving carcasses for scavengers from eagles to microbes. Flora and fauna evolved with this apex predator, and its right to exist feels inalienable to me.

When Doug Peacock was seventeen, he was in Michigan's Upper Peninsula at the Two-Hearted River when he heard a howl. The sound floated across the land, no animal in sight. He stilled, knowing that what enveloped him was vital, was necessary and integral to human wholeness. It lingers inside him, this howl.

Wolves are gradually reentering our lands, accompanied by human argument and discord. Feelings are intense and tension runs high on all sides. Livelihoods are affected and beliefs challenged. Both sportsmen and landowners are forced to modify behaviors because wolves live nearby. More wolves in Idaho ultimately reduces the number of elk on the landscape, at times causing hunters to work harder for their kills. More wolves in Montana increases the likelihood that some will kill cattle. More wolves in Yellowstone means increased revenue from visitors for Yellowstone and for its adjacent towns and enterprises, yet reduced revenues for outfitters who no longer have record-high elk herds migrating from the park each winter. The battle rages over whether the gray wolf should or should not remain listed under the Endangered Species Act. I want a peaceful resolution. I want us to agree on a way to treat wolves that matches their grace and strength, their tenacity, their charisma. A plan that honors the mystery within every living being, whether we understand its purpose, or not.

At the north fork of the Flathead River, high in Glacier National Park, Doug spent most of his day in a tall lookout, up above the trees. It was the late 1970s, and Doug watched for fire. A nearby meadow was a favorite spot to look for grizzlies. A few years earlier he'd seen a mountain lion there. Watched it, one of the world's most reclusive beasts, for a quarter of an hour as it sat, perused, switched its tail back and forth.

But during one visit to the meadow, Doug saw a coyote. The largest coyote he'd ever seen. Ever.

"So I put my binocs on it, and I thought it was someone's malamute. Then two other dark bodies came out from the timber, and they all stood together. Not malamutes. Wolves. That was really something." He looks out the window. His voice softens.

"And all that summer, I knew the places that were prime wolf areas. I'd go there at the end of the day, and stop, and howl." He howls. Unrushed, haunting. It lingers. "I'd howl, there at dusk, in the middle of the park. Sometimes I had to wait five minutes, but almost every time, a wolf would respond. And that carried me for years. Yeah. It carried me through the birth of my children. I really needed something like that in my life."

Doug is a contemplative man who writes, chairs committees, and has founded a conservation organization. He is a wild mountain man who is at once civilized, appropriate, and irreverent. He named his cat Moose, and often calls wolves "woofs." He typed *Grizzly Years* on an old Smith Corona, pecking away in that tower in Glacier National Park. He spent years learning how grizzlies live by observing and sharing territory, respecting them. He wears glasses, had his hip replaced last year, and underwent open-heart surgery just months back. He's spent most of his life fighting like hell to protect the land and wildness that brought him back to sanity after those Vietnam years destroyed him. He has spent thousands of days and nights outside. He is not Hayduke, not a caricature. He is a fallible human who knows the shortest distance between insanity and peace lies across a snow-covered landscape that can only be accessed on snowshoes. A land that for him, these days, lies within the boundaries of Yellowstone.

"What I've seen of the world is not the best. I had to come to terms with death rather early in my life. Not just war, but especially war." Doug came home from Vietnam having lost faith in the goodness of the world. He didn't want to bring children into a society that placed so little value on life. He'd lost too much, and didn't want to lose anything else. But then he began working in Glacier, began bonding with the grizzlies. He claims it's the bears that helped him decide he was willing to be human.

"And then I heard those wolves. Once I had the woofs, I thought it was a good enough world to share with children. My children. That's how they grew up. And that's what they're doing today, pursuit of protection of all things wild. They're going about it in different ways, but it's part of who they are.

"Those three woofs played quite a big role. Their being there let me know it was really okay."

But now, he's not so sure.

"Everything is in danger these days," Doug says. "There's no room for waffling. Or fighting lighthearted, or even for tolerance of that kind of ignorance. It's not acceptable."

Doug's eyes look out from behind the lightly tinted round lenses of his glasses, and they are dead serious.

"Man has changed our environments, and we better damn well wake up, admit it, and start making changes. We argue about how many elk we need for hunters to kill, how to keep cattle safe from bison and sheep safe from wolves, when the entire world is changing beneath our feet. Instead, we should be agreeing on how to best mitigate those changes, and keep our wildlife from increasingly losing their habitat, eventually dying out as species.

"I don't even bother arguing—somebody doesn't believe in global warming, or they're not going to change their life, has that fuck-you, I'm going to keep driving my Hummer, or my oil rig attitude. We're right on the edge here. There's no time for ignorance. Or arrogance."

Back in my car, I left the metropolis of Ennis, Montana—population eight hundred or so—took a right onto Route 287 North, drove sixteen miles to Norris, where I turned east onto Highway 84. A quaint two-lane road winding through farm and ranch country, its surface changed in the blink of an eye from dry to rutted with frozen slush to solid ice, in no detectable pattern. I came up behind an open-bed, wide black truck with ice and snow cemented on its rear bumper. I thought of passing it, then hit a sketchy patch of road that lifted my eyebrows and stole my breath. I changed my mind.

After following the black truck a handful of miles, a large red pickup appeared behind me. Its red and silver grill filled my rearview mirror, then it moved into the oncoming traffic lane and sped past me. As it pulled even with the truck in front of me, the red truck started to slide to the left, then fishtail to the right, and then suddenly it spun like a big red top, kicking up clouds of white snow, obliterating my view. Was it coming back to slam into me? I could see nothing, no truck at all. Abruptly the snow settled and the red truck materialized, skidding off the edge of the road and disappearing. Stunned, I eased onto the narrow shoulder. I grabbed gloves from the backseat and bolted from the car as a blond woman in down parka and jeans slid out from the driver's side of the black truck shaking her head. *Why did he do that? I just know he rolled, oh why did he do that?* Together, we ran back to where the truck disappeared, scanning the gully. Fifty feet down and across a wire fence, the red truck sat upright, its roof undented. The driver's side door opened and a faint, feminine voice floated up: *Call 911.* Another motorist had stopped and was already on the phone. A dark-haired woman climbed gingerly out of the driver's seat and leaned against the truck. *I'm okay. My wrist and my ankle hurt, but I'm okay.* Whew.

I gave my contact information to the blond woman, then said I needed to press on to Gardiner and climbed back into my car. A semi-truck in a ditch. A pick-up flying off the road. What the hell was I doing driving in this snowstorm? I should be home, reading about wolves while sitting in my warm, safe house. Instead I was on these frozen roads, alone, heading to a tiny, anti-wolf tourist town in the middle of nowhere. I reached around and dug into the licorice bag.

The rest of my drive into Belgrade (there are also Montana cities named Amsterdam, Glasgow, Malta, Manhattan) and onto Interstate 90 was mild. No trucks in ditches. I drove a few miles on the interstate before the roads turned snow-packed and icy.

Drivers sped past, spitting snow from rear tires. I gripped the steering wheel. I knew holding on loosely was better. Grip, relax, breathe, grip, relax, breathe. Ridges of frozen slush between lanes grabbed my tires and threw the car into slides, first one direction, then another. I was relieved to finally see a sign for Livingston.

During the warmer months of the year it's possible to reach Gardiner by driving through Yellowstone, but once the winter snows begin the interior park roads close, leaving only the Northeast Entrance Road open, necessitating the trip north to Livingston before coming all the way back down south, to Gardiner. Had I driven to Yellowstone just three weeks earlier, my trip would have been a hundred miles shorter and a hundred times less stressful. However, I was here to see the park in winter, to look for wolves with the Winter Study team. I had signed on for the complete adventure. Trucks soaring off the road and all.

It was nearing five when I exited the interstate at Livingston. The sun had dropped below the mountains. What little light remained hovered, weak as under-brewed tea, seemingly as reluctant to leave as I was to see it go. The short drive through Livingston—population 7,044 in the 2010 census—prepared me in no way for what came next. The two-lane highway to Gardiner was immediately icy, snow-packed, slushy, and everything in between. Five miles later the weak-tea light was gone, and I could see neither the white line delineating my outside border, nor the double yellow line indicating the inner. The reflective patches on the road markers off the right side of the road were my only guide.

With forty miles left to go, the sky was dark. Oncoming headlights blinded me and each time they approached I decelerated, hoping I was somewhere between the buried yellow and white lines, neither too close, nor ready to slide off the road.

Thirty miles from Gardiner, I was exhausted. I wanted to be done. Dark became darker, and approaching headlights now launched a terror that overtook me the seconds before we passed. *Just pull off the road, sit. Quit.* I didn't know whose voice was in my head. Either it was the wise one, warning me I was exhausted and incapable of driving the last few miles safely, or it was the "I told you so" voice, wanting me to fail at the task. I felt tears; I was ready to be done with strong and capable and surrender to weak and inadequate. The car stayed on the road, somehow straight and relatively centered between those obscured white and yellow lines.

Near six o'clock, I was within five miles of Gardiner and my spirits crawled up from where they'd been crouching. The motel would be a haven—I didn't care what it looked like as long as it was warm and my car could sit, parked and silent, out front. The Gardiner Market appeared on my right and I pulled in, having hours earlier realized that I had no scraper for the car windows come morning, nor did I have back-up batteries for my digital recorder. I picked up a plastic packet of foot warmers, and a bottle of wine along with my batteries and scraper, and got back in my car.

I had instructions to turn left onto the street before the Baptist church, then immediately turn right and follow the dirt road into the motel's parking lot. Forget addresses. Bright green, blue, yellow, and red Christmas lights wound their way along the top of the fence around the property, cheery and welcoming. I glanced at the odometer. Five hundred fifty miles of terror, joy, freedom. Beauty.

I was beat. And grateful to check into a warm, clean, one-bedroom suite that would be my home for the next four days. The manager showed me my room, pointing out the large flat-screen television which I told him not to bother telling me how to operate (are you sure?), to the DVD player (we have lots of movies in the lobby you can borrow), to the large bedroom with its own supplementary heater (you shouldn't need this, but), to the tray of organic free-trade coffees and teas on the kitchen counter (plenty more of these if you need, just ask).

I unloaded the car, unpacked. I changed into pajamas, warmed my leftover curry from last night's dinner in Salt Lake. I curled on the couch with a blanket and the latest Sue Grafton novel. Oblivion. No snow-packed roads, frozen slush, sheets of ice. No hurtling trucks, no pickups spinning off the road. Nothing but curry and rice, Kinsey Millhone, warmth. I had no decisions to make except how soon to crawl into bed. 8:30 was the answer, and I set my alarm for 6:00.

I lie in bed thinking about fear. Our most primal fears, of dying. Of being killed, eaten, devoured by wild animals. Wolves, grizzlies, mountain lions. Or by those who love so deeply they want to see inside the one they love. Who expose themselves, sharing grief and disappointments, passions and fears, vulnerabilities. It is death, either way.

11. clear

The world had turned white again. Cold, gray. And then the days begin to lengthen. Journey runs faster, longer each day. He has scoured this land. She is not here. Journey heads north. The snow begins to melt. Clouds depart. Ten miles, twenty miles. Another fifteen. North, true north. Thick groves of pine cover mountainsides. A call sounds in the distance. He sniffs the moist, familiar air. He runs until he stops, exhausted. He curls up, nose on top of tail. He sleeps.

The sharp-edged beep of my alarm clock means home, yet I am away. I'd brought my own alarm clock, a small battery-powered thing that maintains the correct time by regularly communicating with a radio tower in Colorado. No need to worry about power failures. Ever.

I roll out of bed and tiptoe across the cold floor to the coffee maker, fumbling to seat the diminutive filter correctly and fill the narrow water cavity. I'd arranged this visit with Doug Smith, head of Yellowstone's Wolf Project. He'd suggested that instead of trying to meet up with one of his teams in the early morning dark, perhaps I spend my first morning in the park orienting myself. Look for them once the sun was up. Each team drove a white government vehicle—I should look for white SUVs. As I'd unpacked the night before I realized I'd forgotten my hat. My coats have hoods, but I need a hat. I planned to hit the Gardiner Market first thing before heading into the park.

I start layering as the coffee drips. Underwear, long johns, long running tights. Sports bra, base layer, wool turtleneck. Wool knee-high ski socks. I pack my rucksack as I sip coffee and consider the day in front of me. Binoculars, heavy mittens, camera, digital recorder, small bag of trail mix. I spread peanut butter on a whole wheat English muffin, then wrap it in a paper towel and tuck it in a side pocket. Journal, pen, lightweight gloves, hand warmer packet. I fill two water bottles, and prepare a thermal mug of coffee for my drive. I open the foot warmer packet and, following instructions, stick one to the bottom of each sock. Credit card, a few dollars, driver license, lip balm. A clementine.

I slip on wind pants, a light down-filled jacket, a slightly thicker jacket, the outer shell. A purple fleece scarf. After a slight debate, I tug on the smaller boots and decide to take the Sorrels, just in case. I go outside to start the car, using my new scraper to etch away the night's frozen layer of white. It's four degrees. The frigid air attacks my nostrils and my skin tightens in alarm. I blow out breath in short bursts, watching the white clouds sit and then disperse, hover, fall earthward. Still dark, the sky feels close. I can see the mountains to the south in silhouette, Electric Peak sharp, the entire ridge before me darkest black against a sky that is just beginning to lighten. I take a deep breath and cold explodes through my lungs. Adventure, here I come.

I stop at the Gardiner Market just as they open, am greeted by a freckled, cheerful woman bundled in a few layers herself.

"Need any help?"

"I do, I need a hat."

"Right over there." She points to a smallish wire rack in the middle of the frozen foods aisle that is hung with child-size pink gloves and hats, Spiderman mittens, some thick-fingered gloves and perhaps four adult-size hats, two of which are a cadet blue with red trim—ugh—one of which is some combination of primary colors, and the final, a black background with neon pink and green and yellow peace symbols on it. Cait would like this, I think, and decide it's the best of the bunch. Her twin, Allegra, would roll her eyes. I buy it. I ask the woman if she'll snip off the tag, and I pass her my credit card for the $7.99 purchase. I am set.

As I drive toward the park's entry gate, daylight illuminates detail hidden just twenty minutes ago. A few gas stations, beaucoup motels, plenty of small restaurants, a large yellowish log building offering souvenirs and coffee, and one stop sign where Highway 89 comes to a T with Park Road. Though I know Gardiner's residents are vocally anti-wolf, it looks like a typical tourism-driven town. I turn right at the T and round the big U-shaped bend, confronted by the huge, rock entry gate built shortly after Yellowstone first opened, and almost wide enough for two cars to pass. The heater in my car is blaring and I'm sipping on warm coffee as I stop at the entrance gate and pay twenty-five dollars for the privilege of visiting Yellowstone— and Grand Teton National Park, should I so choose—for the next seven days. The ranger who hands me a park map and the fall issue newspaper is a black man, and I can't help but wonder if Gardiner receives him better or worse than they receive wolves. He is the first black person I've encountered in three visits to Montana. I have no idea where he lives, but I imagine that he's one of very few persons of color. I wonder if I'm being politically incorrect, but then Pinkola Estés herself—author, Jungian analyst—would surely find parallels in the oppression of wolves, of black people, of women. It's hard to imagine this wolf-hating town welcoming this gentleman—or me.

Although blacks and women were finally granted equality with the passage of the Civil Rights Act over fifty years ago, and though wolves were reintroduced in the northern Rockies after a decades-long absence, blacks, women, and wolves have

long histories of persecution, and the assumptions and ener-
gies behind those persecutions don't necessarily disappear with
the passing of a law. Women earn seventy-eight percent of what
men in comparable, full time jobs are paid, white supremacist
groups continue to recruit, and wolves retain their vilified stigma in bars and barbeques throughout the West. I'm glad a black
man dares live here, and I'm glad there are wolves on the landscape. And I'm glad I'm a woman. A wild one.

As I drive into the park the day brightens, and I slow and
brake for grazing elk. I take a picture or two as they stare, un-
blinking. Bull elk are everywhere, their antlers huge, imposing,
but where I've stopped to dig out my camera there are only
youngsters. I'm not much of a photographer, but I want a physical, visual record of this adventure in this stunningly beautiful spot of earth. Each breath I take recharges me, renews my
faith in the power of natural beauty to restore. I feel woven into
the splendor, each piece of it a part of me, too. Mammoth Hot
Springs in the early morning of a late November day is a quiet
place, the parking lots empty save a car here or there, the hotel closed for the winter, the visitor center under construction
and temporarily housed in what looks like a double-wide trailer
parked on the grass. I drive through park headquarters and its
sparse village, and turn left onto the only open park road. I am
looking for white government trucks or SUVs. Have no idea
where I'll find them. This happens to me frequently: I set out
on an adventure (road trip, appointment to interview someone,
shopping expedition, new cycling route) without what some
might consider proper preparation. I get the gist, pack snacks
and extra socks, and go. So when Doug told me I'd find them
somewhere, I trusted that I would find them somewhere.

Seven or so miles past Mammoth, having spent a few miles
hugging a hillside and a few more driving a road darkened by
towering conifers, my vista again opens wide and sunlight shat-

ters the snowy hillsides beside me into billions of sparkling particles. The snow is fresh. The storm I'd encountered along my drive through Idaho and Montana yesterday has graced the park with half a foot of snow. I round a bend, the road rises, and off to my right are the first vehicles I've seen since Mammoth, two big white pick-up trucks and two smaller cars, parked in a snowy lot south of the road. Two women in hooded jackets, thick pants, and mittens stand before tripod-mounted scopes, looking toward the southwest mountains. I drive to the far end of the lot in front of the trucks, park the car, and gather my courage from where it tends to rest down by my feet.

"Hi," I greet the women. The shorter one, whose blond hair hangs loosely from under her bright knit hat, turns her head, smiles widely at me. "What're you watching?" I ask.

"Nothing right now," the blond answers while the other woman, dressed in a puffy blue jacket, offers a tentative smile. All of the wolf watchers I've met here in Yellowstone have been generous with their scopes and stories, though during initial conversations, some have been more open than others. The blue-jacketed woman is, at least at first glance, on the less-open end of the spectrum. I tell them I'm looking for the Wolf Project teams.

The one in blue—Ilona, she tells me—says they're up on the knob, nodding to a snub of a hill capped with pines that's further south, away from the road. We decide to hike up there together. It's about a half-mile hike, mostly up, and she carries her scope over her left shoulder and pauses every now and again to catch her breath. She apologizes. Says she's been in Washington the past three weeks, had just returned the day before, and those three weeks at sea level have taken her wind from her. I don't mind the pause. Ilona's pace is just fine with me. We pass over a few dry spots, large rectangular patches of grass, perhaps eighteen inches by three feet, with icy edges where grass meets snow. I wonder if they are spots where elk bedded for the night, but don't want to disrupt our conversation. Ilona's writing a book about wolves. She's been tracking wolves and wolf politics for years. She's on the Bear Creek Council, an organization whose mission is, in part, "protecting the livelihoods of Gardiner businesses by ensuring that Yellowstone wildlife is protected, and that wildlife tourism is understood and valued by the community." In other words, reminding Gardiner businesses just who butters their bread: wildlife lovers and wolf watchers.

We hike up the last few dozen steps to the top of the butte, a tiny hilltop where three Wolf Project watchers have scopes trained on the hillside far away to the southwest.

Brenna, Donny and Kersten say hello, introducing themselves as the watchers of the Blacktail pack. This pack consists of just three wolves, all of which are currently out of sight. The alpha female is a collared wolf, number 693. However, they think she has lost her collar since it has been heard in only one specific location, giving off a mortality sound. Doug and his team believe the alpha female is fine and that the collar has somehow broken and fallen off her neck, but no one has yet been able to locate the collar. A gray female believed to be 693 has been sighted with the alpha, 778, so the concern is not over her wellbeing, but rather, where her collar is. Telemetry can tell you only so much about an animal's position and is not a precise locator. (I later learn that 693 had died, her body found in a remote location two weeks later. The gray female the watchers saw when I was there was 778's new mate.)

Brenna and her team have seen 778 with the wolf they believe to be 693, and a third wolf that has been spending time with them, but this morning the animals moved across a flat, snowy field far across the hillside, then ran into the trees. Brenna waves a hand-held antenna back and forth, then up and down. She picks up 778's radio signal, but we can't catch sight of them anywhere.

"Why do you move the antenna in different directions?" I ask.

"When we can't catch a signal on horizontal, we'll try vertical, and sometimes you can hear it that way."

The technicians hold the directional antenna—a contraption perhaps twelve inches by eighteen with a short handle—and lift it skyward, waving it slowly left to right, horizontally. They'll then turn it forty-five degrees, and perform the same left to right scan, searching for signals "on vertical." Because of the way radio waves travel, at times the signal from a wolf's collar can be heard more easily on vertical, especially if the wolf is in a narrow canyon or ravine where signals bounce from hillside to hillside.

"Where did you catch that signal?" Donny asks.

"Just to the left of where we saw them running into the trees." Brenna points for Ilona and me. It's one of those "follow that taller tree up until you see a hollow in the land, then look to the left of the snow patch and find the next group of conifers and then it's right there," explanations. I'm lost. Brenna says, "Look to the right of that area of region, and see that little arm of snow that grows larger as you move right, and it's over there." Region, I don't know what region is. No one else questions her, so I sit with it for a while. Finally I have to know.

"Brenna? What's region? I don't know that term."

"Oh, no problem. See how this area has all these dead trees, left from the fire? Well, all the new growth started at the same time, so all the trees are almost the exact same height, so we just call that the area of regen, regeneration, a patch where everything's the same height."

Oh, regen, not region.

Donny's down jacket has a two-inch square piece of duct tape on the back left shoulder, and I've already noticed the bottom of Ilona's sleeve is wrapped in duct tape, too. Before my trip is over I'll have seen duct tape holding boots together, patching seats, and plugging rips in more down jackets. Back home they sell duct tape in camouflage, hot pink, stripes, and every school color you can think of, but here, like in Missoula, it's silver or it's nothing. Donny has the radio, and it crackles to life—Doug Smith's voice. He's up in the plane, searching for the Eightmile pack, letting ground teams know what's visible from above.

"We're next," Donny offers. Soon we'll be able to scour the sky for the small, yellow Piper Cub. It's the first Winter Study day that Doug's been able to fly, the weather until now having been inclement at best. Enthusiasm peppers his voice. I wonder what it's like to fly above these valleys and knolls, buttes and hollows, searching out the wolf packs you've known and followed for almost twenty years. I hear the thrumming, 150-horsepower engine. The plane is just a yellow dash against a mountainside when I first see it. Doug blares again, and we listen as he looks for the Blacktail wolves in the area of regen where Brenna lost sight of them two hours earlier.

"I see them, they're in the trees—you're going to have a hard time seeing them from where you are, they're moving south . . ."

The news from the plane isn't encouraging for wolf viewing. But watching the plane fly over the trees, its wings throwing flashes of sunlight back in my eyes, is thrilling. I envision loping wolves, seen from the free-flying plane, grounded yet part of the sky above.

A crackle. Doug's voice, loud and clear: "They're in there, just in the trees. We're heading your way. We'll try to locate 693's collar, but I think the signal's gone."

The small yellow plane is heading straight for us. It buzzes over the five of us standing on South Butte as we wave wildly at Roger, the pilot, and Doug, in the tiny seat behind him, the two men filling the cabin. With a final swoop they head off to the east, taking with them, possibly, the last excitement of the day. The wolves may bed in the trees for hours, or they may pop out again. The watchers settle in. They scan the distant hillsides. Brenna stands and waves the antenna back and forth, but now there are no beeps at all.

"Have you tried catching them on drift?" Kersten asks.

"What's on drift?" I'm lost again.

Brenna fiddles with the dial. She explains that temperature and battery fluctuations can affect a signal, so the techs try searching for a specific wolf's signal a few kilohertz on either side of the assigned frequency. To catch a wolf's signal on drift just means something in the atmosphere is affecting reception.

No beeps. The wolves have either moved far away, or are hidden by something which blocks the radio collar's signal.

When I ride my bicycle, I take my phone. Only one canyon, Millcreek, refuses entry to cellular waves. On every other ride, I can always be located. I am a mother: I might be needed.

Reality, though, is that Jake needs me less. His latest surgical scar has healed. Even without the Baclofen, he is mellow, though his limbs are tight again. Beau, beginning high school, tolerates each hug and every goodbye kiss. He lives behind his bedroom door. He doesn't ask for help. Allegra and Cait are in middle school. Cait is compliant. Allegra is belligerent. Angry. Taking every pain and secret of our family and making it her own. She draws pictures of Little Joe, hangs them on her wall. She awakens grumpy, stomps off to school, drags herself home. Pounds the piano. Slops her way through homework. She needs me more than anyone else, but her porcupine skin won't let me close.

It's 2011, and wolves have been delisted in a land mass covering Montana, Wyoming, Idaho, a corner of northwestern Utah, and parts of eastern Washington and Oregon. They are prolific, intelligent, hardy. But they're also hated and vilified, and not likely to be well protected by the legislatures in many western states. Montana, Wyoming, and Idaho sell licenses to kill wolves. Conservation organizations step up their activities arguing for continued protection, and hunting organizations fund lobbying to fight against it. The wolves have no idea. In this way they're like Jake, whose world intersects with ours, but who is so self-contained, he's completely unaware of anyone's ideas or activities, or plans for him. The wolves live up in the hills, the mountains, in valleys—hunting, mating, raising their pups—with no understanding at all of what we are planning to do with them.

All three of the Blacktail watching team have black, insulated backpacking chairs: two attached squares of cushion encased in ripstop polyester that open at right angles to each other, held by a strap. More often the trio fold these up and stand on them, stopping heat loss from boots on snow. It's ten degrees, and the butte top is only about twenty feet by fifteen. Not enough room to run laps. We're atop South Butte—Brenna tells me that the creatively named North Butte is just a few miles across the road, north of us. Kersten offers Ilona and me, at different moments, everything from some of the tea in her thermos to one of her packs of hand warmers. It's clear we both find the thought of accepting anything ridiculous: we are short-term visitors, while she has the rest of the day to contend with. My car with its fabulous heater is just half a mile away. I'm beginning to think of returning to it, after more than two hours of no wolves. Ilona mentions she might be ready to leave, and we say goodbye, trudge downhill together. I'm ready to search for another one of Doug's teams, and apparently she is, too. I don't want to glom onto her side, but the wolf researchers in this small section of park that's open aren't something either of us can hog to ourselves.

"Do you have a scope?" she asks as we reach the elk beds, those brown, grassy rectangles sticking out from the snow like postage stamps on white envelopes.

"No," I reply, shaking my head.

"You might want to consider renting one, just for the experience of it, learning to work it—they're not that hard. But it would be good to have your own instead of relying on other people's."

I nod, wondering if she's suggesting I'm a freeloader. I came without plans to rent a scope. Daniel's colleague lent me a pair of binoculars for the trip—they were in my backpack—but even binoculars intimidate me. I experimented with them at home, twisting lenses left then right. The trees and fence before me leapt in size and green filled my sight, fuzzy and indistinct. I lowered the binoculars to assess what the branches and wood really looked like, all of it completely unrecognizable through the eyepiece of the binoculars. I'd brought them with me, but was unexcited about using them. I didn't think I'd fare better with a scope.

"I work part-time in a gallery that rents scopes. You could just rent one for a day or two, see what it's like."

I reluctantly ask her which gallery and where it is, and she tells me the name—which enters and promptly leaves my mind—and that it's in the tallest building in Gardiner, I can't miss it. No address, just the descriptor. When we reach our cars she gives me her email address and an invitation to the Bear Creek Council holiday party, then says she's going to stop at the Tower Junction pit toilets. I feel like a kindergartener following my teacher around. I have to pee, too.

At Tower Junction, I get out of my car and start attacking the icy buildup that's still so thick inside my wheel wells that my tires screech madly every time I turn. I chip away a quarter inch, then another, and Ilona comes out of the toilet, telling me she's going to head on down the road, looking for the next crew. I thank her again, tell her I won't be far behind.

"This toilet's much nicer than that one," she offers, pointing to the one farther to the right, and I grin and wave her off. I move to another wheel well. Break off another quarter inch, amazed at the mass of frozen, dirty snow adhered to the metal. I thrust the scraper a few more times into the fourth wheel well, then toss the tool into the car and head to the nicer outhouse.

Last summer, Mark, Kirsten, and I camped at the Towers campground, just a few miles uphill from the Junction toilet, where I now hover, unwilling to touch my thighs to the frozen seat.

We three had sat at our weathered picnic table, conifers on all sides shooting skyward. We talked about wolves. The extirpation, the resolve to restore them to their original territory, the political upheaval. The angry hunters and weak state agencies. About Wildlife Services shooting wolves from airplanes, using public money, on public lands. About powerful lobbyists representing ranchers and hunters. I'd tried to understand the argument against wolves, to be open-minded and to listen. Yet it's uneven ground.

Mark cautions against false equivalence—comparing two sides of a debate when one is a denialist position, or a position with inconsiderable substantiation. When one side is supported by evidence—as is the pro-wolf position—and the other is not, there is no logical equivalence between the two arguments. One is backed by science and data, the other isn't. Researchers have demonstrated that ecosystems benefit when elk herds are trimmed. Evidence shows that killing wolves does not prevent future livestock predation. However, it remains to be proven that society is damaged when a hunter cannot find an elk to kill. Science supports the wolf, not the other side. But the other side has a bullhorn, and the debate doesn't sound balanced.

I had asked Doug Peacock how he deals with people who won't accept that data and science don't support their positions, who cling to ignorance like a life raft and insist on the false equivalence.

"They can't be reached," Doug says. "They just can't be reached. So I don't try. I don't seek out that population of the world. It's everywhere. I'm too old to fight, after this heart job. I'm going to focus on the ones who at least will open their minds a tiny bit. You've got to find a little basin of sunshine, tell people about it, keep it shining. Fight like hell to protect it."

Yet I know the lines can't be easily divided: ranchers, hunters, and politicians, versus conservationists, biologists, and animal lovers. We are too complex. There are biologists who support wolf hunts. And there are hunters who embrace smaller elk herds, with the resultant greater challenges. There are organizations of backcountry anglers and hunters who are vocal about hunting ethics, who aren't troubled by wolves on the landscape. Some ranchers—and ranching communities, like the Blackfoot Watershed—are predator friendly. They're willing to utilize calving barns, more sheep dogs, fladry, range riders. They bring their dogs in at night. They take responsibility for their lives, their businesses.

"You take domestic animals and put them out in wild places—do you expect them to defend themselves?" WildEarth Guardians' attorney Bethany Cotton fires. "Of course not. So yes, it might cost a little more to protect them, but that's part of the deal. Every profession has its dues and expenses. And most of us aren't subsidized, as are those who have public grazing allotments like so many of these sheep and cattle producers do. And reimbursement programs—all of us are paying for these. We all are subsidizing ranchers. There's a farmer in Idaho who filed a claim—for almost thirty thousand dollars—because elk have eaten his wheat! Elk are hanging around, the elk herd numbers are too high, and they're eating to their heart's content because there's no threat from natural predators."

The argument over wolves involves, on one side, scientific data and the ethics of the Endangered Species Act, and on the other side, an uproar based on misinformation and conspiracy theories. Science and logic are on the wolf's side, and it's only the volume of the opposing clamor that makes it appear to be a valid debate.

Back on the road after visiting the restroom, I'm a mere mile or two past Tower Junction when I see Ilona's car parked next to a smallish white SUV and a huge sable brown pickup in a freshly plowed pullout. The white SUV has an orange bubble light on its roof. I park and walk over to the group, which could be captioned "four women adoring a Jesus-like figure." It's Pete Mumford. His long blond curls, mustache, and neat beard are as attractive now as they were five months earlier. I meet Sara and Lizzie, Pete's teammates, and a tall young woman named Cheyenne, who is assigned to another project in the park. Cheyenne's long auburn hair is braided into a rope that reaches her middle ribs, and her snow boots have a pale pink inset under the crisscrossing laces. She's one of those fortunate few whose nose doesn't turn bright red and run in the cold, whose skin doesn't chap, whose long limbs look slender in insulated clothing. Lizzie is petite with sparkling eyes and a knit hat with ear flaps. Sara's lightly freckled skin retains a bit of summer tan, her front teeth overlap a smidgen. Everyone is wearing a hat, standing in the sunshine, the temperature hovering near twenty. It's almost balmy.

"Yeah, on his flyover Doug said our wolves are so out of sight we might as well call it a day and go home," Pete laughs, leaning back against the white Equinox, folding his arms against his chest. With a nod to winter, he's wearing pale green ski pants with the same acid green down jacket he wore the June morning I met him. Banter flies between the four of them. Ilona waves off, I thank her again, and the remaining five of us talk a bit longer. Doug has warned them that I will be trailing them for a few days, exploring the wolf controversy. Cheyenne asks if I'm talking to people other than park people, biologists, and wolf watchers. I tell her about the ranchers and outfitters I've spent time with, the hunters. She is visibly pleased, glad that I'm probing more than just one side of the issue.

"I'm a peacemaker," I tell them. "I think the issues are workable."

They all smile, and Sara points to my hat. "We can tell." My hands fly to my head and the black hat with neon peace signs all over it. I hadn't thought twice about it. I wear my intention like a badge.

Cheyenne teases Pete about the orange bubble light on top of the Equinox, and everyone laughs. Doug Smith rounds up vehicles from wherever he can for the Winter Study, and no one's exactly sure which federal department owns a Chevrolet SUV with an orange bubble light on top, or why. Maybe it's DEA. I ask Pete if I may join them the next morning.

"Sure, we meet at the Tower ranger station at 6:30. Just meet us there. We listen to see where the wolves are, then try to get there and get set up so we can see them soon as the sun comes up."

"How far is it from Gardiner to the ranger station?" I ask.

"About twenty-five miles, but you should probably allow an hour. Roads are sketchy right now."

Back in my Subaru, I contemplate my next few hours. Vacant, thanks to the elusive nature of wolves. Cooke City is a few miles outside the northeastern park entrance, and I consider driving there to visit the bakery I'd loved back in June. A thirty-three-mile drive, which doesn't sound too terrible. I back out, turn the car eastward. Maybe I'll see something along the way. At the least, I'll see the Lamar Valley in winter. I drive through open land, acres and miles of it, sagebrush-dotted and snow-crusted land. Winter-burdened rivers sludge through, banks and edges already frozen, the rivers themselves full of swirled and stacked ice floes, clear and white and a curious blue-green that dazes me. I stop to take pictures. I open, my ribs separate. A drumming, inside, pulses with the earth. The Absarokas soar. Land spreads before and behind me. It bumps and lifts high. I stand where it is smooth, undisturbed. I hear, from within, a howl. I see me, across the river, on the ground, cross legged. Hands in lap. I wear heavy, coarse linen, a shawl woven of rich aubergine and loden and indigo. My hair is twisted behind my head. Eyes closed. I sit, one with the earth, the valley, the world. I hear me, I thrum and drum with the rhythm of the earth. My howl sings out over the valley.

I am moving closer to being her.

Again in the Subaru, I turn the car around. I've convinced myself that Ilona's correct, I should rent a scope. Learn the tricks of it, spend time sighting it, view the wolves through my own instead of those belonging to others. The drive back into Gardiner takes longer than seems possible, and I see no white government trucks except the lonely one parked in the lot at the base of South Butte. I hope Brenna's team has found some wolves to watch. I decide to return at dusk.

The gallery is chock full of artwork, jewelry, sculptures, and photographs, and the woman who greets me, coming down the stairs from above, tells me if I give her a minute, she'll put the art lights on for me. I say no, that's fine, I'm just here to rent a scope. She moves around the counter to help me. I'd driven all the way through Gardiner, almost to the outside limit, looking for the tallest building in town, as Ilona had told me to. Not a single roofline looked significantly higher than all others, and

I finally stopped at the big yellow log building on Highway 89 (Hot coffee! Gifts and sweets! Chocolate! Laundromat!) and asked the jolly man behind the counter if Ilona worked there. No, he shook his head thoughtfully, I think she works at the Yellowstone Gallery, down on Park Street. Thanking him, I looked longingly at the cases filled with chocolates, caramels, turtles, truffles, and said I might have to come back for some chocolate. He said he'd keep an eye out for me, and I slipped out the door and drove around the corner and down the block, locating the gallery, parking in front. Stepping back, I assessed rooflines, and had no idea why Ilona would have called it the tallest building in Gardiner. If it was, it was by no more than three inches, and I wouldn't even place a bet on that. I drew a mental line from the top of its pointy façade to the roofline of the building next door, the Montana Saddlery, and called it even.

Music plays in the gallery, a man's voice, a baritone. It has a bluesy feel to it, or maybe it's downright country, but it's gentle and so easy I have to ask who it is.

"Keb' Mo'," she tells me. "Isn't he great?" The track playing over the gallery's impressive sound system is John Lennon's *Imagine*. Smooth, so mellow. We complete the rental agreement for the scope and I sign the charge slip.

"Do you have the CD we're listening to? I think I need it." She smiles and sorts through a pile on the counter, then moves to a wooden display case where more CDs are arranged.

"Yes, here it is." She hands it to me. The word "Peace" is spelled out in fat white letters on the blue cover. I smile. Of course I need this album.

I pay again, and she gives me directions for returning the scope Sunday on my way out of town, when the gallery is closed—her house is up the street next to the Yellowstone River Motel. I look doubtful. She tells me not to worry, people do this all the time.

I place the scope with its collapsed tripod legs in the back seat of the Subaru, and prepare to head back into the park, making sure gloves and hand warmers are accessible. I'll climb South Butte again. See if the wolves make an appearance. Dawn and dusk are the best times to catch wolves on the move. It's just past four, and the sun will be down by five or shortly after. I drive back through the entrance gate, wave my pass at the same ranger. I reach the parking lot where the white truck sits. Earlier I carried my backpack full of supplies, but this time I climb the hill without any accoutrements save my camera. I know the way. I step through the spots where elk bedded, and I follow boot prints up the side of the butte. When I crest the hill, the three watchers remain in position, two seated, one standing.

"Did the wolves ever appear?" I've surprised them, and they welcome me back like the diversion I am.

"No, not a thing, nothing at all since you left." After friendly glances, they turn back toward the scopes. They must be so cold, and so tired from a day spent in limited motion. Watching for wolves is indeed romantic, but also, at times, tedious. The sun has dropped below the mountain range before us and light is steadily vanishing from the skies. Shadows deepen and patches of regen fade into dark blurs against ghostly pale snow. The three begin loading their backpacks. They attach camp seats with carabiners. They look around to be sure they've collected everything brought up to the knoll ten hours ago. I take a few pictures of Electric Peak and of the tiny shack that supports a large telemetry antenna.

"There's a sleeping bag in there," Donny tells me. "And a desk."

Amazed, I open the door to see. Sure enough, there's a platform built across the back side of the four foot by six foot shack, covered by a red sleeping bag. A small window faces Electric Peak, and below it a platform juts out so that one could sit on the bed and write, while looking out the window. An old, red machine sits on the floor behind the door, a gasoline heater perhaps, and I look at the aged, dry wooden walls of the tiny structure and shudder.

"What's the story of this shack?" I ask. Brenna answers.

"Oh, we inherited it from an old coyote study. We use the antenna now for the wolves sometimes, but yeah, I guess someone has stayed here." The antenna mounted atop the roof of the jerrybuilt shack is huge, at least five feet wide and seven feet across, and can be manually rotated to search for signals. I imagine nights spent in the shack, listening to coyotes howl and documenting the experience, all alone in the wildness of the park. Lonely, a bit eerie. An experience I'm not sure I have the courage for.

The three hoist backpacks and strap them on, lean scopes across shoulders. We begin our descent in the near twilight. At the parking lot I thank them, and wish them better luck the next day.

I'm cold again, and trembling as I await heat. The seat-heat button has remained in the On position since yesterday morning in Salt Lake. It has yet to generate too much warmth. It's been a day. I haven't seen a wolf, but I'm not worried. Doug Smith warned me some days are good, and some days are fabulous. I have three more days to look for wolves. I drive slowly northwest toward Mammoth, my headlights flashing on snow, on icy patches, on the fairy tale trees that line my path. Heading to my temporary home I am pleasantly tired, ready to snuggle on the couch with my blanket and book, some soup, maybe a glass of wine. The elk herd I saw on my way in this morning is now gone, or perhaps just far enough off the road that my headlights don't capture a one. Dark has dropped over the park, into every valley and crevice. I pass a small herd of antelope, each motionless as a statue. I continue out through the massive stone gate built so long ago, and wonder that I am here in this mostly silent, placid national park.

In my motel I shower, standing under the streaming hot water until my skin turns bright pink then red. I've turned the heat up to seventy-five, and I pull on fresh wool socks, my pajama pants, and two tops before I open my soup and heat it in the microwave. I chose the Arrogant Frog pinot noir in part because it was in a bottle with a screw top. That, and frogs hold a special meaning for me. Years ago, while I was questioning my life's direction, I was introduced to the phrase *leap and a net shall appear*. Frogs don't need nets, but I do. I've leapt a few times and managed to miss the net, but more often than not that net seems to show up and save me. Or perhaps when I thought I missed, I was actually saved by a net of a different kind. For here I am, still.

I find a glass in the cupboard and pour myself some pinot, grab my bowl of soup, and head to a corner of the couch where I pull up my legs, balancing the soup bowl between chest and knees. I'm ravenous. I eat a small container of Chinese rice crackers, and an English muffin. A mini donut and a handful or two or three of trail mix. I finish my wine and look at the time. 8:30. Time for bed. My alarm is set for 4:45, to leave by 5:30. I turn down the heat, and crawl between the sheets.

12. cold

Journey crosses the grassy meadow, trots up the draw. Aspen leaves flutter, pale green, tinkling like bells. The night is cool, but the ground remains soft. He crests the draw, lifts his nose. Deer, elk, coyote—a conflagration of scent. His ears point forward. Wolf. He searches the land for movement. Brown, tan. Gray. He walks between trees, the game trail narrow and leaf-strewn. His hackles rise. His feet pad. His eyes flit left, right. A howl splits the air and he freezes. Another howl, a series. A warning.

Journey creeps forward, curious, hungry. He moves into a trot. He follows the echoing howls. The trail bends. He rounds a hillside. The scent intensifies. Wolf, wolves. He runs. Beyond the trees, into a sage field where a black wolf stands rigid, his tail long and straight. Journey halts. A gray wolf, another. Five. The black howls, and they tear forward, leaping, slicing the distance between them, teeth bared. Journey wheels around, hind paws digging into dirt as he runs for his life.

I am awake two minutes before the alarm will blare. Press the button to turn it off. I don't want to leave my warm bed. Heat turned up, coffee brewing, I pull on wool socks and my first two layers. Pour coffee into a mug, add milk and a touch of sugar. Holding the mug is fabulous, inhaling, heavenly. I sit at the table, turn on my laptop. Always one of my favorite parts of day, this is a time of gratitude for simple things. Warmth, coffee, being alive. I sip as I check the forecast, which hasn't improved since I last checked. It's negative five, warming to a high of eighteen. With wind chill I'll feel like it's negative fifteen. I sip more coffee. It's 5:20 when I remember to go start the car and chip ice off its windshield, hoping all the hunters staying here won't be tempted to steal my idling car. They won't. Real Montanans drive trucks. And sometimes go sliding off the road. I pack more layers and some food, fill my thermal mug with coffee, and tuck behind the wheel.

My drive through the park is unnervingly spooky. My headlights catch and reflect ice and eyes of elk, outline towering trees in their narrow slices of light, inadequate in these huge spaces. I feel small on the empty road, the temperature in negative numbers, the sky still deepest ink.

After forty minutes of driving, I see the lights of the Tower ranger station, drive past, and turn into the restroom stop two hundred yards down the road. I'm in the ranger station lot three minutes later. I park facing east to watch the continuation of the morning's gentle, and as yet subtle, sunrise. A few minutes later, the white Equinox with the orange bubble drives up next to me. Pete opens his door to tell me they're heading to Hellroaring Overlook; they've picked up signals from their pack toward the west. I follow the Equinox down the road, back a few miles toward Mammoth.

At the small Hellroaring Overlook pullout I set up my scope. Pete and Lizzie do the same. Sara has the day off. The sun, still nowhere to be seen, has sent its first harbinger far and wide, and a gentle glow illuminates the mountain ridges across the valley from us. We can see each other, trees, hillsides, snow, but the world is still soft-edged and rounded. Before any of us have the wolves in view we hear howling, a chorus of howls, echoing across the valley between the wolves and our roost. These are the first wolf howls I've ever heard. I'm listening to a hymn. Magical, spiritual, spine-tingling, it's all of these, all at once. A great knot of joy jams my throat. Pete and Lizzie have the pack sighted in their scopes, and I am working on it, the wolves straight across from us, diminutive bodies moving through snow and sage fields. Lizzie offers to find them for me, and lets me look through her scope as she adjusts mine. I see wolves, moving wolves, howling wolves, incredible creatures not of myth and fable but of flesh and fur and bone. We trade scopes and here I am, watching a wolf pack on the hillside, minus five degrees, my scarf stretched up over my nose and my peace sign hat yanked down below my eyebrows. Barely able to inhale, floating on the sound of a handful of wolves howling their greeting to the day.

There are four Winter Study teams: one each for the packs with territory near the road—Junction Butte, Blacktail, and Eightmile—and a final team called the Cluster Crew. This latter team tracks the spots where GPS-collared wolves spend more than one hour within a range of a hundred meters. The GPS collars collect data which the biologists can download remotely, to track where the wolves have spent time. Every thirty minutes the collar stores a location. When this information is downloaded and studied, "clusters" are determined by the proximity of location points. Downloads are done weekly. When locations are plotted and clusters labeled, the Cluster Crew heads out to search the location and determine why the wolf spent so much time there. The crews usually discover carcass remains, which help increase understanding of wolf predation—the ultimate purpose of the Winter Study.

I'm with the Junction Butte team this morning, and after an hour or so at Hellroaring Overlook our wolves have settled down and are bedded on the hillside across the way. The Cluster Crew—two wiry young men who look totally stoked to go on twenty-mile winter hikes whenever asked—arrives and holds excited conversations with Pete. Lizzie and I watch balls of fur nestled in gray sagebrush. I overhear "the perch" and suddenly everyone is packing up. The Cluster Crew tears off in their small white SUV, and Pete tells Lizzie stay here, no, come on, let's go. I follow. We head further west, another mile or so. We pull off the road, park, and gather things for the hike to the top of the hill.

"It's in the shade, and we might be up here for a few hours, so bring whatever you need," Pete tells me. Hmm. Not sure what more I could bring to help me stay warm. My car says it's now only negative two, but hell, temperatures less than zero steal right into my core. A game trail takes up from the road-side, steep and brown, snow not yet sticking to the south-facing dirt path. Pete and Lizzie head up, telling me I can follow their tracks, as I sit in the car absorbing as much warmth as possible before I venture out. My backpack still contains everything I started the day with. I remove the plastic water bottle. I won't want cold water while I'm up there. I eat a cereal bar. I ponder my wimpiness. I reluctantly put gloves back on and get out of the car. I swing my backpack into place, pull my arms through the straps. I lock my car and tuck the key in my pocket, where a hand warmer rests, radiating just enough heat to remind my fingers to circulate blood.

Nudging boot toes into the frozen earth, I make my way up the narrow trail to where it crests, then follow the boot tracks of others around to the left as Pete told me to. The ground is lumpy with grasses and small plants and the snow is only an inch or two deep here, so boot tracks are at times difficult to follow. Other tracks cross the path. Elk and bison and rabbit are all I discern, though others are bound to be there as well. Pine marten. Wolf. I keep my eyes peeled for boot marks, and follow where they lead. Pete's given me a general idea of where the perch is, so when I reach a small open meadow I don't worry so much about the crisscrossing tracks, knowing I've got to head up the hill and to the left, to where pines stand tall and I can see the hillside drop away before them. I find boot prints again and follow all the way to the top, where the perch unfolds before me, a small opening between conifers with a grand view of the hillside we'd been staring at from a different angle all morning. Sun is unlikely to ever hit this spot, north-facing as it is, and our breath hangs in front of us for moments before it breaks and falls apart. Their scopes are trained on the wolves, and I set up mine, extending its three legs and locking them in place then peering through the eyepiece, trying to recognize at least one feature of the hill before me. I look away from the scope and up at the hill with my naked eye, trying to memorize a feature and its position—the dry, sage-covered bump halfway down from the top, a singularly narrow tree—then search for it with my scope. I sometimes succeed, sometimes fail. I'm not yet ready to ask for help. I'm caught between wanting to curse Ilona for the added stress and to thank her, knowing her suggestion is making me toughen up. It's good to be tough. Uncomfortable. Annoyed.

Each Winter Study team tracks the wolves of its pack, documenting the wolves' positions and activities whenever possible. Each team member has a digital recorder into which they speak observations: 9:34, wolves milling, 9:35, black pup urinating, 9:43, wolves nesting, 10:02, wolves howling, 10:03, wolves traveling. I listen to them and picture them transcribing this, later, in the evenings as they sit around in pajamas and eat, trying to warm up. Then I envision Doug Smith receiving all these reports, reading them: marking territory, sleeping, howling, milling, traveling. He is dedicated to his work, a true biologist. Probably a bit of a science nerd. My interest is caught by what color the wolves are, how their howls sound, their grace in movement. Wolves nesting, 10:08, I hear Lizzie whisper into her recorder.

Pete exclaims about how cold it is, even though today he has a heavy camouflage jacket zipped over his green down coat. He tells Lizzie he's going to jump, so it's on her to keep her eye on the wolves. He moves back from his scope and begins jumping, knees high, exhaling loudly with each landing. Whew, whew, whew. I tread lightly in place, and Pete turns back to me and says, you have to make it big! Get that blood pumping! I jump a bit higher, telling myself I'm not that cold. Yet. When Pete's back on his scope, Lizzie takes a minute to jump and run in place, then she comes to reset my scope on the wolves. I can barely see them. They're nested in the hillside and obviously not in need of warming the way we are. Men are always warmer than women are, so I'm relieved that Pete feels the cold, too. I run in place and lift my knees higher. I jump.

Wolves' fur is really a double coat, the top fur or guard hairs resting on an undercoat. The guard hairs repel dirt and moisture, growing more thickly during the winter, shedding during spring as temperatures rise. Guard hairs are actually hollow, facilitating their action as insulators, and they function much as umbrellas do, keeping moisture from penetrating to the undercoat. Wolves are made for cold weather. A wolf will curl up with his head between his rear legs and cover his face with his tail, tolerating temperatures as low as negative forty degrees Fahrenheit. The coats of Alaskan wolves are even denser, and they can withstand temperatures that would claim my life in about thirty minutes.

The Junction Butte wolves are nestled into their hillside and do not seem interested in moving. And then they're up, going after a bison, chasing a small herd of elk. Returning to rest again. Then traveling. Then resting. Pete talks to them, no, don't go after that bison! You'll never get it, don't do it. Lizzie's eyelashes keep sticking to her eyepiece, and I am constantly wiping the ice off my own eyepiece as it freezes, beginning at the outer edge and bit by bit working inward until everything I see is a beautiful kaleidoscope of color and shape. Don't do it, Pete tells the wolves. Our eyes are tearing from the wind and cold, and I can feel my eyelashes freezing together, but they haven't managed to stick to the eyepiece yet. I jump again. My car is just half a mile or so below; I could go down to wait there until Pete and Lizzie have had enough. I am frozen. They've discussed heading back east, to watch the pack from a different vantage point, but haven't yet moved to do so. I jump some more, then begin covering my scope's eyepiece and lens, telescoping its legs back to their compact positions.

I tell Pete and Lizzie I'm headed back to my car, where I'll wait for them. They nod agreement, and I head left, following the path we made on our way up. Moving warms me a smidgen.

Dropping over the first edge is easy, since there are no tracks but ours on the shallow white snow. But as I approach the meadow, other tracks enter and leave, and suddenly I've lost the boot prints. But I know where I am. Sort of. I came up this hillside just two hours earlier, and I know it eventually curves around the ridge of land and heads down to the road. I walk back into the spot where all the tracks converge and search for boot prints, but now see my new tracks as well as everything else, and have no idea where the tracks are that I am supposed to follow. I strike off toward the ridge I think we came over, and when I reach the top and look down I see nothing like a road, no brown dirt game trail, but only more snow-covered ridges. How can this be? I look in the direction we were looking from our perch, then to the east, and everything is white and winter grassy and hilly and pine-covered. Okay, I'm not truly lost. I just need to climb back up to the perch and start all over again. I'm all right; I'm not truly stranded in a meadow in this all-but-deserted national park.

I'm on my way back to the perch, crossing through that bewildering, well-traveled meadow, focusing on my feet when suddenly I hear the sound of fabric brushing fabric and I look up: there are Pete and Lizzie, thirty feet above me on the hillside, traversing to the right, using the trail I should have found. Hey! I yell, Here I am! They don't hear me. I run up the hillside as best I can, desperate to follow their tracks and not make another wrong turn. I'm sweating with a peculiar mix of panic, relief, and exertion when I hit their trail and discover it's easy to follow, noting their bobbing heads just forty feet in front of me. They crest the ridge and disappear but I know I'm okay now, and I travel across the ridge and then down the earthy game trail. They've reached the cars by now and discovered mine to be empty. They look back up the trail and I wave. I took a shortcut, I say, one that got me lost. They don't seem to be worried, which is more than I can say for me. I just learned a lesson. I tend to be overly confident, at times, in my ability to handle whatever's thrown in front of me. Sometimes I should be more careful. Sometimes it's wise to be worried. Or even better, cautious. Or to at least know where you are.

Jake is leaving home. I pack his clothes, his—my—favorite stuffed animals. Blankets, a royal blue one with red toy soldiers and his name knit across the bottom, over and over. A pale blue one with a satin edge. A red fleece one, his name and a heart embroidered in a corner. I pack his CDs, forty of them, from Tchaikovsky to Chopin to Il Divo. A kite to hang above his new bed. A handheld massager that an aide might use. There is little else.

I am in agony. I grasp onto the idea that I am sharing Jake with others. That, just like any child, he needs to have more experiences outside his home. For almost seventeen years, I've kept Jake mine.

Guilt sits under the surface of my skin. Loss, overwhelming loss, an emptiness in my house, in my heart. And air, lightness.

I sleep nine hours a night. I take naps. I've chosen a care center where he is one of the youngest, the quietest. I visit him. One day I learn that they will send him on a bus to spend the day at my house. I take Jake to get a bus pass. We arrange a weekly trip. The city para-transit bus delivers him by 9:30, and I bundle him up to go back at 4:30. While he's home he hangs out on the couch. I hold him. I play music. I buy new CDs.

Jake seems to have transitioned without difficulty. When I visit him at the center, he rests, a bolster under his knees, or propped on his side like I arrange him at home. When he spends the day with me, he is content. He does not rage, or cry, or moan. He does not laugh as much, either. As the months go by, he seems to draw even further inside, though this hardly seems possible.

After a year away from home, Jake is even less present than he used to be. His eyes are less blue. I wonder if he's trying to decide just how much longer he wants to do this. Stay at the center. Travel back and forth on the bus. Be rolled, propped, moved, fed. Breathe. Be human.

We head back over to Hellroaring Overlook. It's just after 10:30. Sunlight hits the edge of the pullout. I look for a spot in the brilliance. Finding one, I work on aiming my scope at something that might be a wolf. I think I know where they are—the pack is settled on a bump of the hillside that is sage on the left and snowy on the right, with a rounded top—but I'll be damned if I can find that spot, so easily seen with the naked eye, through the eyepiece of my scope. Back and forth I look, finally locating the bump through the eyepiece, and if there are wolves there they are successfully hiding from me. Pete and Lizzie joke about the languid, nesting pack. I ask Lizzie to come make sure I'm looking at the correct spot of hill. Pete's radio crackles and I hear Rick McIntyre's voice, his distinctive intonation and verbal gait. Yes, he says, his voice fractured by spits and hisses, the rangers have moved a carcass over by Tower, and the Canyon pack is in the area. We'll probably see wolves feeding over there in not too long. Pete acknowledges the message, tells Rick the Junction Butte pack is nested on the hill, unmoving. They end the call. Alpha 8-9-romeo, signing off. Turning toward me, Pete suggests I head over to Tower Junction. It might be the best chance I'll get for seeing wolves today. With a thanks, I pack up my scope and place both of us in the car for the drive east. I turn the heat up, full blast.

I was single last week, for two and a half days. Daniel and his son moved out. We were on the phone, making plans for him to come pick up some furniture, clothes, various sundries, his books. We discussed pans. I told him to take the new pans we'd bought last winter, that I would use the old ones we'd put aside to give my son when he moved into an apartment. He said, what will you cook with? I replied, a pan is a pan, I don't really care. And, somehow, the pan conversation led to a more serious discussion about how we had ended up where we were. Which led Daniel to ask, can we talk about it? When I'd told him three days earlier that I wasn't happy and didn't want to continue, Daniel blurted *we never should've gotten married*, and *if I could, I'd move out tomorrow*. And he'd found a way to move the next day, taking his son, his dog, enough clothes for five or six days, out and into a Residence Inn fifteen miles away, near his office. After he left I took deep breaths, I lost myself in a mediocre novel, I sat quietly by myself and felt my own being. I'd squished her for a long time, and I was letting her fill back up, be who she really was. Is.

Two days later we talked, his talk sweet and apologetic and convincing, mine agreeable—nice—and we decided to put more effort into fixing our relationship. *I screwed up, I know I did, I will do anything, I promise, I love you and we can do better. I will do better.* I ached to believe him. I placed my foot in the trap, and I was tethered again. I'd tried to run with the wolves, to set free my wilder self, but succumbed to the pressure of commitment, working harder, guilt, what a nice girl should do. And a desperate belief that he was the person I imagined him to be. *I will do what you're asking, I will do that too, I can see our future, let us try again. I've let you down, let me fix it.*

That night everything came back—the son, the dog, the clothes, the marriage.

I needed more of him. I needed the deeper places inside to be available to me. Before we married, we'd talked about it.

"I don't want to change," he said. "I like myself, I'm a good person."

"I'm not asking you to not be you. I'm just asking you to go deeper into you. Are you willing to do that?"

He'd said yes, he was.

But he wasn't.

For whatever reasons, Daniel had put up walls and barriers all around himself. He was better defended than the Federal Reserve Bank of New York, eighty feet below the street, fifty feet below sea level, continually guarded by marksmen. He claimed he wasn't, that he knew he had some form of a shell he wore in public, but that he didn't wear it with me. I said he did. And I can't completely and safely remove my own protective barriers and show the jelly inside with someone who can't do the same in return. We had no emotional intimacy. I wanted to know what was in his heart; he said he didn't know what I meant. We'd battled this for years, while on the surface our relationship was mostly easygoing and intellectually pleasurable. I thought we'd made a break-through right before we decided to get married, but I was learning his words were rarely followed by action. He may have wanted to share himself with me, but those walls were impenetrable from either direction. I need to let my own wild nature be free, and I needed Daniel's to be unleashed as well. I need to love deeply, wholly, wildly. And I want that in return. I'd been talking about these issues over the entire length of our marriage—and in our dating days beforehand. And I thought I could create what I needed. I thought my tenacity would eventually pay off. In the meantime, my soul was drowning, my heart imprisoned by my inability to give up, my voice silenced because I'd forgotten—if I'd ever even learned—how to howl.

I have a wolf guide, within. She is spirit. She knows me, who I've been and who I will become. She is what I'm able to access when I let loose the leash and give up who I think I need to be. She is utter truth. Infinitely patient and wickedly wise, she lets me walk a path that bends far, far out of my way before she'll find a way to nudge me back. She knows what fuels me, ignites my passion, soothes me, fills my heart with joy. She knows that when I dare allow myself these things all of the time I will create, I will sing, I will dance and weep with delight.

She knows that when I'm filled with fear I am as far away from her as a mountain peak is to a lake in the valley below. But she also knows that we two are connected, just as the peak is to the lake. By not only land, but also by a journey that once set out upon is behind me in an instant. Once completed, the journey becomes but a memory, a moment of history, an event that time has collapsed into a speck of existence. It lives within me, proof of my strength, my resolve. My commitment to being who I am at my core, that place where a bit of wild flicks its flame.

Years ago I'd begun to practice a form of meditation a true master wouldn't recognize. I'd close my eyes, work on eliminating everything but nothingness, and try to be tranquil. A friend had once offered that three minutes of meditation was better than none, and I'd clung to that. I was lucky to get half a dozen seconds of true blankness before thoughts and words and things would enter. I'd thank them for visiting and kindly send them away. New ones tiptoed in. But I added it to my repertoire of life practices, and those minutes spent in meditation-like non-activity benefited me. I became calmer, less reactive. Less anxious, more fearless. And yet every time I'd sit there with closed eyes and as much nothingness in my mind as I could summon, it felt as if I wasn't achieving as much as maybe I could be. Then I began asking for a guide, asking a wolf to come join my meditation, come show me something. It came. And things changed. It spoke to me, through me, wordlessly, but always with a message. Sometimes humorous, other times thought provoking. Supportive. Or surprising. It took me on journeys, opened my eyes.

My wolf knows me better than I know myself, and she loves me. She knows my scars, wants to challenge and support and adore me, and is committed to helping me live the life I have the opportunity to live. I need her to be free.

I need to free her.

When I reach Tower Junction I see no cars, no carcass, no wolves. Not even a circling raven. Stumped, I drive another half mile, then execute a three-point turn on the narrow road, and head back toward the junction. As I pass the intersection of roads I see the old white Mercury Marquis that belongs to Cliff, a Silver Gate resident I introduced myself to the day before. Grizzled and frequently in and out of his car as he follows wolf activity, Cliff keeps his eye not only on the wolves in the neighborhood but on the watchers of the wolves as well. Cliff is a staple of the watching community and knows more than he will ever tell.

Cliff has pulled off the road. He looks to be setting up a scope, so I turn into the Sinclair gas station, forsaken in this dormant season, and leave my car to join him. As I trudge over to where he's stopped, I see he's talking with the driver of a small gray SUV. Nearing them, I recognize Rick. Cliff moves north of the road to set up his scope. Rick steps out of his car to greet me. As I say hello a honking sound erupts from the sky. Higher-pitched than the call of the Canada geese that fly through our valley at home, a fuller sound than that of the seagulls who frequent our ponds and the Great Salt Lake. Looking up, I see striking white bodies moving in a vee, their snowy feathers brilliant against the blue sky.

"What are they?" I whisper to Rick, who quietly replies, "Trumpeters." I count one side of the vee, nineteen birds, while listening to their overlapping honks. I'm spellbound. I've never seen trumpeter swans in flight, have only seen them once in a marsh, near the elk refuge outside Jackson Hole. I watch, speechless, until they become small dark dots and the calls disappear into the endless cold air.

Rick and I cross the road and set up our scopes near Cliff, facing north, pointing at a slight rise where, astonishingly, I see a pack of wolves. Some standing, some resting on the grass, all facing me.

I have the white wolf in my scope. Her gaze is focused—directly at me, it seems—her posture alert, her fur the color of unpolished alabaster. Winter white, softer than the crisply vibrant feathers of the trumpeters. To her left are two black pups, her youngest, and a toast-colored gray wolf from a previous litter. To her right, stretched along the ridge, are two more grays, their fur umber, ochre, tan. Her mate, the black alpha male, is not in sight. The wolves are so close that I can see only two or three at a time, and must pan the scope to see them all.

They are spread out along the ridge as if it is theirs, five or six feet between them, except for the two pups who lie close enough to reach out and swipe one another with a paw. They are less than two hundred feet away and the scope brings them right to me—I can almost see the twitch of a nose.

Rick tells me this is the Canyon pack, whose territory is further south and west, but who sometimes come up to this part of the park during the winter. The alphas are both eight and a half, old for wolves in the park, and have kept their pack together since 2008. The male, a black wolf, is collared, but the female, he tells me, isn't collared; Doug Smith didn't want to destroy her beauty by placing a clunky dark collar against her rich white coat. I'm watching the wolves, enthralled, when I realize that Rick is packing up his scope, saying something like "move down the road." He's suggesting we go around the bend, closer to the carcass, since the wolves will be heading that way. I hurry to put the covers on my scope and fold its legs. He's in his car and driving away as I walk to the Subaru. Cliff's car trails the SUV.

Around the bend, I park and unload the scope. Rick points out where the elk cow carcass is—just south across the road and east fifty yards, perhaps a hundred yards away—and then turns north again.

The white wolf starts down the hillside and my heart quickens. She's coming our way. Sure-footed, she moves smoothly down through clumps of sage and patches of snow. She is headed to the carcass. She will traverse the road far enough away that I am not in her path. A gray follows her, less easily spotted against the still-brown hillside with its intermittent dustings and clumps of snow. They're moving east, away from us, to a place the ground slopes and eases them across the road. The two disappear from sight, then reappear on the opposite side of the road where I can see only their backs, the top of a head, a quick movement through the brush. And suddenly the wolves are there, by the barren tree that rises from the ground like a vision from a witch's cauldron, its trunk and branches gnarled, dark, twisting this way and that, awaiting naught but ragged-winged vultures. Beneath the tree lies the carcass. Ravens, not vultures, light on the blackened branches and wait their turn.

Ever wary, the wolves examine wind and landscape, noses quivering, ears and tails alert, before dropping their muzzles to the dead cow elk. Their bodies nearly fill my scope. I watch the white wolf rip meat from the cow elk carcass, her muzzle first pink then red. She lifts her head between bites, eyes scanning bushes and rises. She tracks us humans as well. The gray tears into the flesh a foot to her right, and as he devours great chunks of meat and bone the same pink colors the fur of his muzzle. More ravens flock to the twisted tree and perch mere feet above the two wolves. I count seven ravens, eight, ten.

"Look," Rick whispers. His fingers lightly touch my arm. I turn. He's pointing back behind us, to the hillside the white wolf and her yearling traveled before crossing to the carcass. The black wolf—the alpha male—his ebony fur silver at the tips, moves downhill. A gray wolf trails him by twenty feet, picking his way down the same slope. We watch without scopes; they are close enough for us to see—to touch, it seems.

"Notice how gray the black is? That happens as they age. This black and his mate, the white, have been together a long time, raised many pups." His voice is low. We try to be unobtrusive, given our cars and scopes and bodies, all conspicuous, marring this environment.

The black has neared the bottom of the grassy hillside and instead of traveling east as his mate did, he cuts back west. He moves through the grass directly to our left.

"He's going to circle around us," Rick murmurs.

The black wolf trots through sage and shrub, occasionally turning his head toward us, while the gray follows behind. They could be dogs on the hillside, shepherds, huskies, approaching smoothly through the grass. Graceful, steady, intent.

He's within fifty feet of us, forty. I rotate on my boots, eyes glued, as he circles past us. He cuts across the road to the west, the gray yearling trotting a dozen yards behind. They widen their circle, no rush to reach the carcass.

There are four wolves now, all across the road, all within a few hundred feet of where I stand, all visible as I move my scope. More ravens have joined the few in the tree, and I lose count looking at them. Ten, maybe twelve. I center my scope back on the wolves at the carcass. They are eating, still.

I try to locate the black and his companion. Grass and shrub are thicker where I last saw them, and it takes me a few minutes to find the wolves. They have halted, and appear hesitant. Awaiting a signal from the white wolf? Or maybe the black is just leery of all the people, the vehicles. Cars have collected, all parked along the edges of the road, and watchers have focused their scopes and cameras on the tableau. No one speaks. A park ranger has arrived and set up bright orange cones and a sign warning visitors not to park between them. He's designated a road-crossing path for the wolves to return to the northern hillside after they're done with the carcass, a natural depression, the path the white traveled when she first came.

I move my scope back to the white, see that she and the first gray still rip mouthfuls of flesh then pause. I return my eye to the second pair of wolves, who are moving closer but haven't yet approached the elk's body. The wolves are so large in my scope I can see only one at a time.

Though I cannot detect a swollen belly, the white wolf has apparently had enough, and she turns east and leaves the carcass. Her yearling trails after, and before the ravens can react, the black male and his follower are at the carcass, tearing the remaining flesh. The alpha tugs hard enough that the entire carcass moves. There is little flesh and meat left on the bones. They eat for less than ten minutes, then they, too, depart. The wolves are barely three steps away when the ravens swoop down, stepping across the elk's ribs and hip bones, inserting their black beaks into cavities, feasting on fat and sinew, shreds of meat, muscle, marrow.

The naked tree is once again barren, lifeless.

I wanted to see wolves on this trip. I hadn't imagined how many, how close, how often, what color, engaged in what activity. I just wanted to see wolves. Up close. And now I have. I am amazed by the serenity of the entire scene. The wolves are steady and determined, patient. Calm. They come, eat, vigilant the entire time. They leave. No rush, no ceremony, simply an awareness, a hunger felt and satiated, a return to the place from which they came.

Rick quietly explains that alpha males appear to do less disciplining than the females, suggesting that they might hold back for fear that their strength is too much for the pups. They play with the pups, though, don't they? I ask, and he tells me that they do, that one of the park's most famous wolves, number 21, would tussle with his pups, pretending to lose, falling down and playing dead from a slight tug on his leg. However, alpha males are out searching for food so much of the time, working hard to make the kills they do, that when they're back with the pack they often just need to sleep. The yearlings, the older siblings, often fill the role of pup-watcher and playmate. Pups are nursed, weaned, fed, nurtured, and taught the ways of the world by the entire pack. Step-parenting comes naturally to wolves, and parentless pups are always taken care of by the pack. Even powerful alpha males accept the progeny of other male wolves. It takes strong, healthy alphas to lead and guide a pack, and the Canyon pack is led by two who have years of experience.

The black and the gray move toward the ridge via the same route they used on the way to the carcass. They move past me, forty feet from where I stand. They avoid us, seeming to focus on the path before them, but I sense they are aware of every one of us, each vehicle, how many large, circular tubes are pointed their way. Their bodies move sleekly through the shrubs. Their paws lightly touch the snow-dusted ground.

They continue up the hillside. They traverse the rise. At the top, the two wolves pause and look back toward us. A tail flick, a lowering of a nose, and then the black wolf whose fur is gray with age and experience disappears over the edge and the younger, brownish-tan gray wolf follows his father and is, in the blink of my eye, gone.

"Did that scare you, the wolves being so close?" Rick asks, still quiet.

I look up in surprise. "No, not at all."

I hadn't even considered it. I was mesmerized, thrilled with their proximity. And I know enough about wolves to know that they do their best to avoid us, and would never attack a human when another food source is readily at hand, would prefer not to come anywhere near us. Had those wolves been grizzlies or mountain lions, I would have been terrified.

Rick nods approval, one corner of his mouth lifting slightly.

I'd read Rick's book, *A Society of Wolves*, which lies on my living room table. With photographs that bring you eye to eye with wolves, facts and history that elucidate, stories that entrance and amaze, the work is filled with not just his research but also his experience. He's spent his adult life working in national parks. Rick knows wolves as well as most wolf experts in the world. He knows their patterns and behaviors, their stories, their charisma. I'd heard stories about Rick's dedication to the Yellowstone Park wolves from researchers and wolf watchers, including the fact that he is out in the park tracking wolves every day of the year. But nothing, not even meeting him last June, has prepared me for what I'm about to discover about Rick in the next few days: he is an entertainer who enjoys making people laugh. His spontaneous roadside speeches—he's given over a thousand in the past six years—are peppered with cultural references to engage his audiences. He'll joke about how nothing will scare bears away better than country western music, and refer to a park wolf as "the Angelina Jolie of wolves."

However, now Rick is quiet. The wolves are gone, and the vehicles that had gathered are dispersing, one by one. I hadn't noticed them collect, and am surprised to realize how many cars are here besides Rick's, Cliff's, and mine. It's as if a secret code was transmitted: carcass at Tower Junction, head there now.

Rick is heading back west. Laurie Lyman, who compiles daily data from the army of wolf watchers, needs a ride. Rick's eager to move and keep tabs on his wolves, so he asks if I'll give Laurie a ride when she's done packing up. Sure, I say, and he pulls out. I clean off my front seat, moving my rucksack and everything that's sprawled out of it into the back seat. I open the hatchback for her scope. She climbs onto the passenger seat and we drive west, back to Hellroaring Overlook. Laurie and her husband, Dan, live in Silver Gate, right outside of the park's northeast entrance, but Dan had to return home to meet the furnace man; Laurie will catch a ride home later with Rick, who is a neighbor. If I lived in Silver Gate, I wouldn't want to miss an appointment with the furnace man, either.

Laurie posts her notes daily on a website called Yellowstone Reports, where a dozen or so contributors post information about wildlife in the park. Laurie's been watching wolves consistently since she moved here from California more than half a dozen years ago, a retired schoolteacher who fell in love with the wildlife in the park. Laurie knows the stories of these wolves better than most everyone except Rick. She's spent enough time watching them to gain a sense of how they work together as families, how they nurture their young, how they teach. Nose nudges, eye contact, shoulder to shoulder rubs, demonstration, and howls communicate what young pups need to know to become self-sufficient, to perhaps one day lead their own pack. We talk about tourists and hunters and politicians and wolves, then collar numbers, names, litters. Laurie defends these wolves through the spread of information about them, hoping that education will guide society to decisions that better protect wolves.

I drive until I find Rick's SUV, then park and open the back for Laurie to grab her scope. Rick is reconnoitering with Pete and Lizzie. I arrange to meet Lizzie and Sara—Pete is scheduled off—the next morning, at 6:30, at the Tower Ranger Station.

I'm still thrilled, flying high. Wolves, so many of them. So close. Wild, yet focused and calm. Savage, aggressive. Or just hungry.

Jake is home for the day. He's cold, dressed in long johns under his jeans and turtleneck, a snug hat pulled down to ears and eyebrows. He rests on my lap, a blanket wrapped around him. I hold him. He sleeps a lot these days. His body temperature rarely climbs above ninety-six. He's leaving soon. I know this, I will it and accept it, and I resist it with everything I possess. I've held him for more than eighteen years, this boy whose wrist I can encircle with thumb and index finger. For the past year I've told him he may go, anytime, that I will be all right. He's done his job. And he's begun his transition, his body cold, the continual naps, the curling inward.

13. gone

Gray storms. Journey wanders, staying far from wolves in the dis-
tance. He follows a river upstream, his stomach still full from yes-
terday's kill. The valley is wide and he scans the tree-lined edges.
He smells no prey. Lifts his head. Howls. The wind behind him, he
runs again, an even trot.

The river bends. Journey curves with it, a hummock on his right.
He rounds the embankment and faces a wall of wolves. They
growl, teeth and eyes flashing. Journey's paws plant in the soft
riverbank. He watches their eyes, noses, tails. A big gray steps for-
ward. Journey tenses. The alpha male takes another step. Journey
holds firm. The big gray advances and three wolves follow. Jour-
ney stands motionless as they come closer, then sniff and circle
him. Snarls and barks erupt and Journey rockets away. He runs
to the top of the hummock, looks down at the wolves. They don't
pursue. They watch. One of the wolves, slightly smaller, steps to-
ward Journey. His yellow eyes meet hers.

I park at the ranger station a minute or two early. I face east.
I want to catch the sky in the process of changing, which I
cannot seem to do: suddenly it's a shade lighter than it was, and
I failed to see the transition. Minutes tick by, and my nerves
tingle. Where are they? Have I missed them? I start the engine
and drive forward so that I have a view into the residential area,
where red taillights cast a glow into the sharp air and, as I creep

further forward, I see headlights, too. It's the white Equinox, warming up. Relief. I don't want to have screwed up, been at the wrong place. Misinterpreted. I turn my heat on high and let the engine idle for another minute or two, then turn it off. It's 6:40, and then 6:45. At 6:50 I turn the car on again for heat, and at 6:57 they finally pull up in front of me and Lizzie leans out of the vehicle, apologizing. She and Sara both smile at me guiltily.

This morning we turn right, heading east, driving past the skeleton of the cow elk. Sara has the antenna out, scans for signals. What she hears is faint, difficult to pinpoint. We're trying to locate 869, a yearling male, one of the youngest in the pack. "They're traveling," Lizzie says. This fascinates me, that the trackers know this, though it's really quite simple: the strength of the signal is strong to the east, then it fades and becomes stronger further west, then it fades and becomes louder even further west. The wolves are moving. We stop twice to listen along the road, then drive to Hellroaring Overlook.

Our scopes are focused on the hillside. Lizzie and I stamp our feet while Sara waves the antenna back and forth, searching for those scratchy beeps. Rick McIntyre pulls in, then Laurie Lyman. I hear another car pull into the small half-circle lot, the snow beneath its tires squeaking like manhandled Styrofoam. Silence. A minute later a man's voice cuts the frozen air.

"Getting any signals?"

Lizzie shakes her head and responds with a chipper no. It's still early.

"Ah," he nods his head. "We'll find them soon enough, I'm sure."

Clad in a royal blue, to-the-knee down jacket and wearing a gray knit toque, the newcomer expertly sets up his scope and is scouting for wolves within seconds. Though I've never before met the man, his voice is immediately familiar and a bit whimsical. I swear I hear a bit of Minnesota in there. He's in his late fifties, perhaps, and though it's difficult to tell because of the puffy down jacket, my guess is that he may be a bit thick through the waist.

I turn to him and introduce myself, and he tells me he's Doug McLaughlin. Doug is another wolf watcher, as well-known as Laurie. I smile as I let him know how glad I am to meet him. Even if both our noses are red and running, and there are no wolves in sight.

Doug manages a lodge in Silver Gate, spending as much time as he can out looking for wolves and documenting them with photographs. He was a pioneer of the digi-scoping technique that allows photographers to capture images seen through a scope, and loves nothing more than taking pictures of the wolves he spends hours watching. Except, perhaps, his big German shepherd, who sits in Doug's car. I startle when he tells me the dog's name is Jake.

I'd visited the gift shop in his lodge last June, wandering through aisles stuffed with huckleberry taffy and syrup, Yellowstone Park t-shirts and caps, snack foods and pocketknives, beautiful leather goods made of buffalo hide, and Swarovski scopes. As a Swarovski dealer, Doug always has the newest scope.

Doug is in the middle of a story when we leave Hellroaring Overlook to look for the wolves further east, and in our new location I set my scope next to his and he continues. I am delighted to be listening to this warm-hearted man who spends most of his free time tracking animals. The next story he tells me sends a shiver along my spine and makes me long for such experience.

Maybe.

At his lodge they'd had a guest who'd gone skiing, alone, one afternoon. When it grew dark and she hadn't returned, they called the rangers. It was close to midnight when, just as the searchers set out from the parking lot where her car was, they saw a dot of light coming down the hill, a headlamp. "I'd gone further than I'd thought," the woman said, "and lost track of time. I'd just started back when I heard a faint rustling behind me. I couldn't see what it was, and I kept going." She heard more rustling, was spooked by it, but still couldn't see anything in the darkness. "When I heard it again, I turned, and this time I saw eyes—an ember-like glow—and realized it must be a wolf." She skied on, listening carefully, knowing the wolf was still following. "After a while I relaxed a little, and even got to a point where I felt he was watching out for me." The park rangers hiked up to her ski tracks, followed them by flashlight until they found wolf prints. "You're a lucky woman," they told her. "You had some good protection there."

My scope has been positioned to view a portion of hillside spotty with sagebrush, where some of the wolves are supposedly bedded. Gray-brown wolves lying down, nose to tail, among clumps of gray-brown sagebrush, is a visual challenge, much like the Magic Eye drawings where you stare forever at an illustration, waiting for your eyes to release and go fuzzy so that you can see the hidden image within. I try this with my scope; still no wolves. Fortunately I'm not alone in this, and the other watchers chat quietly, return an eye to a scope, then again back away. It's lupine nap time.

Doug tells me about a book his friend Brian Connolly wrote, based on the Hayden wolf pack that formed a dozen years ago, a book written for middle schoolers.

"The book is about a wolf pup and his adventures, and it gives a real good sense of what it's like for the wolves here in the park. The pup he based his story on was collared, number 638. He disappeared in the summer of 2009, hasn't been spotted since."

Hopes are that he started his own pack somewhere outside

park boundaries, but chances are high that he met his death out there instead. A while back Doug started a non-profit, and one of its activities is handing out bookmarks to youth who visit the park. Most of the dedicated wolf watchers in Yellowstone are of middle age and older, and Doug realizes it's today's youth who will eventually be making better decisions for our wildlife. The bookmarks are imprinted with a Farley Mowat quote: "We have doomed the wolf not for what it is, but for what we have deliberately and mistakenly perceived it to be—the mythologized epitome of a savage, ruthless killer—which is, in reality, no more than a reflected image of ourself."

"Ar, ar, arooh," a bark-howl floats across the valley toward us. My eyes light and I look at Sara, who smiles and nods her head. We think it's coming from the black pup, searching for the rest of its pack. I want to answer it, but I'm not yet comfortable throwing my head back and letting out a howl. Even if it were permissible. Wolves will often respond to human howls, but human howling is prohibited in Yellowstone National Park. I hadn't known of this restriction until I read the park's newspaper the day before, where imitating wolf howls is listed along with travelling off road, camping outside of designated areas, and imitating elk calls, as a forbidden activity. The top cause of death for adult wolves in the park is attack by wolves from rival packs. If you're a wolf, going about your business, napping, chasing mice with your pups, and you hear a howl you don't recognize, it will put you on alert and likely cause stress as you consider outsiders invading your territory. I will sacrifice.

While the wolves lounge and nap, the wolf watchers disperse, all but Lizzie and Sara, who have no choice. I decide to head east, try again to visit the Bearclaw Bakery.

The drive is longer than I remember, the snow thick and

deep as I climb in elevation to 7,300 feet. It's between Yellowstone season and snowmobiling season, what resorts call the shoulder season, and Silver Gate is shuttered, not a soul in sight. There are a few cars in the parking lot of the dark, wood-sided church near the west edge of town, and as I turn to look at what might be causing all the excitement I catch sight of the church's sign, the Chapel of Peace. Of course. If you keep looking, you eventually find what you seek.

Main Street in Cooke City is snow-packed, and I drive carefully because snowmobiles share the road with me. I wedge the little Subaru between pickup trucks and huge snowmobile-hauling trailers, and am excited to see the Open sign in the bakery window. I enter the same room I did last summer, only now, instead of a crush of visitors, a single table is occupied. The waitress from last summer is seated there, dressed in jeans and a sweatshirt, and of the three others at the table, a bearded man looks like someone I saw in here last June, too. Locals. Everyone looks up at me and the owner says hi. I needlessly ask if they're open.

"Yes, breakfast, a limited menu," the owner tells me, the same blond woman I remember.

"That's fine," I respond, more concerned about what's in the baked goods case than what's on the menu. She lets me choose a table, and offers coffee.

"Decaf?" I ask.

"No problem."

She makes me a decaffeinated Americano at the espresso machine, and I ask for a big splash of milk. The bakery case is empty, and the glass jar on top holds fat chocolate chip cookies, which are just not the same as cinnamon and gooey caramel rolls. I morosely choose something from the menu, the Sammie I a.m., asking if she could substitute a biscuit for the croissant. Ham, scrambled egg and shredded cheese on a split biscuit should fill me up, at least until I go stand in the cold for another few hours.

The entire kitchen is visible from the tables, the two areas separated by the glass-fronted baked goods display case and a small set of shelves. Her espresso machine is sleek and efficient, and her four-burner stove is miraculously capable of putting out seventy to a hundred breakfasts on busy summer mornings. Today is opening day for the season at the Bearclaw Bakery.

"Yep," she tells me. "I went to Bozeman, shopping, yesterday, and I decided to just do a limited menu today. No baked goods yet—" my heart falls, I'd been hoping some were hidden in the back— "and not everything I usually do. The season'll pick up soon, but not yet."

I ask her about the name of the breakfast I ordered, the Sammie I a.m., and she blushes.

I ask if it was named for a person, and she says, "Well yes, in a way, because the snowplow driver, who's from Ohio, would always come in and ask for a 'sammie,' his name for a sandwich."

I love it. Reminds me of the small town I grew up in as a teen, where the shopkeepers knew all the regulars by name.

I don't ask her about wolves. The flyer from Wolfwatchers. org is still taped to the back of the cash register as it was last June, and that suffices.

I wrap the uneaten half of my biscuit and tuck it in my backpack, knowing I'll be starving again soon, and pay my bill.

Back in the car shivers shake my entire body, because it is just plain old cold. I flip a U-turn, and then halt in the middle of Main Street to let four snowmobilers, their brightly graphicked snow gear covering every inch of skin and scalp, enter the road from behind the bakery, and track down the street a quarter mile or so before turning off between two motels. It's pure pleasure to be patient, to let them go before me, to be on this snow-packed road in Montana where snowmobiles have just as much claim to the path as I do. I've driven snow-mobiles, experienced the exhilaration, but now prefer the silent smaller footprint of snowshoes. Cooke City is a big snowmo-biling town, while Silver Gate remains quieter, less motorized, during the winter months. The latter community is probably more my kind of place.

Heading west, I reach Silver Gate within a few minutes, and again note the shut-in feeling of the tiny burg. One source states the Silver Gate population is twenty, with a total combined population in the two settlements of 140. I've met five of Sil-ver Gate's twenty in the past few days, dedicated wolf watchers all. A few homes are visible, nestled in trees or plunked by the road, and I try to imagine living here, the quiet, the solitude, the densely packed conifers. The tourists driving through in summer, the snowmobilers in winter. The only access all winter being through the park—the Beartooth Pass Highway connect-ing these hamlets with points east is closed—which means the nearest shopping is almost an hour and a half away, in Gardiner. The reliance on the plow driver, and most likely, neighbors. I don't know that I could live here, but I'm intrigued by those who do. Perhaps they gather for potluck dinners and attend the Chapel of Peace church. Maybe they live for the quiet, or per-haps they fill their homes with the sound of television, movies, music. Or do they hole up by themselves each afternoon as the winter sun drops behind the mountains, hibernating each night until the indigo dawn?

I am at the top of a roller coaster: the park road west of the entrance station descends immediately and sharply. I let the car's weight pull me down the icy road. I coast, holding my breath. When the valley opens up, I search for wolves. I see only a few deer—not even the small herd of bison I saw on the way to Cooke City. The park is teeming with wildlife, and the fact that

I don't see creatures is a testament to their own marvelous camouflage, and my impatience. Were I to sit for hours, the world before me would change.

A few miles before I reach Tower Junction I begin looking for government vehicles, or Rick's vehicle, or even Cliff's or Laurie's or Doug's. I'm not particular. I'd just like to view a few more wolves. I pass the junction, continuing west until I find the Equinox with the bubble on top at the Hellroaring Overlook pullout. I join Sara and Lizzie, sighting my scope on the opposite hill, where the Junction Butte wolves are lounging, again. While it's quiet, I ask them about their wildlife tech experiences, how they came to be here this winter. Sara calls her life path to this point serpentine, and I envision my own crooked path. Some find their passions more easily than others. It is said, when we are born, our work is placed in our heart. I love this for its inevitability; if you listen to your heart, you'll find what you are meant to do. Sara first earned an art degree and taught ceramics for a decade, until she spent time with friends in the Canadian Arctic and met a team of sled dogs. This unleashed in her a desire for more education, this time veterinary school. However, after a few years of working on research projects as a wildlife tech to help pay the bills, she decided that her real passion was wildlife, and that a veterinary degree wouldn't provide the opportunities she most desired. Her first wolf study was on the Nez Perce Reservation in central Idaho with a population of captive wolves—behavioral research. The next was in Algonquin Park in Ontario, a hybridization study of wolves and coyotes. Arizona was her next move, working for the Game and Fish Department, tracking Mexican wolves using telemetry, with a goal of reducing human-wolf conflict. After spending seven months there, she moved on to Minnesota, working with the U.S. Geological Survey on a wolf-deer study run by David Mech. This study entailed traveling the boundary waters, setting traps on portages to find and collar wolves. Sara and a partner traveled the waters by canoe, going out for two weeks at a time, checking traps daily.

Working here in Yellowstone is her fifth wolf study. She hopes there will be more. Born in New Hampshire, Sara has been drawn to canids and to carnivores, and her life path seems to be settling into a firm pattern. One of travel and adventure, and for this study, lots of unbelievably cold weather. I've only seen her wrapped in hats and scarves, have no idea what color or length her hair is and would probably not recognize her dressed casually in a restaurant.

I turn to Lizzie. She's from North Carolina, where she worked with captive red wolves at a sanctuary. "We'd get wolves from people who thought, hey, it'd be fun to have a wolf as a pet, then it bites someone, and needs to be removed from the owners… I spent a lot of time educating people. Wolves do not make good pets." While earning her wildlife biology degree from Colorado State at Fort Collins, she worked as a tech on a small-mammal trapping study ("blinging" mice and chipmunks by putting small metal tags on their ears) and on a mule deer study. Her most recent adventure was a three-month-long internship with Jim Halfpenny, a botanist, ecologist, and naturalist who lives and works in Gardiner and teaches animal tracking and natural history classes all over the world. Lizzie's eyes sparkle, her laugh is a polite and feminine guffaw, and it's obvious that doing the work she does with wild animals puts her exactly where she wants to be, regardless how freaking cold it is.

I ask what they know about howling, and Lizzie tells of the Red Wolf Coalition, a group that takes people out on "howlings" during summer evenings at dusk. A telemetry tech with antenna searches for wolves in the area, then lets people howl and listen for responses from the wolves. Sara's work in Arizona utilized howling studies as a tool to search for wolves not yet accounted for. A strict protocol was followed whereby a technician would howl for so many seconds in a small crescendo, once in each cardinal direction, then would begin a new cycle for so many seconds in a longer crescendo, again in each direction, trying to elicit return howls. Before I knew of the prohibition, I had been hoping the team would help me work on my howl. Doug Peacock told me it ain't rocket science—you don't need a degree from Julliard—any approximation will do. I practice a brief howl in my head, ar-ooh, letting it gently fade away. Mm. Not too bad. Maybe even okay. Maybe almost wild.

As the afternoon deepens, watchers come and go. The three of us keep our scopes focused on the sedentary wolves. Rick arrives. He walks to the very edge of the pullout to set up his scope. He sights on the distant hillside. I am positioned five feet behind Rick and Amy, a committed wolf watcher from Livingston. I overhear part of their conversation—the words don't register until I hear Rick saying, "…tried to watch Kesha's reality show last night."

I think I've misheard. But then Amy says something about the show, and the conversation continues. Yes, Rick McIntyre, Pied Piper of wolf watchers in Yellowstone Park, must spend his evenings at home, watching reality television. I can't accept this. Rick turns around and asks me if I know who Kesha is— I've heard of her. He tells me that she was here in the park a few weeks ago, filming part of her reality show. Five vehicles, a swarm of cameramen, sound technicians, makeup artists, gofers, all here at the very same small asphalt apron we're now standing on. I sigh relief. Cameron Diaz was also here, he says, and I agree with him that they're both beautiful women. He moves past me to his SUV, and returns with an eight-by-ten photo of Kesha, standing by a scope here in the park, her eyes dramatically made up, her clothes nothing like the outerwear we're all bundled into today.

"Do you think that's make-up?" he innocently asks, pointing to the thick dark lines around her eyes, the shiny blue, the lengthy eyelashes.

"Mm, maybe?"

"Wolves have natural eyeliner, did you know?"

I look at him, wide-eyed.

"Take a closer look at pictures of wolves, you'll see a dark line around their eyes."

"Males, too?" I ask.

Rick smiles.

Everyone has left but Lizzie, Sara, and me, gone to look for wolves from another pack because ours are so languid. It isn't too long before Rick returns, though. He parks, walks up to the three of us.

"Hey, Lizzie, Sara, have the rangers been by yet?"

They shake their heads.

"We haven't seen any rangers, not all afternoon."

"Well," Rick says, "apparently they're on the lookout for two young women because they've had reports of these women harassing men throughout the park. Giving the men a hard time, flirting, being inappropriate."

It takes a moment for the light to dawn, and then we're all laughing. Rick teases Lizzie about her lazing wolves, her note-taking, her gullibility. He suggests that she buy a share in his tapioca mine down in Florida, which earns him a split second of silence followed by one of those polite guffaws. The Pied Piper is in possession of a keen, slightly goofy, very dry sense of humor.

When the wolves are at peace, Rick is, too. And maybe he does watch reality television at night. Maybe he joins others for those potluck dinners. I don't know. But what I do know is that

Rick has over ten thousand pages of notes, observations about wolves in the park. Travels, fights, hunts, kills. Playfulness, mating, births. Death. Creation of a new pack, the end of an old.

Jake is home for Christmas, and we listen to carols all day long. His presents are wrapped and under the tree with everyone else's. I bought him a stuffed felt toy to rest in the crook of his arm, which is always bent, and a bright red scarf, soft as a puppy's tummy. My other three children shop until the last minute and wrap presents only hours before we unwrap them all. Jake sleeps through the opening of gifts. After bagels and fruit, Beau, Cait, and Allegra leave with Bob to celebrate with his family, and Jake and I are alone. This may be our last Christmas.

I could have been a better parent. Maybe I should have fed him more, sung and read to him more often. Discovered other things that made him happy. Tried harder, somehow, to ease his discomfort, stop his seizures, straighten his spine. What he's given me is so much more than I've ever given him. I light cinnamon candles. Amidst all the torn wrapping paper and abandoned ribbons, I hold Jake on my lap, let him rest against my chest. I whisper to him, *It's okay. You can go. You have been my greatest gift, you have taught me grace. I will see you, on the other side, one day. We will look into each other's eyes. I will see you, and you will see me. You will tell me stories. You will tell me what it's been like, all these years, inside your body. You will tell me about Little Joe. I will lose part of my heart when you go, but you can keep it for me. Give it back when I see you. And you see me. You can go, Jake. You can go.*

Sunday. This is it. I feel a pull from home, yet am reluctant to leave the park and its wolves behind when I drive away a few hours from now. I'm meeting the team again at the Tower ranger station. I'll spend a few hours with them, hoping to see and hear wolves before I have to leave.

I try to memorize the road and terrain. I want to remember headlights bouncing sparkles and prisms back from the snow and ice. The fairy tale trees towering above and at times enveloping me, creating a tunnel of pre-dawn magic. I round each bend leaning with the curve, I accelerate on flat dry stretches and brake in anticipation of ice. I watch for critters, though I see none. I thank God that I am here, and I thank the universe for arranging it. Filled with vistas, individual trees, wolf lore and actual wolves, howls and people and stories, I am rich. Sated. Yet eager for more, perplexed to think I won't do this again tomorrow. I am part of this ghost park, and at the same time nothing but a momentary visitor.

Each morning I've watched the sky move from dark to dawn, and each morning I've tried to put it into words. It's like a sheet of dark blue construction paper in front of a light bulb that steadily draws closer and closer; it's like a deep blue balloon, slowly filling with air and lightening shade by shade. This morning as I sit at the ranger station and watch frozen willow branches sparkle, I realize how foolish it is to try to describe nature in terms of the synthetic. Why am I using art supplies and electricity to describe something completely natural, non-replicable by artificial means? The sky is simply brightening, so gradually and imperceptibly that the change from one shade of indigo to the next is impossible to catch, yet incontrovertible. Dawn is arriving. As much as I thrill to its appearance, I am sorry that it draws me closer to my departure. I will not be here tomorrow to try again, and fail, to find perfect words.

Pete and Sara drive up and tell me they're heading east, where they've picked up a few signals. We head toward Slough Creek. We pull off once to listen with antenna and receivers, then again a half mile later. The wolves are traveling. Pete and

Sara unload scopes at the second pullout. Before they take the protective covers off eyepieces and lenses, more telemetry and a brief radio conversation with Rick McIntyre inspires them to continue further east. They're listening for 869 and 870, the only wolves in the pack that are collared, and they're not hearing 870. The male, 869, is sending out a signal that comes and goes. Each collared wolf has a specific assigned frequency, which the technicians know by heart and search for with their radios and antenna. They keep these frequencies protected to prevent illegal telemetry searches for the park's collared wolves.

"Can you catch them on drift?"

"I'll try," Sara answers Pete. She twists the antenna's dial.

Wolf 869 beeps, faintly and to the east. We pile back into our cars and take off for the next observation spot—another knoll, but one easily seen from the parking area. One I can hike up to and down from without becoming lost. I trail behind Pete and Sara, having again lingered in my car for a few extra moments' warmth. Reaching the top, I extend the legs of my scope's tripod while they begin to remove lens covers.

"Oh, what?" Pete's face screws up into a smile. He peels tape from the end of his scope, first one side and then the other, loosening the piece of paper that had been taped across the lens. He turns it to us: *Happy Birthday! Lizzie.* It's written in a decidedly feminine hand, curlicues replacing serifs.

"That is so like Lizzie, a totally Lizzie thing to do." Sara smiles and shakes her head, adjusting her scope.

Pete tucks the note in his pocket and a few Hey, happy birthday comments float his way. The search is on for 869, and if all goes well, the rest of the pack, too.

We look out over the narrow valley Slough Creek anchors. A sturdy hillside rises to the north, on our right. A smaller knoll rises west of us—Bob's Knob, named for wildlife filmmaker Bob Landis—and the creek runs between the two. The creek is the size of a Utah river, a good fifteen to twenty feet across, though in sections a frozen crust stretches from one side to another. I sight in on the valley a few hundred yards in front of us, using the river as a reference point, searching to match a bend I see unaided to the vision I see through the tiny eyepiece. I find the bend, then pan to the left, across the river. I see four or five elk, grazing. I hear that 869 is across the river bank from the elk, and I pan back to the right, meticulously searching the snowy edge of the creek, looking for this brown-gray wolf that blends into every background I see. I pop my head up to make sure I'm looking where I think I'm looking, but can't even see the elk. Well, maybe those stubby brown dots are elk. Eye back to the eyepiece, I gently move the scope back and forth, searching for wolves. I keep seeing those grazing elk. Even when I think I'm looking at the far side of the river, I suddenly see elk. The scope makes a jerky jump as I pan and suddenly there's a wolf in the middle of my lens: I am looking at 869. I did it. I have a wolf in my scope. He's still on the far bank of the creek, but now in a place where an ice bridge has formed and I watch him pick his way across, toward the grassy ridge where the elk graze.

Everyone is watching him—the rest of the pack members are out of sight—wondering if he'll try to attack an elk. Doug McLaughlin is beside me, Pete and Sara to my right. A man who drives a Jeep and whom I've seen at many pullouts the past two days is a bit to my left, as are the dad and son who climbed the knoll and settled in shortly after we did. Dad has two days' growth on his cheeks and chin, dark, and the hair sticking out from the bottom of his son's cap is the same almost-black color. The boy's cheeks are rosy red and he must be about ten, young enough to admire and imitate his dad without caring who sees. They both look through their scopes, both trained on the wolf. He moves easily along the bank until suddenly he's gone from my sight. It's quiet. Am I the only one who's lost him? I move my scope left to right, not finding the wolf anywhere. Damn. And then I hear, "Anyone have him? I lost him in the grass there."

A chorus of similar comments rises into the air on white breath that immediately disappears, and I lift my eye from the eyepiece, hitting my hands into each other and stomping my feet to send frozen blood back into circulation. It's damn cold. Doug's nose is running. Pete's mustache has frozen crystals along its edges. With 869 out of sight everyone moves, shakes limbs, stomps feet, wonders aloud where the rest of the pack is. Most turn their scopes somewhere else, searching hillsides and gullies for any sign of life. Doug points to a spot on the hill north of us.

"See that stretch of pines, oh about halfway up, on the left, that's Diagonal Forest. And to its right is Horizontal Forest, then below that, see where that golden area is, that's Lion Meadow. That tree down there, that's Marge Simpson Tree, it's shaped like her hair—I was here the day that name caught on—and then there's Round Tree, and over that way," he points to the south, "is Southern Round Tree." Who assigned these names, I wonder. They're captivating, romantic. With each name I learn, the more I'm drawn into my environment, the more I wish to preserve.

"I went into Gardiner yesterday," I tell Doug, "and bought *Alphie*, the book your friend Brian wrote."

"Ah," Doug smiles. "It's a good book. It's a good thing." He nods at the young boy with his dad. "It's his generation, you know, who will do the right thing. They'll understand. And books like *Alphie* will help."

That generation—my children's—is going to help. They're already changing things, and doing it beautifully. When Bob announced that he was gay, our girls were eleven, and Beau was fourteen. I feared other children in the school would tease them mercilessly, that they would be harassed and belittled. It didn't happen. Being gay no longer carries the tremendous social stigma it used to, not for them. My children's generation has decided there are better things to worry about. And Doug is hoping that today's young people will view *Canis lupus* as another wild animal, one with as much right to be here as any other, and offer the wolf shared space in our environments. Peace is possible.

I don't see 869 again. I don't see any other Junction Butte wolves, nor any more wolves at all, not here in the park, not this visit. I've been monitoring the time. I know I have to leave soon to make it home to Salt Lake before bedtime. I collapse the tripod's legs, compacting it back into its two-foot-long form. I re-velcro the lens covers, check my pockets for the car key. I have to leave this knoll, these people, the park, Montana. I have a forty-five minute drive out of the park, then I'll return the scope to the gallery owner's home. Then I'll head north, then south, on my nine-hour drive, my gradual transition from wolf watcher in Yellowstone to everything else I am when I'm in Utah, running my business and home, being mom to my children, trying to be a wife.

I offer goodbyes and words of appreciation and gratitude. I take Doug's business card and tuck it safely in a pocket. It's hard to look Pete in the eye, he's so damn good-looking. I have Sara scribble down her email address so I can check in with her later. I walk down the winding trail inhaling the park into my body, wanting to take something home with me—the expanse, the beauty, the fragility and the enduring majesty of it all, the silence, the trumpeter swan's honking calls and the howling, oh the howling. I don't want to let any of it go, not even the frozen toes, the iced eyelashes, the bloodless fingers. I am wiser. More grounded. More wild. I hold on to what wolves demonstrate: strength, competence, tenacity. And commitment—wolves only give up when the only thing to do is give up.

As I round each bend I look for critters. I'm awed by snow-dusted trees. And I brake before driving onto snow-packed, icy stretches of road as they appear around curve after curve, all the way out of the park.

I am alone in the house, and in between chores and computer work, I pace the hardwood floors in stocking feet, silent and stealthy. I returned from my winter Yellowstone sojourn almost six weeks ago. Yesterday I removed my wedding ring.

This is day two. Or day three, if you're counting by calendar dates—yes, it's really the third day. But I told him two days ago, in the morning. I'd come home from my workout, sent the kids off to school, let him take a shower and get ready for work. Then I'd told him. We talked for an hour, maybe more, it might have been less. At one point he got up and came to me, took my head in his hands and kissed my hair and said, I'm sorry, I'm beating you up. He'd been arguing with me, telling me how I hadn't ever been committed, how I hadn't been willing to move to his part of town, hadn't made room for his car in the garage, hadn't let it be our way, that it always had to be Susan's way.

Years ago for Christmas I gave him a metal cuboid engraved with the words It's All About Me. I wanted him to speak his truth, ask for what he wanted. Stand up for Daniel. His standard answer, anytime I asked what he'd like to do, was, I'm with you.

He told me, after that kiss on the head, that my decision was wrong. That he'd honor it, because he had no choice, but that it was simply wrong. We sat next to each other on the couch, perpendicular, my toes tucked under his long legs, pressing against his hamstrings underneath sturdy denim jeans. *Your toes are cold, it's not cold in here.* My toes are always cold.

He didn't explode, he didn't threaten. He argued and accused me of not trying, but he didn't say the things I'd put in his mouth when I'd envisioned this. I was prepared to be dismissed, belittled, browbeaten, renounced. I'd had to practice using my voice, speaking my own truth, telling him what I wanted, standing up for myself. Howling. I was nowhere near wild, but I said, aloud and with conviction, that I could no longer continue in our marriage.

The first day I took the dog for a long walk, I did laundry, I kept my hands and body busy. I wailed inside, I questioned every thought and feeling, I considered how much truth was in the words he'd spoken. I wondered what it meant that I couldn't move to his part of town, to suburbia. Was the fact that I wouldn't leave my neighborhood an indication that we shouldn't have married? I imagine a relationship—loving, trusting, reciprocal, warm, satisfying—with someone who lives twenty miles away in stucco suburbia. I don't think I could. I can't howl in suburbia, I can't be fully me. I'd be a trumpeter swan without a marsh, a mountain with no spring or stream or lake. It wasn't about Daniel, the inability to move, it was about me knowing me.

The second day I worked. Busywork, handwork, moving around the house as often as possible. He and his son went to a hotel for the night. I kept reminding myself that my decision was long considered and thoughtful. That I'd explored all other options, that I'd tried, that we had tried. I howled in the car.

Today, I remind myself again. This morning I cleaned, organized, threw away, made pesky phone calls I'd been dragging my feet toward. I was gentle with myself. I lit candles. I told myself repeatedly that this is best for all. I paced. He sent me an email: *Watch your step—if you see a small piece of my heart lying around the house, please don't step on it. It's the only whole piece of my heart that's left.* I don't want this, but I realize I made an offer that wasn't accepted. He's not yet ready to join me on this path—he didn't understand what I was offering, couldn't accept. I am on the wild path, and he, as of yet, is not. I don't want to howl alone. I can't be in an environment where I'm the only one howling. I need a mate, I need my pack.

A week later he comes over to get some of his things. He's settled on a townhouse, leased it, is settling in. He saw a therapist two days ago, had an epiphany. He gets it, he understands what he's been doing all these years, he understands he needs to dig into why he decided to live life without emotions. He knows he needs to change. *I'm so sorry I fucked everything up.* I'm sorry, too, I reply. I feel a bit of wonderment: he has crashed through the floor and come out on the roof. He has a lot of work ahead of him, but he genuinely seems to understand that his life has to change. We are tender with each other, we cry, we hug and kiss and then I help him carry things out to his car.

Sometimes the damage we cause is irreparable. What has been rent cannot always be mended. We create dust bowls and cause animals to go extinct, we let cattle destroy riparian areas so that they can no longer be home to songbirds and beaver. We destroy relationships through ignorance, through that same refusal to acknowledge truth.

An aide from the care center calls in the middle of the night. They're taking Jake to the hospital. He's having difficulty breathing. By the time I get there, he's been diagnosed with pneumonia. It's early on a Monday morning.

"Oh, this will be your most boring hospital stay ever," the nurse reassures me. "You basically just sit around, wait for the antibiotics to kick in, let him sleep."

I am relieved, settle in. I spend the morning. He opens his eyes just once, for a moment. He sleeps. I kiss him goodbye. I return the next day, prepared. I've brought work with me. I stay most of the day.

Wednesday morning I am dizzy. Lightheadedness comes and goes. When it comes, it hits me like an amusement park fun house: the floor tilts, the room darkens, and I don't dare move. Bob drives across town to pick me up, takes me to the hospital.

I lie down on the bed with Jake, close my eyes.

All is fine until today's doctor walks into the room. She does not smile.

"It is not good. Your son's kidneys are failing, and you need to make a decision about what you'd like to do. We will need to intervene, if that is what you wish. Would you like some time to talk this over?"

Early in Jake's life, we questioned his doctors about what came next. None would suggest how he might develop. When Jake was a few days old a neonatologist told us it was likely Jake had cerebral palsy, which could manifest in a wide range, from tremors in a single hand to complete body involvement. We hoped for finger tremors. But by the time he was fifteen months, it was clear his life would not follow the trajectory of a healthy baby's. Wouldn't even trail it. His developmental delays—not being able to roll over, track objects with his eyes, grasp for a toy—were diagnosed as cortical blindness and spastic quadriplegia. The cerebral hemorrhage had injured so much brain tissue Jake had almost no voluntary control of his body. His scoliosis compromised his lungs, both squished in a narrow chest, his right side pulling hip and bottom rib impossibly close. By age two, his limitations were clear, and our pediatrician told us Jake was unlikely to make it out of his teens. *It's usually a pneumonia that takes kids like this.* The implication: and that is when you will let him go.

But Jake is healthy—has never had the flu, barely ever a cold. He'd contracted pneumonia at two and a half, while recovering from his gastrostomy tube placement. That pneumonia had resolved itself naturally—though during its stay I'd hear Jake's rasping breath from across the house and pray, wildly and constantly, for its departure—and he'd not had another since.

He's just months away from turning nineteen.

This isn't the first time I've had to decide whether or not to let Jake die. Each other time tore my being, and occurred only after hours—sometimes days—of excruciating soul-searching, examination of my faith, visions of life without him. Preparing for the inevitable occurs in waves, each lap against shoreline followed by a recess. Acceptance, resistance. Intellectual knowledge dragged back under by emotional denial. Pain. Love.

But this time, the decision is thrown at me by a white-coated, caramel-skinned woman with long dark hair in a neat braid, someone so matter-of-fact and severe that the decision seems purely medical, a simple yes or no. *His kidneys are beginning to shut down, and we either need to operate, or you can withdraw treatment.* And this time, I'm more prepared. Jake's been leaving for quite a while. And now the antibiotics have failed to fight off the infection coursing through his body. Bob and I may choose the operation, or we may leave the hospital, taking Jake home with us to die.

The people from hospice talk with us. They will provide a bed, oxygen, medications, a nurse every other day, a daily aide to help bathe and care for him.

The nurse removes Jake's IV and leads. She quiets the monitors. He is so small, no longer attached to anything here at all.

I've been dating Daniel for nine months. He comes to pick me up. I wrap Jake in a huge white flannel blanket the hospital gives me. I sit in a wheelchair, holding him, as a nurse pushes us down the hall. At the hospital doors I stand and carry Jake to the car. I push the seat back as far as it will go. I sit, Jake on my lap, and buckle the seatbelt around us both. Daniel drives us to my house. Home.

Candlelight, shadows dancing on the ceiling. Music. The oxygen machine is behind the laundry room door, across the house, its mechanical wheeze muffled. I sit with Jake, I read. Meditate. Sing under my breath. Bob has moved in, leaves each morning for work, sleeps on the couch. Beau talks to Jake each time he walks by. Cait and Allegra change the CDs in the player. Kenny Loggins' *Return to Pooh Corner*, Jewel's *Lullaby*. Allegra curls up with Jake, her head with his on the pillow. My mother and step-father visit. Bob's mom, siblings. Friends stop by, bringing dinner. We retain the nurse but dismiss the daily aide: I don't need help caring for Jake. I give him water with each dose of medication until the nurse tells me Jake doesn't need more water. My chest hollows, presses against my throat, throbs. I give him morphine. He sighs, sleeps, opens those huge blue eyes, closes them. His black, curling lashes lie against skin so pale, so translucent, I can trace veins underneath, follow them to his heart.

The figures are tall, narrow. Obelisks. Shadows, gray against the unlit walls of my living room on this January evening. They stretch to the ceiling, bending, as if they are too great to fit, but unwilling to come any closer or take more space. Jake is leaving; they've come for him. He's been with us five days, resting, sleeping, disappearing. The nasal cannula pushes oxygen into his nostrils. We send morphine into his gastrostomy tube. His ribs poke. Violet shadows lie beneath his eyes. He opens those startling blue eyes and searches the ceiling, the high corners of the walls, with intensity, his jaw rigid. Then he relaxes, closes his eyes, returns to where he's been. But this is it. Each breath is ponderous. Lengthy. I haven't seen his eyes for hours, maybe since morning. And when the shadows come I know. They hover, shifting like candle flame. But they are resolute. When they finally disappear, I know they've taken Jake with them. I let the candles burn, I close my eyes against the tears, and I curl next to his body. Jake's heart keeps beating. He breathes until the next afternoon, his heart beating torpidly, then irregularly, then not at all. But he was already gone. He'd left. They'd taken him, gently, on tall gray shadows.

14. peace

Flames leap. They twist and dance, and the faces of those sitting across the circle from him hide, then reappear, tinted orange and bronze. Eyes gleam, bare skin glistens. Be-shup's eight-year-old eyes shine. Shells and teeth catch firelight, fling it into the night air. Feathers blur and soften the edges of shoulders and heads, blending them with the night. Excitement flutters in his belly, for he knows a story is coming. His mother touches his knee. Her face glows gold, and her smile passes through skin and into his chest. He has the most beautiful mother of all. His father sits across the flames, next to the elders. He sits tall and proud, as should the best hunter of the tribe. Be-shup is a lucky boy.

Between the fire circle and the deep night sky rises a mountain. Its rocky slopes are masked by pines and quaking aspen. Ridges, each filled with dens and nests, fall away, leading down to the valley. Be-shup hunts for rabbits near the base. His father prowls higher, returning with deer, sometimes an elk. It reaches higher than any other in sight. It is called Big Mountain.

A chant begins, soft and deliberate, men drumming the rhythm. *Thum, thum, thump, thum, thum, thump.* He pats his knees with open palms, mouths the words, adding sound as the volume grows. His whisper becomes song as words lift into the air and the drumbeats echo from tree trunks and rock. Song jumps from star to star, finally falling back down into the flames as words return to chant, then whisper. Drumbeats soften to a hum. The fire spits and pops. In the silence, Be-shup nestles sit bones into the earth. Story is next.

The elder's face moves in and out of shadow, but his voice is deep and smooth as deerskin.

Once, upon our land, long, long ago, when those with four legs had voice, Wolf, the great creator, was challenged by Coyote. Coyote was a trickster, and not to be trusted. Our great ancestors stayed far away from Coyote, who was always up to no good. Our people, the Neme, did not want to be double-crossed, or tricked into losing something.

Because our people treat Wolf with reverence, Coyote resents Wolf. One day, Coyote decides it is time to teach Wolf a lesson, a lesson that will cause our great people to dislike Wolf.

On this day, Coyote and Wolf talk about the people of our land, how they are part of the land. Wolf claims if one were to die, he could bring the person back to life by shooting an arrow underneath them.

Coyote says to Wolf, if people were to die, and you were to bring everyone back to life, the land would soon be filled, and there would be no room left. Once someone is dead, Coyote says, they should remain this way. If Wolf takes this advice, Coyote tells himself, the Neme people will come to hate Wolf.

Wolf does not speak, but is tired of Coyote's lack of respect toward him. He nods his great head, and decides to teach Coyote a lesson.

After the sun rises and sets again, then again, Coyote's son is bitten by a terrible rattlesnake, something no creature can survive. Coyote runs to Wolf, with great panic and fear.

Please, Wolf, bring my son back to life, as you said you can do. Shoot your arrow underneath him, return him to this world.

Ah, Coyote, says Wolf. You yourself told me that the dead should remain dead, that I should no longer interfere. I will no longer bring anyone back to life.

And this, my people, is the day that death came to our land. Coyote's son was the first to die, in punishment for Coyote's sly and troublesome ways.

Wolf never again raised someone from death, and our great people soon learned sadness and grief. However, Coyote's trick failed, for our great people continued to respect and revere Wolf, his strength and power, his great wisdom. Today, we honor Wolf, and consider sadness, death, and grief to be our greatest gifts to those we love.

Ay-yo. A hushed call begins with Be-shup's father, then circles through the men of the tribe. Flames have quieted, and their shapes, orange tipped with blue, shift back and forth between the disintegrating logs.

The storyteller lets his head fall back. He lifts a gentle howl into the sky. Be-shup tenses muscles, holds his breath. The snap of burning wood. A pulse of wind. He releases his breath, draws in another gulp and waits.

Ar-roo. The answer floats high over the creek, the blaze, and Be-shup, whose body responds with a shiver.

15. howl

Journey is old for a first-time father. Five. But it comes naturally. He hunts, brings food back for the family. For his mate, their three pups. They are tucked in the trees, hidden in a hanging valley in the midst of a mountainous national forest. When the pups are old enough to be left, his mate will hunt with him. They'll hunt elk. She is swift, fierce. He had traveled over three thousand miles in search of her. He wandered scorched earth and frozen terrain. Slept alone, hunted alone. The echoing howls of his birth pack traveled with him. He heard a song, a song of the land, whispers of whistling wind, crashing water, and heat waves dry as dust. The song lived inside, pressed him forward. Painted pictures, drove his feet.

Mythologist and writer Joseph Campbell believed that the very experience of being alive is what the human psyche desires—not an understanding of the meaning of life. Furthermore, Campbell didn't believe life has a purpose. He described life as "a lot of protoplasm with an urge to reproduce and continue in being." However, he continued, "each incarnation, you might say, has a potentiality, and the mission of life is to live that potentiality . . . there's something inside you that knows when you're in the center, that knows when you're on the beam, or off the beam." Work, connection with others, love, and adventure keep me on the beam. And often, I'm so engaged with the experience of being alive—swooping on my bicycle, inhaling fresh cedar in the mountains, watching wolves lope past me, feeling a rush of desire to howl—that I float above that beam.

I'm still perfecting my howl. I work on it only when the house is empty. I'm embarrassed, a last vestige of un-wild me clinging to my structure. I've tried it in my car, but find driving difficult with my head tilted back, neck elongated. A howling fest might be the perfect addition to an upcoming dinner party, after the first, or possibly second, round of cocktails. I recently searched online to find a video, wanting to listen to a howl over and over again, and found a site that's had over four million views since it was posted in 2008. I'm not the only one interested in the howling of wolves.

Researchers and wildlife watchers assign meaning to howls based on behavioral observations. When I asked Sara, the wildlife technician, if she knew why the wolves on the hillside across from us were howling, she took a moment to answer, then said no. I want there to be an answer, yet I am grateful for her willingness to admit ignorance. How can anyone know what's in the mind and heart of a wolf? We suggest, we guess, we deduce, we assume. I hear people say two wolves fell in love; I'm not sure I can accept as fact that wolves experience love. I'm leery of anthropomorphizing wild creatures, but perhaps love is not reserved for only human beings. The mother bison that stood over her dead calf for a day and a half: maybe I can allow what exists between her and her calf to be called love. Allowing your progeny to nibble at your ears, jump on your back, nip and tease, and to respond with nose rubs and gentle rolling of bodies with paws, surely seems like love. Perhaps I need to adjust my understanding of love.

Bonds begin with identification. I start by relating to those who look like me, who behave as I do, vote the same way, choose similar activities. As I expand my awareness, I search for deeper connection—people who share my beliefs and desire comparable emotional experiences. As I evolve, I identify with all, for I know that within myself lies every aspect of life, from feelings of fear, anger, and hurt to joy, passion, and compassion. At this highest level I identify with all sentient beings for I understand that I am no different but for unique arrangements of genetic material. Within each of us lies a beating heart, and a spirit. Unquantifiable, the spirit is not exclusive to humans, but something possessed by all living creatures.

In the Sierra Madre of Mexico it's said the spirit of a wolf will always remain in the world. Perhaps we, too, possess this gift. Maybe our spirits remain always in the places we've lived and loved. My grandmother's spirit would be in Estes Park, out in the field, feeding apples to horses, rubbing their flanks, brushing the tangles and knots from their manes. My grandfather's spirit would hover in music rooms, above pianos, in hard-sided violin cases lined with crushed blue velvet. Jake passed from this life four years ago. His spirit is in my house and wherever I go: his spirit stays with me. The spirits of thousands of wolves would rest in wooded hillsides and vales, high on mountaintops, at the edges of hidden lakes and hanging valleys, alongside riverbanks and aspen groves, tangled in juniper branches and rustling in tall sedge grasses. If all that ever lived leave behind a spirit, the richness of our environments increases by the millionfold.

Perhaps, at times, wolves feel the presence of those spirits, spirits of their ancestors and of their foes, and howl. Sensing those who lived before them, acknowledging wisdom or strength or cunning or great leadership, honoring the past. Some howls are to collect pack members strewn out upon a mountainside or over a meadow. Perhaps some howls bind what exists now with what lived before, salutations to guidance passed along through genetics, through flesh and fur and bone.

Just as what I suggest is, in ways, a paradigm shift in the way we view humans in relation to creatures, in *Rambunctious Garden* Emma Marris contends that it's time for a paradigm shift in the environmental world, that we release our dream of saving pristine wilderness and accept that humans have changed landscapes since they first walked the earth, and begin to work more effectively with what we have. She argues that "We must temper our romantic notion of untrammeled wilderness and find room next to it for the more nuanced notion of a global, half-wild rambunctious garden, tended by us." Marris sees this garden in existence everywhere, on green rooftops and in national forests and in city block backyards, providing us opportunities to healthily manage the nature around us. She suggests we move forward, adjusting, sliding gently closer to the edge of what is next. Marris concedes that seventy-five percent of the world's ice-free land "showed evidence of alteration as a result of human residence and land use," but she offers an optimistic treatment plan. Creating more rambunctious gardens everywhere bridges the dichotomy between urban settings and wilderness, and offers more people an opportunity to connect with nature. It's impossible to return ecosystems to how they once were—we can only begin from where we are, accepting some loss, working toward better solutions as we move forward. However, Marris hopes we retain scads of unmanaged land to, in part, ensure that future generations might still be able to get lost.

Ecologists define a novel ecosystem as one that contains a human-influenced combination of species. In working with such environments, biologist Joe Mascaro learned he had to let go of value judgments and assess instead with objective measures. Just as a forest fire isn't a catastrophe, a new form of ecosystem isn't necessarily bad, only different. Mascaro suggests the value lies not in nature being exactly as it was centuries ago, but in our ability to observe it operating naturally, without human beings controlling its processes.

We have changed the earth in uncountable ways, and eco-systems continue to adjust in response. In its resilience, balance, and ability to connect us to a greater consciousness, wildness remains our most compelling teacher. However, for us to continue to learn from it we must have access to it. Marris suggests it's possible to have spiritual and aesthetic experiences in more humble natural settings—that we don't need to be in the Himalayas or the Grand Canyon to be awed—and this might be the greatest reason of all to create natural settings everywhere we can. Nonetheless, we must still protect every bit of wildness that remains. And when we find ways to correct past mistakes, we must act—as we did by returning wolves to wilderness.

Physician and psychoanalyst Donald Winnicott developed the theory of a good-enough mother. He believed it possible for children to thrive, even without perfect parenting. If enough people are good enough parents, children benefit and our society is enriched. I want to be a good-enough inhabitant of our world. There are no perfect stewards of the land, and I might not be a perfect environmentalist. I don't spend all my energy fighting for pristine wilderness, arguing against all that injures the environment, rallying people to vilify cars, motors, sheep, cows. I'm not always certain of what the best answer is to every environmental dilemma. Nevertheless, perhaps I can be a good-enough environmentalist. Being aware, considering the effects of my choices, using my voice to educate others; these pieces matter. Maybe if enough of us are willing to be good enough, our environment will benefit. At this juncture, our ideas of perfect ecosystem management must be adjusted. Work to ensure that best science is used, but allow the process to unfold without expectations of perfection. Keep wilderness. Add some rambunctious sanctuaries.

While having access to wild places is ideal, the existence value of places and creatures matters too. Marris recognizes this, acknowledging that we benefit from merely knowing something exists. Places and things we can hold in our minds, dream about, expand our realities by considering. Actual places: Yosemite. Alaska. Antarctica. Amazonian rain forests. Critters and creatures: Elephants. Tigers. Polar bears. Dolphins. Environments where coexistence reigns: The African savannah. The ocean. The Blackfoot watershed. My not-so-wild Big Mountain.

Max Planck, originator of quantum theory, suggested that a conscious, intelligent mind lies behind the force that holds the atom and all its compositions into greater matter together, and that the ultimate mysteries of nature cannot be solved by science because we humans are part of nature, part of the enigma itself. At some point it's enough to be intrigued, to honor similarities, be astounded by complexities, and revel in the creatures that inhabit with us this earth. From manatees to wolverines to pink fairy armadillos, our world is filled with diversity that originates from the same matter that created us all. From complex arrangements of atoms come snakes that grow new skin, salamanders that regenerate limbs, three-toed sloths, and wolves.

Journey of the Universe, a documentary film that with breathtaking visualization tells the story of our universe and its present trajectory, explores the question of our human role. It suggests that "over the course of fourteen billion years, hydrogen gas transformed itself into mountains, butterflies, the music of Bach, and you and me . . . the body of the universe gave birth to our bodies. The self-organizing dynamics of the universe gave birth to our minds. We belong here." Because we share our origins with those mountains, those butterflies, that music, we are drawn to them, astounded by them, made curious by their inconsistencies, foreignness, and, paradoxically, what we have in common. If all that inhabit the universe share a common origin, we are connected in ways we cannot yet truly fathom. Our draw to nature, our wonder regarding the natural world, are indications of an innate awareness, a truth that our bodies know more than we do about who we are, where we came from, where we belong. Brian Thomas Swimme and Mary Evelyn Tucker, authors of the *Journey* book and film, tell us that wonder will guide us, and ask, "the human species has a genius for becoming astounded by almost anything in the universe. What can this mean?" They answer that it means we are meant to be drawn, we are meant to be filled with wonder and awe. We are meant to respect, exist side by side, and be thrilled by our amazement.

To know there are unexplored places throughout the world, and within. As microcosms of the world in which we live, we are filled with complexity and mystery. There is more to discover, the expedition is nowhere near over.

To know there are beasts and songbirds: mountain lions and grizzly bears capable of ripping us to shreds, wolves, tanagers and orioles and warblers. There are butterflies and dragonflies, moose that can trample, deer that woo. Creatures exist that scare us, return to us our humility, thrill, amaze. And the same lies within. We each have parts that threaten, frighten, soothe, relax and stump.

To know that upon lands both wild and tame live creatures both feral and domesticated, and to know that ecosystems survive with and without our interventions. Even most of the environments we have messed up horrifically are finding new equilibriums. Coexistence is the law of the land whether we acknowledge it or not. The grizzly, the wolf, the elk and the bison live side by side, as can the rancher, the hunter, the conservationist and the predator. As Solzhenitsyn penned, it is time in the West to defend not so much human rights as human obligations. Management is necessary, education vital, empathy crucial.

It is awe that saves us. At the end of December I stand in silence, snowshoes strapped to boots, looking out over white hillsides sprinkled with pines, the creek far below, icy at its edges and dark, flowing gently over the time-rounded rocks that line its bed. On a warm January day I bicycle to the reservoir, one end of it solidly white, the opposite end unfrozen, the swath in between a brilliant mix of swirling, semi-frozen, glassine-like mirror. The surrounding hillsides and mountain peaks that move southward in layer after layer after layer are white, densely white, and I am immobilized by awe. It is this awe that makes me howl, makes me defend the wildness, helps me fight to keep these places alive, healthy, functioning in ways that create this landscape, this experience that cannot be found anywhere but right here, this experience that will continue to be found in pockets everywhere we allow them to remain.

I've explored Yellowstone, Missoula, the Blackfoot Watershed, the Gros Ventre Valley, Paradise Valley, hundreds of miles of Idaho, Wyoming, Montana. I've seen wolves. I've heard them howl, I've watched them tear carcasses apart. I've read books and spoken with more people than I can count, and I know that nothing I've read or been told comes close to the experience of standing in wildness, breathing it in, letting its richness, its wholeness, seep into my pores and remind me of who I really am, who I can be when I have the courage to say yes to that person. I say yes. I howl.

It begins with a howl, but that isn't enough.

Carrying capacity refers to the ability of an environment to sustain life, an equilibrium between creatures and the food availability, living space, conditions of the environment, and water supply they need. The carrying capacity of a particular watershed might be ten thousand elk, and when elk numbers grow to exceed that maximum, limited available resources will cause that population to decline, eventually returning to the environment's maximum carrying capacity for elk. Ponds, lakes, streams, land itself, all have maximum carrying capacities for specific critters and creatures.

Caring capacity is the human ability to care about an issue, which also must retain an equilibrium and not surpass its maximum. For myriad, varied reasons, we stop caring about issues. I can become overwhelmed by information, facts, and options. I might be uncertain that providing funding—often the easiest way to use my voice—will truly support my position, and not just someone's lifestyle. I may simply be too busy focusing on my own life, children, business, and recreation. I might stop believing I can make a difference, or I might decide it's plain old hopeless. A physical therapist who helped me heal after my bicycle crash asked numerous questions—does this hurt, can you do this, what does it feel like when I push here—and told me that *I don't know* is an okay answer. It is. And we might resort to that at times. But eventually we're spurred on to do more research, brainstorm options, and narrow it down to what we're able to do, anyway. We have limited resources, just like the environments that support life, and we need to make wise use of what we have. Our task is to decide how to best move forward, focusing on what matters to us, living our lives authentically and with meaning.

Making decisions can twist our innards, can cause breakouts of rashes and hives, can immobilize us. Sometimes the best thing to do is just make the damn decision and move on. Usually we know in our gut what the right decision is. We, like a pup with a stick, toss the pros and cons around, send them skittering in one direction then another, grab hold the dilemma and worry it, gnaw it, maul it again and again. And eventually utter yes, or no, the decision our gut told us to make eons ago. And the decision here is clear. Wolves belong on our landscapes. Wolves deserve our commitment to a peaceful coexistence.

Nonetheless, arguments continue to arise, and not all researchers agree that wolves can revive ecosystems. Biologist Arthur Middleton, a postdoc fellow at the Yale School of Forestry, refutes the trophic cascade theory of ecosystem benefit from the presence of wolves. He claims the tenet that wolves keep elk nervous, moving, and at lower population levels, thus benefitting the land, isn't necessarily true. His research at the University of Wyoming shows that elk do not modify their feeding behavior when wolves are present. His study, however, took place over a period of only three years, which is likely too short of a time to thoroughly understand behavior patterns of creatures in the wild. Middleton goes on to clarify that what he most takes issue with is that we've latched onto one story, one conclusion, without considering all the other factors that play into change within an ecosystem. He fears we lose sight of the science when we try to "sell" the wolf by claiming it is a hero that's saving landscapes. Middleton suggests that for scientists to claim the wolf will revive ecosystems is akin to the bitter ranchers and hunters propagating myths—the reintroduced wolves' larger size, devastating effect on elk numbers, disease-spreading, evilness—about wolves. He suggests we all look at the situation more clearly, with less hyperbole. The wolf is neither savior nor spawn of Satan, it is a top predator whose behavior affects prey in ways researchers don't yet completely understand. Middleton's research might not support Doug Smith's research, which might not always agree with that of David Mech or Rolf Peterson. Wildlife biology cannot be studied in a sterile lab, ecosystems differ across time and space, and the people who live closer to the land than any of us, the Inuit, know that the most accurate answers to questions about the wolf involve the word *sometimes*. In focusing on individual pieces and parts we become blind to the panorama spread before us, and forget to trust in its design.

I had known since Jake weighed less than ten pounds that he was likely to die young, and that I was likely to outlive him. I began releasing him when he was five months old. And so the stabbing pain, the walloping loss, the elephant-sized hole in my life after he died, were a shock. I sleepwalked through the funeral, the hugs from friends, schoolteachers, physicians. I took Jake's urn of ashes home with me. I had little to say to anyone. I functioned, but with a heart so devastated it beat in fits and starts. In knots. In lumps and jumps and screams.

I slept. I made lunches for my children, sent them off, then napped while they were at school. Weeks passed, and I napped less, spoke a little more. And then one night I dreamt.

I arrive at a house. Once inside, I discover that it's positioned on a hillside, its entire backside opening to the valley below, stairs and windows and floor below floor offering rooms, nooks, crannies, views of what goes on forever and ever. There are young people in the house, all glowing with peace, enlightenment. My guide is a young man, slender, light-haired, who is gentle in manner and voice. He walks with me up and down stairs, along hallways, introducing me to spaces I'd never imagined. We talk. He explains to me that the rooms, the spaces, all have different functions. They are for resting, reading, drawing. Painting, sculpting, writing. Creating. Healing. Each room is unique, and beautiful. I realize, after some time, the young man is weary, and I feel a tremendous love for him. A sisterly, motherly love. I am much older than he is. I offer to massage his shoulders. He removes his shirt and at once I see how painfully thin he is, his shoulders tightly hunched. They are distorted, thin, poking, one higher than the other—they are Jake's shoulders.

I wake, clutching the blanket he last used, which still smells of him. The white blanket from the hospital. It's dark, I'm alone. I just had my first conversation with my son.

Living my most powerful, most human life requires a willingness to be awed. By nature, by wildlife, by creatures and critters and exquisite flora and tenacious vines, and by other humans. We're here to work together, and challenge each other. I won't settle for ignorance and denial. I want to be aware, to truly see. I want to breathe deeply, to accept weaknesses and difficulty, to lift myself. We breathe awe in, we give it back. When we're willing to recognize it and coat our lives with it, we find it everywhere.

Nature doesn't pretend. It doesn't deny or defend itself. It simply is. Wildflowers, creeks, fish, grubs, wolves. The stream flows without worrying about the bends, rocks, and logjams in its future. Lilies toil not, they simply grow. Lilies know their place. We humans struggle to know our place. We've been questioning it as long as thoughts have been recorded, and while some factions know we are here to dominate, others of us know we are here to live in respectful, integrated awe. Still others ponder, and sit on wooden fences, pigtails in their hair or battered cowboy hats on their heads. It's time to get off the fence. It's time to acknowledge our role in creating the current environment, and focus on mitigating the damage we've done, preserving what we can to keep wildness alive.

Awaken to awe. Love who and what you love. Let us listen, let us love, let us howl.

I suggest that your environment matters. That those grassy meadows, trees, streams, pastures, red rock deserts, lakes, mountains and valleys affect your life more than you might know. And that when you find a way to spend more time in the wildest place you can find—whether it's up a nearby canyon, down by a lakeshore, alongside a stream, out in a forest, in your neighborhood park, digging in the pots where you grow your terrace garden—you will rediscover a vital piece of you. Maybe through an owl, a grasshopper, or a minnow. Dirt. Sun-warmed stones, the north-facing moss-covered bark of old trees. Songbirds. Chattering squirrels, racing geckos. Regal elk. And if you're incredibly lucky, a reclusive wolf.

The more you find yourself in wildness, the more you understand how crucial it is that we have it. Children need it; adults need it too. Hone in on your favorite places of wild, and determine how you can best support them. Learn more about the ecosystems important to you. Buy a National Park pass, buy a seasonal pass to visit local canyons, learn to leave your motors in parking lots and use your legs. Bicycle. Hike. Leave the smallest, lightest footprint you can upon the land, but dare to make those footprints, allow yourself to make those footprints, encourage others to place theirs alongside yours.

Use your voice to speak up for what can't. Recognize when people and groups are voting for laws that serve their own agendas and not those of a healthy environment. Write a letter to the editor. Join an environmental group that resonates with your values. Dare to question. Know that you have a right to your opinion, you have a right to your own experience, you have the responsibility to speak for what it is you want and need. The millions of us in this world who understand that both peace and wisdom are found in wildness are more powerful than the millions who disrespect the earth and its inhabitants; we just haven't realized it yet. I ask you to realize it.

Decide what it is you're willing to care about. I hope it includes green things—trees and lush grass, piñon pines and pungent sage—and waterways. I hope it includes critters and creatures, those that screech and whistle, chatter and howl. I hope it includes healthy land, and places that are at least a little bit wild.

I hope it includes a guide, inside, whether it is an eagle, a bear, or a jackrabbit. I hope it includes a conviction that your presence on this earth is purposeful, and meant to be at one with nature. I hope you find your voice, that you practice howling, and that one day you pull on your brand new cowboy boots and unleash that howl upon our world.

I ride my bike. Jake is with me. In the wind, in the moose in the hollow. In frozen swirls on the reservoir. In red dirt, in oak leaves, in quivering hummingbird wings. He is everywhere. As am I.

Acknowledgments

With deep gratitude to all who trusted me with their stories: Kris Murri, Denny Emery, Michael Powers, Jim Hester, Sabine Kallas, Tiffany and Jimmy Wiser, Ilona Popper, Terri Smith, Laurie Lyman, Seth Wilson, Eric Graham, Stephen Speckert, Liz Bradley, Ralph Maughan, Barry Lewis, Denny Iverson, Jim Stone, Dan Pocha, Bob Roland, Tracy Manley, Nathan Rott, Pete Bengeyfield, John and Mary Theberge, Bob Brister, Bethany Cotton, and Anna's dad. Even more gratitude to Doug McLaughlin, and his Jake.

Rick McIntyre shared his experience, jokes, and insight, and offered—gently—corrections and guidance. Doug Smith was generous with his time, knowledge, and experience, as were his many Wolf Project scientists: Pete Mumford, Sarah Eto, Lizzie Cato, Cheyenne Burnett, Donny Eaton, Kersten Schnurle, and Brenna Cassidy.

Kirk Robinson welcomed my inquiries and continues to keep me informed of all things carnivore.

Kathryn Miles, Marybeth Holleman, Michael Soulé, Mary Ellen Hannibal, Renée Askins, Clarissa Pinkola Estés, Stephen Trimble, and the estimable Barry Lopez all provided inspiration.

Doug Peacock, by inviting me into his home, scared and delighted me. I am honored to share small pieces of his experience on these pages.

Tremendous appreciation to Bob Rolfs, who passed along the wisdom to just start writing; to Jeanne, who always reads what I ask her to read; and to everyone in my family, who let me tell the stories.

I am eternally indebted to Mark Bailey and Kirsten Allen, who planted and nurtured the seed. This book is a result of their commitment to furthering discussions of landscape, life, and ultimately, love. As well, Kirsten had the fortitude to guide me, often over the same territory, again and again, and these pages reflect her knowledge, skill, and talent as an editor. She reined me in, kept me on the right trail, fed me, and challenged me to be worthy of speaking for those who can only howl. Anne Terashima's intelligence, keen eyes, and perceptive nature have added (and often subtracted) precisely what was necessary.

Mary Sojourner, master storyteller, helped me sharpen both pencil and eraser.

With humility and awe for her myriad intuitive gifts, I thank Amy Irvine McHarg for envisioning a different book, and helping me discover a way to write it.

Perhaps most integral is my gratitude for the thousands of people who've been part of returning to the landscape an animal that roamed the earth long before man—and woman—stepped foot upon it.

ABOUT SUSAN IMHOFF BIRD

Susan Imhoff Bird finds inspiration in Utah's stunning canyons, valleys, and water-sculpted rock. A mother of three and owner of a gratitude-based business, she is fascinated by human interactions. When not writing, reading, trying to meditate, or attempting yoga asanas, she can be found on her bicycle or snowshoes, absorbing the wisdom of the natural world. And occasionally howling. She lives in Salt Lake City, Utah.

SusanImhoffBird.com

Torrey House Press

The economy is a wholly owned subsidiary of the environment, not the other way around.
—Senator Gaylord Nelson, founder of Earth Day

Love of the land inspires Torrey House Press and the books we publish. From literature and the environment and Western Lit to topical nonfiction about land related issues and ideas, we strive to increase appreciation for the importance of natural landscape through the power of pen and story. Through our *2% to the West* program, Torrey House Press donates two percent of sales to not-for-profit environmental organizations and funds a scholarship for up-and-coming writers at colleges throughout the West.

Visit **www.torreyhouse.com** for reading group discussion guides, author interviews, and more.